A Seat at the Table

A Seat at the Table

Congresswomen's Perspectives on Why Their Presence Matters

KELLY DITTMAR

KIRA SANBONMATSU

AND

SUSAN J. CARROLL

Oxford University Press is a department of the University of Oxford. It furthers
the University's objective of excellence in research, scholarship, and education
by publishing worldwide. Oxford is a registered trade mark of Oxford University
Press in the UK and certain other countries.

Published in the United States of America by Oxford University Press
198 Madison Avenue, New York, NY 10016, United States of America.

CIP data is on file at the Library of Congress
ISBN 978–0–19–091573–5 (pbk.)
ISBN 978–0–19–091572–8 (hbk.)

9 8 7 6 5 4 3

Paperback printed by Webcom, Inc., Canada
Hardback printed by Bridgeport National Bindery, Inc., United States of America

CONTENTS

ACKNOWLEDGMENTS

This book would not have been possible without the assistance of numerous people and organizations.

We are very grateful to the Political Parity Project at the Hunt Alternatives Fund for its generous financial support. We greatly appreciate the support of the staff there, as well as their confidence in our ability as members of the Center for American Women and Politics (CAWP) to interview a large number of women members of Congress given the difficulties researchers often encounter in trying to conduct interviews on Capitol Hill. We extend special thanks to Swanee Hunt for her leadership and vision, and her long-standing support of work to promote women's political empowerment.

We are deeply indebted to Debbie Walsh, director of CAWP, who contributed to this project in so many ways. Debbie believed in the importance of the project and worked hard to secure funding. As a co-principal investigator on the grant with the three of us, Debbie contributed significantly to the conceptualization and design of the research. She willingly called upon her wide network of political contacts to help us secure interviews with congresswomen, and she agreed to be part of our interviewing team. She traveled to Washington on several occasions alone or with one of us to talk to congresswomen.

We are grateful to Cathy Wineinger, our graduate research assistant on this project, who conducted more than her fair share of interviews with women members. Cathy also provided willing and critical help with a variety of less glamourous tasks related to the project. Kathleen Rogers's assistance was also invaluable, from her meticulous reviews of the manuscript to her substantive input on early drafts.

Several colleagues at CAWP lent their valuable expertise to this project, including Ruth B. Mandel, Gilda Morales, Chelsea Hill, and Linda Phillips. We are especially grateful to Audra Lubiak, who so adeptly handled the scheduling of interviews and made our travel arrangements. The high participation rate among congresswomen can be largely credited to Audra's tenacity and persistence. We also are indebted to Kathy Kleeman, whose superb editing skills improved the quality of both our interview transcripts and the book manuscript.

Several current and former members of Congress, congressional staffers, organizational leaders, and other friends assisted us with outreach, encouraging women members to speak with us. We are incredibly grateful for their efforts. Our thanks go to former senators Olympia Snowe and Mary Landrieu for their willingness to make a joint appeal to congresswomen to participate in our project. The co-chairs of the Congressional Caucus for Women's Issues in the 114th Congress, Representatives Kristi Noem and Doris Matsui, as well as their staffs, also took time to advocate for our project to their colleagues. Democratic Leader Nancy Pelosi and her deputy chief of staff, Diane Dewhirst, lent their time and influence to our outreach efforts and no doubt bolstered our participation rate. Outside of Congress, we extend our thanks to organizational leaders and friends who tapped their own networks and vouched for our work. These women include Dianne Bystrom, Julie Conway, Cindy Hall, Susan McCue, Stephanie Schriock, and Candy Straight, among others. We are especially grateful to Rutgers's vice president for federal relations, Francine Newsome Pfeiffer, who was an essential resource to us in Washington.

We received valuable criticism and feedback from several scholars who read all or part of this manuscript. In particular we would like to thank Tiffany Barnes, Janet Martin, Michele Swers, and two anonymous reviewers, who provided detailed feedback. Additional thanks to members of the Brigham Young University Political Science Department for comments and recommendations provided at a research workshop where part of this work was presented. The eleven students in Sue Carroll's graduate seminar on gender, race, and representation also provided thoughtful reviews. Additionally, we thank Craig Volden and Alan Wiseman for their early feedback on this project. The manuscript has been strengthened as a result of the comments and suggestions we received from all of these scholars.

We have been very fortunate to have Angela Chnapko as our editor at Oxford University Press. We are grateful for her enthusiasm, support, and efficiency.

Kelly extends her thanks to her own support system—family, friends, and colleagues—whose understanding, encouragement, and welcome distractions from work were key to her sanity and the project's success. Kelly's time as an American Political Science Association Congressional Fellow also provided her invaluable insights that informed this work, as well as regular reminders—often thanks to her boss at the time, Representative Rosa DeLauro—of why women's representation matters in Congress. Finally, sincere thanks is offered to Sue Carroll and Kira Sanbonmatsu for the confidence they have placed in their former graduate student; it is an honor to call them colleagues and co-authors.

Kira thanks Tim and Vanya for their patience while she traveled to Washington and for their good company—both of which contributed to the book's completion. She also thanks her family and friends for their support and their interest in this work.

Sue is grateful to her canine companion, Sadie, whose demands for walks and attention keep her from spending too much time in front of her computer, and to her tai chi and qigong instructor, who has taught her to maintain better balance in her life.

Finally, we are ever so grateful to the women serving in the 114th Congress who generously shared their time and their insights with us. We hope that their words as reflected in this book will inspire others to follow in their footsteps.

A Seat at the Table

1

Introduction

When Senator Lisa Murkowski (R-AK) took to the floor on Tuesday, January 26, 2016, she noted that something was "genuinely different" about the chamber. "As we convene this morning, you look around the chamber," she observed. "The presiding officer is female. All of our parliamentarians are female. Our floor managers are female. All of our pages are female." Due to a blizzard, very few members made it to work that day, leaving Murkowski and Senator Susan Collins (R-ME) alone with the women on staff. Asked to explain the gender disparity in who showed up that day, Murkowski posited, "Perhaps it speaks to the hardiness of women—that 'put on your boots and put your hat on and get out and slog through the mess that's out there' [attitude]." Perhaps that hardiness is evident not just in women's journey—whether literal or figurative—to the US Congress, but also in the way they navigate an institution that has long been dominated by men and is frequently characterized as broken.

In this book, we examine how the women of the 114th Congress (2015–17) attempted to have a meaningful impact on public policy and provide effective representation in an institutional and political environment characterized by gridlock and party polarization. Through interviews with more than three-fourths of all women members, we provide first-person perspectives on their representational roles, discuss what motivates their legislative priorities and behavior, detail the ways in which they experience service within a male-dominated institution, and highlight why it matters that they sit in the nation's federal legislative chambers. We describe the strategies they employ to "slog through" any challenges they confront, including those tied to gender, race, and party polarization, in order to get things done. Many accomplishments of women—and men—in the 114th Congress received little attention in the press, but suggest the need to look beyond the headlines and measure more than successful legislation and vote counts to understand how women represent multiple constituencies in the daily business of the US Congress.

The women we interviewed fervently believe that their presence matters. Consistent with the findings of previous studies of women public officials, these congresswomen assert that their experiences *as women* provide them with perspectives different from those of their male colleagues. They describe the ways in which those experiences both fuel their passion to address issues affecting women and provide a gendered lens that they apply to their work on a variety of other public policy concerns. Many congresswomen also see themselves as a voice for the voiceless, advocating for individuals and groups whose interests are underrepresented in Congress, including the economically disadvantaged, children, citizens not represented by lobbyists, and the unborn.

Our interviews with congresswomen also demonstrate that race and ethnicity and partisanship exert powerful influences on their views and priorities. Women of color bring their perspectives and experiences to bear in expanding policy agendas to reflect intersectional realities. Ideological differences among Republican and Democratic women influence the positions they adopt even when they share a commitment to the same issue.

Importantly, according to the women we interviewed, the significance of their congressional presence is not limited to their direct influence on public policy and legislative debates. Many expressed the view that women have a distinctive work style that prioritizes results and values collaboration and consensus. Repeatedly, these congresswomen emphasized that their primary motivation is to get things done in the face of hurdles to achievement. Most of the women we interviewed see women as more likely than their male counterparts to both create and capitalize on opportunities for bipartisan collaboration, including opportunities emerging from single-sex networks and activities.

Congresswomen take seriously their responsibility to serve as political role models for other women and share a commitment to increasing women's political representation. And they understand the challenges that can accompany women's election to office. Those we interviewed frequently told us that overcoming obstacles to running was more difficult than navigating a male-dominated institution once they were elected to Congress.

They assured us that they are both accustomed to navigating gendered and raced terrain and more than capable of clearing hurdles to their congressional leadership and success. Despite gridlock and party polarization, they feel a strong sense of accomplishment—that they are getting things done. And while their perspectives, experiences, and influence are neither uniform nor interchangeable, these congresswomen believe their contributions are of great significance to the institution of Congress and to the people they represent.

GENDER AND REPRESENTATION

Foundational literature in political theory and American politics explores the most basic debates over representatives' autonomy from and accountability to their constituents, and these debates continue (e.g., Burke 1790; Madison 1787; Mill 1861; Pitkin 1967; Dovi 2007). Moreover, scholars have devoted volumes to discerning *who* are among the constituents that legislative representatives are meant to—or choose to—serve (Pitkin 1967; Fenno 1978; Lublin 1997; Williams 2000; Mansbridge 1999, 2003; Dovi 2002). These questions are complicated by identities that representatives bring with them to legislative settings, which contribute to representational relationships that cross district, state, or even national borders (Mansbridge 2003). In scholarship focused on identity and representation, a common distinction—drawn from Hannah Pitkin (1967)—is that between representatives "standing for" and "acting for" the people they represent. But it is the relationship between these behaviors that has been the primary focus for scholars of identity politics, including scholars of women and politics (Carroll 1994; Thomas 1994; Dodson and Carroll 1991; Carroll 2001; Beckwith 2014; Escobar-Lemmon and Taylor-Robinson 2014; Thomas and Wilcox 2014). More explicitly, does the presence of women legislators—in numbers alone—substantively change outcomes due to differences in women's representational behaviors and/or priorities? In understanding who representatives believe they "stand for," we can better identify who they "act for" and why.

Much of the research to date on women in Congress has used quantitative measures of legislative behavior—from bill sponsorship to roll-call votes—to identify gender differences in legislative priorities and decision-making. While some studies have found evidence that women and men in Congress vote differently on issues of specific interest to women, those differences have waned in recent years as the two parties have become more ideologically polarized (Dodson et al. 1995; Dolan 1997; Norton 1999; Swers 2002; Frederick 2015). Moreover, analyses of roll-call voting across issues reveal that party affiliation and constituency demands typically supersede gender in shaping how legislators vote (Schwindt-Bayer and Corbetta 2004; Frederick 2009, 2010, 2011, 2013; Simon and Palmer 2010). Emphasizing the importance of analyzing gender differences across the entire legislative process, Swers (2002) argues that women's influence is most distinct at the bill sponsorship stage, a finding that has persisted over time (MacDonald and O'Brien 2011; Volden, Wiseman, and Wittmer 2016), within congressional districts (Gerrity, Osborn, and Mendez 2007), in the US Senate (Swers 2013), and on global issues (Angevine 2017).[1]

Beyond giving priority to legislation that matters most to women, scholars have found that women members are more likely than men to invoke gendered rhetoric when they speak on their chamber's floor, demonstrating the distinct value of women's voices in congressional

1. Volden, Wiseman, and Wittmer (2016) find that most women's issues are raised more frequently by women members (House 93rd–110th), but women's proposals meet with less success than those of men.

debate (Levy, Tien, and Aves 2001; Swers 2002, 2013; Osborn and Mendez 2010; Pearson and Dancey 2011; Swers and Kim 2013; Dietrich, Hayes, and O'Brien 2017). These analyses of gender differences in rhetoric begin to capture the more nuanced ways in which gender shapes legislative behaviors in Congress, but remain limited in their examination of the motivations behind women's legislative behavior.

In the early 1990s, the Center for American Women and Politics (CAWP) took a different approach to investigating the relationship between descriptive and substantive representation among women in Congress. Through interviews with 43 of 54 women serving in the 103rd Congress and 38 of 58 women serving in the 104th Congress, CAWP identified multiple ways in which gender shaped the experiences, approach, and impact of women in office (Dodson et al. 1995; Hawkesworth et al. 2001). For example, CAWP found that nearly every congresswoman interviewed reported feeling a special responsibility to act on behalf of women. In addition, women introduced new issues to the congressional agenda and brought their distinctive life experiences and perspectives as women to their consideration of legislation (Dodson et al. 1995; Hawkesworth et al. 2001; Carroll 2002). This research provided key insights into some of the ways women's increasing presence in Congress—and in elected office more generally—can make a difference.

Our current research on the 114th Congress builds on CAWP's previous study of women in Congress, focusing on congresswomen's own perceptions and views of their jobs and their contributions in a different era and political context—one characterized by extreme gridlock, intense partisanship, proportionately few women within the majority party, and a high level of public disapproval of Congress. Increased partisanship has empowered party leadership and centralized legislative decision-making, further limiting the ability of individual members to influence the policy process. We examine gender dynamics in what can be considered a very hard test case for finding evidence that gender matters—that is, in a congressional environment that makes it especially difficult for women (or perhaps any member of Congress) to provide effective representation and have a meaningful impact on public policy.

RACE, INTERSECTIONALITY, AND REPRESENTATION

Some past scholarship has focused on race/ethnicity and representation. Initially concerned with whether Black legislators were best situated to advocate for constituents of their shared racial background, this literature has expanded to encompass other minority groups, most notably Latinos (Swain 1995; Canon 1999; Tate 2003; Casellas 2011; Minta 2011; Hero and Preuhs 2012; Rouse 2013; Wallace 2014; Wilson 2017). The expectation that descriptive representation by race has substantive consequences has largely found confirmation. Moreover, minority officials can affect public attitudes and participation directly and indirectly (Bobo and Gilliam 1990; Gay 2001, 2002; Bowen and Clark 2014).

Scholars focused on the behavior of women of color in politics have found that typical studies of either gender and representation or race and representation fail to account for the experiences of women of color; most work takes either gender or race as the central category of analysis. Yet these categories are usually operating simultaneously, meaning that legislative life and the representational relationship cannot be fully understood without attention to both categories.

Beginning with Kimberlé Crenshaw's pathbreaking work (Crenshaw 1989, 1991), scholarship has increasingly applied an intersectional lens to a wide range of political phenomena, including legislatures. Such works often treat race and gender categories as analytically inseparable and even mutually constitutive (King 1988; McCall 2005; Junn and Brown 2008), although some scholars have allowed for the effects of race and gender separately as well as intersectionally (see, e.g., Weldon 2006).

A growing body of work investigates the unique ways that women from minority racial and ethnic backgrounds run for and win office, as well as how they behave once elected (Bedolla, Wong, and Tate 2014; Bratton, Haynie, and Reingold 2006; Fraga et al. 2006; Bejarano 2013; Minta and Brown 2014; Brown 2014; Brown and Gershon 2016; Hardy-Fanta et al. 2016). Such work demonstrates that neither gender studies nor race/ethnicity studies adequately capture the experiences of minority women

(Cohen 2003; Fraga et al. 2006; Reingold and Smith 2012; Rouse, Swers, and Parrott 2013; Brown and Gershon 2016); these works also reveal the prominence of subjects who are either non-Hispanic White women on the one hand (in gender research) or men of color on the other hand (in race/ethnicity research). It would be a mistake to treat women of color as a monolithic group, however. Indeed, Nadia Brown (2014) has shown that Black women bring a collective identity as Black women, as well as their unique personal identities, to their roles in state legislatures.

Other works have further complicated the concepts of gender and race by investigating the ways that race and gender shape life within legislative institutions with consequences for power, influence, and policymaking (Smooth 2001, 2008). Interviews from CAWP's study of women in the 103rd and 104th Congresses were used by Mary Hawkesworth to detail the "silencing, stereotyping, enforced invisibility, exclusion, marginalization, challenges to epistemic authority, refusals to hear, legislative topic extinctions, and *pendejo* games" to which congresswomen of color were subject (2003: 546). Describing these processes as key to the "racing-gendering" of Congress, Hawkesworth illuminates the different ways in which institutional biases alter women's congressional experience, power, and influence.

More women of color served in the 114th Congress than served in the mid-1990s, when the interviews Hawkesworth (2003) analyzes were conducted. In fact, women of color represented just less than 40% of Democratic women in the 114th Congress. With a record number of women of color serving in Congress today, we have an unprecedented opportunity to understand their perspectives and draw comparisons across subgroups of women. We attempt to illustrate the ways in which they contribute to all aspects of congressional deliberations. We also try to highlight the ways in which they bring perspectives that often diverge from those of other women, both as women of color whose intersectional identities and experiences differ from the intersectional identities and experiences of the White women with whom they serve and as members of distinctive racial and ethnic minority groups whose experiences differ from each other.

Institutional Presence and Power

For 128 years, the US Congress was a political institution exclusive to men. Jeanette Rankin (R-MT) was elected to the US House of Representatives in 1917, becoming the first woman to serve in Congress three years before women had the right to vote nationwide. Between Rankin's swearing in and the 114th Congress, 307 women served as voting members of Congress.[2] That number is just 2.5% of the 12,177 members who had served since Congress convened in March 1789.[3] Of the 307 women members, 198 were Democrats and 109 were Republicans. Fifty-four were women of color, with the first woman of color, Patsy Mink (D-HI), elected to Congress in 1964. Still, Black, Latina, and Asian American/Pacific Islander women represented just 6.2% of all members serving from 2015 to 2017 (see Table 1.1). As of 2017, two states—Mississippi and Vermont—had never sent a woman to Washington, DC.

In nearly 100 years of service, and especially in the past few decades, women have made important strides in congressional representation and power. Just 30 years before the 114th Congress began, women were less than 5% of members; two women served in the Senate and 23 women served in the House. At that time, just one woman of color, Katie Hall (D-IN), was a member of Congress. When the 114th Congress convened, 20 women served as US senators, 84 women as US representatives, and four as nonvoting US delegates. Women of color represented just under one-third of all women members, including the first Black Republican woman, Representative Mia Love (R-UT), who was elected in 2014. All but one of the women of color served in the House. Senator Mazie Hirono (D-HI) was the only woman of color in the US Senate in the 114th Congress and only the second woman of color ever to serve in that chamber.[4]

2. Five more women have served as nonvoting delegates.

3. This does not include statutory representatives, such as resident commissioners and delegates. http://history.house.gov/Institution/Total-Members/Total-Members/.

4. Carol Moseley Braun (D-IL), a Black woman, was the first woman of color elected to the US Senate, serving from 1993 to 1999.

Table 1.1. WOMEN IN THE 114TH CONGRESS BY RACE/ETHNICITY, PARTY,
AND CHAMBER

	House		Senate		Total	
	Democrat	Republican	Democrat	Republican	Democrat	Republican
Asian/ Pacific Islander	5	0	1	0	6	0
Black	17	1	0	0	17	1
Latina	7	2	0	0	7	2
White	33	19	13	6	46	25
Total	62	22	14	6	76	28

SOURCE: Center for American Women and Politics. Nonvoting delegates are not included in these counts. Representative Colleen Hanabusa (D-HI) is also not included but served from November 14, 2016, to the conclusion of the 114th Congress after winning a special election on November 8, 2016.

Despite increases over time, the progress of women's numerical representation has been slow. As a result of the election in 1992, popularly referred to as the "Year of the Woman," women nearly doubled their representation in Congress. However, that election's increase remains the largest jump in women's congressional representation to date. As Figure 1.1 shows, the number and proportion of women in Congress have risen incrementally since 1993. While the number of women members reached a new high in the 114th Congress, their presence increased by less than one percentage point from the 113th Congress, and they remained less than one-fifth of all members.

As the 114th Congress convened, gender disparities in representation were apparent across the two political parties. Figure 1.2 shows that these differences are consistent with the trends over time; the number of Democratic women has outpaced the growth of Republican women members for the past few decades. Although the total number of Republican women increased by two in the Senate and three in the House from 2014 to 2015, women remained fewer than 10% of all congressional Republicans. The number of Democratic women dropped by

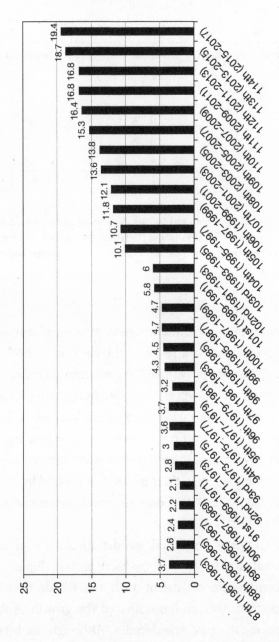

Figure 1.1 Percentage of Women in Congress, 1961–2017.
SOURCE: Center for American Women and Politics.

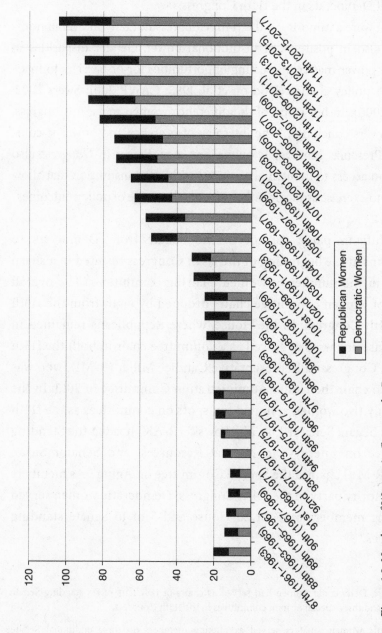

Figure 1.2 Number of Women in Congress by Party, 1961–2017.

SOURCE: Center for American Women and Politics.

one following the 2014 elections, but women nevertheless constituted one-third of all Democrats in the 114th Congress.

Women were a minority in the 114th Congress not only in overall numbers, but also in positions of institutional power. Gender disparities in positional power matter in creating opportunities for or barriers to institutional or policy change (Dodson et al. 1995; CAWP 2001; Swers 2002; Dodson 2006). In her study of the difference women make in Congress, Michele Swers concludes, "The interplay of presence and power is complex . . . Presence, however is only a first step. Power in Congress also depends on access to influential positions within the institution that allow members to exercise strategic influence over the shape of policy outcomes" (2002: 134).

The shift in party control in the Senate from Democrats to Republicans at the beginning of the 114th Congress resulted in a sharp decrease in the number of women chairing committees. The overall number of women committee chairs dropped by eight from the 113th to the 114th Congress. In the House, where Republicans remained in control, just one woman served as a committee chair in both the 113th and 114th Congresses: Representative Candice Miller (R-MI), who was selected to chair the House Administration Committee in 2013. In the Senate only two women assumed top spots on committees as the 114th Congress began; Senator Lisa Murkowski (R-AK) headed the Standing Committee on Energy and Natural Resources, and Senator Susan Collins (R-ME) chaired the Special Committee on Aging.[5] As members of the minority party in the 114th Congress, Democratic women served as ranking members on 7 of 20 House and 5 of 16 Senate standing committees.[6]

---

5. In contrast, Democratic women had served as chairs or co-chairs of six standing Senate committees and three special or joint committees in the 113th Congress.

6. Democratic women senators served as ranking members on three additional Senate committees in the 114th Congress: the Select Committees on Ethics (Barbara Boxer, CA [co-chair]), Intelligence (Dianne Feinstein, CA), and Aging (Claire McCaskill, MO). Senator Amy Klobuchar (MN) and Representative Carolyn Maloney (NY) served as the ranking Senate and House Democrats on the Joint Economic Committee.

Representative Nancy Pelosi (D-CA) retained her position as House Democratic Leader in the 114th Congress, and Representative Cathy McMorris Rodgers (R-WA) served as House Republican Conference Chair. In the Senate, Patty Murray (D-WA) served as Democratic Conference Secretary, the only woman in either party to hold a top party leadership post in the Senate. In addition to the leadership positions listed for both parties by the House and Senate clerks, congressional party caucuses select members to serve in lower-level leadership posts. Whether by serving on whip teams, steering and policy committees, electoral committees, or in similar roles, women in Congress have found additional opportunities for gaining influence.

Party Polarization in Congress

Scholarship on the partisan nature of Congress has focused extensively on the concept of party polarization, sparking debates over how it is defined and measured and seeking to evaluate its effects on congressional processes and outcomes. David Rohde's (1991) study of partisanship in the House of Representatives was among the first to comprehensively evaluate the presence, measures, and outcomes of party polarization in Congress. According to his concept of conditional party government, the degree to which parties matter in congressional business is related to the level of homogeneity or consensus among party members. Growing internal consensus, and thus strength, can fuel and be fueled by parties' ideological separation. As Marc Hetherington argues, strong party government is characterized by wide separation between parties and high homogenization within them, yielding party voting as a bloc and increased polarization overall (2009: 201). Keith Poole and Howard Rosenthal refer to this as the "spatial theory" of party polarization, whereby parties are polarized when they are "far apart on policy issues, and the party members [are] tightly clustered around the party mean" (2007: 105). They evaluate this theory by using their DW-NOMINATE scores of congressional roll-call votes, identifying the ideological positions of individual members over time.

Using these data, Nolan McCarty, Keith Poole, and Howard Rosenthal (2006) found that the parties in government were farther apart than at any point since the US Civil War. That separation has continued, with more recent evaluations revealing even larger gaps between party means and "asymmetric polarization" where Republican members have moved even farther to the right than Democrats have moved to the left (McCarty 2012; Theriault and Rohde 2011; Theriault 2006, 2013). Sean Theriault confirms that "polarization in the Senate almost perfectly reflects House polarization," demonstrating that this reality is not distinct to Congress's lower chamber (2006: 484).

Hetherington concludes, "Little doubt remains that elites are polarized today," but emphasizes that these data reflect the growing starkness of party differences, not necessarily clustering at the poles of ideological distribution (2009: 415). This point is important, as it has led to scholarly debate over whether or not the phenomenon we are both observing and evaluating is better termed "party distinctiveness" instead of "party polarization" (Lee 2015: 263). As Frances Lee summarizes in her review of existing literature:

> The evidence for increased party distinctiveness is unequivocal and ubiquitous, as well as highly consequential for the operation of the U.S. political system. But whether the parties have polarized in the spatial sense of the term is far more ambiguous. (2015: 267)

She offers a more complicated definition of party polarization in Congress, arguing that polarization can be amplified in practice (e.g., message votes) even if members and parties are not any more polarized in ideological positioning (Lee 2015: 263). Overall, the loss of ideological overlap among members of Congress, tied to party unity in voting, has been the clearest indicator of party polarization in the modern Congress (Theriault 2006; Pew 2014; Lee 2015).

While party polarization in Congress may be greatest—at least by these measures—in recent history, many scholars have noted that its presence may be the norm rather than the exception in congressional history (Lee

2015: 262). Han and Brady (2007) argue that it was the relative lack of party polarization in the postwar period of the 1950s and the slow replacement of members that followed it that created the "unusually bipartisan era" of the middle to late 20th century. They show this by using DW-NOMINATE scores, wherein median differences between parties declined immediately after World War II but were restored to prewar levels in the 1980s (Han and Brady 2007: 509–11). Sarah Binder notes that by 2012 the distance between parties was nearly equivalent to what it had been before the 20th century, concluding, "It is not clear whether current levels of polarization are going to subside anytime soon" (2014: 17).

THE 114TH CONGRESS AND PARTY POLARIZATION

Just as Senators Murkowski (R-AK) and Collins (R-ME) encountered a new type of US Senate on a cold day in January 2016, they faced a new institutional reality a year prior when the 114th Congress convened on January 6, 2015. For the first time since 2007, Republicans held the majority in the Senate. They also retained and expanded their majority in the House,[7] marking the first Congress since the 109th (2005–2007) in which Republicans controlled both chambers. But hopes for a more effective Congress[8] were short-lived, as the 114th Congress proved to be the third

---

7. The 114th Congress opened with the largest number of Republican House members since 1931. The Senate had the most Republicans serving since 2001.

8. Entering "America's New Congress," as GOP leaders called it, Senate Majority Leader Mitch McConnell (R-KY) and Speaker of the House John Boehner (R-OH) vowed to "get Congress going." They published a joint op-ed in the *Wall Street Journal* the morning after Election Day 2014, vowing to "prove the skeptics wrong" and "restore an era . . . where members of the minority party in both chambers are given the opportunity to participate in the process of governing" (Boehner and McConnell 2014). Senator McConnell (R-KY) pledged to return to a five-day workweek, allow for more floor debate, and restore power to committee chairs. He promised in his first postelection press conference, "We're going to pass legislation," adding, "This gridlock and dysfunction can be ended" (Hulse 2014). Even some Democrats shared their hope for a more effective Congress in 2015. Senate Minority Whip Dick Durbin (D-IL) told reporters, "We want to reach agreement as much as possible," but remained skeptical of McConnell's promise of a more open legislative process (Howard 2015).

least productive Congress in nearly seven decades, enacting fewer pieces of legislation than every Congress between the 80th (1947–48) and the 112th (2011–13) ("Vital Statistics" 2017). In its first year, the 114th Congress passed some major pieces of legislation, including an overdue reauthorization of the Elementary and Secondary Education Act, a five-year transportation funding bill, the USA Freedom Act, a long-debated bill fixing the formula for Medicare repayments, the Justice for Victims of Trafficking Act, and a bill giving trade promotion authority (known as "fast-track") to the president that would prevent Senate filibusters of trade deals. In its second year, the most notable achievement came in the session's final days; passed in a bipartisan fashion, the 21st Century Cures Act provided the National Institutes of Health with additional funding for medical research and innovation and included resources to target the opioid crisis, cancer, and brain diseases like Alzheimer's.

The unexpected resignation of House Speaker John Boehner (R-OH) in October 2015, coinciding with the run-up to a highly contentious presidential election and a forthcoming congressional election, contributed to greater unpredictability in House and Senate business in the second session of the 114th Congress. In September 2016, members barely avoided a government shutdown when they approved a stopgap funding bill (in the form of a continuing resolution) instead of a formal budget resolution for fiscal year 2017, ensuring that early promises by Senator Mitch McConnell (R-KY) that the congressional budgeting and appropriations processes would proceed in "regular order" in the 114th Congress would not be kept.

Partisan politics remained more common and characteristic than bipartisanship in the 114th Congress, creating conditions more conducive to gridlock than productivity. Party unity in member voting remained high ("2015 Vote Studies" 2015; "2016 Vote Studies" 2016), but votes are not the only measures of polarization. Gridlock was also evident in bringing bills to the floor. Perhaps the clearest and most public examples of this type of partisan gridlock concerned gun control legislation, which the Republican leadership refused to schedule for a vote, and confirmation of

President Obama's nominee for a vacancy on the Supreme Court, which Senate Majority Leader Mitch McConnell refused to move forward from the time of Merrick Garland's nomination in February 2016 to the end of the Congress in January 2017.

Partisanship was also on full display amid a series of investigations that persisted throughout the 114th Congress, including those conducted by the House Select Committee on Benghazi, focused on potential wrongdoing by Hillary Clinton while secretary of state, and the Select Investigative Panel on Infant Lives, launched by the House leadership in the fall of 2015 in response to videos (later determined to be falsified) accusing Planned Parenthood of selling fetal tissue. Some observers saw both investigations as efforts motivated by electoral politics leading up to the 2016 elections that detracted from congressional business.

Finally, the polarized environment in Congress was arguably fueled by, or at least reflective of, greater polarization among the electorate. In a 2016 report, the Pew Research Center found significant jumps in citizens' unfavorable evaluations of the party to which they did not belong. In fact, 45% of Republicans and 41% of Democrats told Pew that the other party "threatens the nation's well-being." These ratings increased from 2014 to 2016, demonstrating a growth in mass partisan polarization (by these measures) over the course of the 114th Congress.

WOMEN REPRESENTING IN AN ERA OF PARTY POLARIZATION

How do women navigate a polarized political context like that of the 114th Congress? The popular narrative that women are more likely than men to work across party lines stems, at least in part, from some of the prominent successes women earned together in previous congresses, particularly on gender-specific issues (Dodson et al. 1995; CAWP 2001). This narrative also comes from women members themselves, who identify collaboration and collegiality as among their distinctive strengths. Finally, both members and media share stories that detail both causes and effects of women's bipartisanship.

Perhaps the most frequently cited evidence of women's bipartisanship in recent years is the role women senators played in ending a government shutdown in 2013. One week after the shutdown began in October 2013, Senator Susan Collins (R-ME) took to the Senate floor, asking her "Democratic and Republican colleagues to come together" to "legislate responsibly and in good faith" (qtd. in Newton-Small 2013). Two other women—Senators Barbara Mikulski (D-MD) and Lisa Murkowski (R-AK)—spoke up after her, expressing their support for a bipartisan compromise. Over the next week, a group of about 13 senators worked on a plan to reopen the government. Women, who constituted just one-fifth of all members of the Senate, made up about half of the working group (Weisman and Steinhauer 2013). Most important, they were credited with getting the ball rolling, offering a substantive solution, and expressing an openness to collaboration that benefited from the relationships they had developed with each other over years. News reports detailed how the Senate women held one of their famous bipartisan dinners the night before a group of Senate women spoke in unity on the chamber floor. The women also credited each other in post-shutdown interviews, noting how they worked together to break the impasse. Similarly, their male colleagues praised women for being key actors in getting Congress back to work, fueling the narrative that women are more likely than men to prioritize productivity over partisanship.

This example points to the value of relationship-building as a potential antidote to partisan polarization, but scholars have cautioned against overstating that effect. In her study of women in the US Senate, Swers emphasizes, "While women may socialize and periodically collaborate on policy across party lines, Senate business is organized and dominated by the political parties" (2013: 243). Lawless and Theriault distinguish legislators' propensity for collegiality from their likelihood of forging compromise. Analyzing participation in social activities alongside members' willingness to present obstacles to legislating via procedural votes or amendments, they conclude that while women are more likely than men to engage socially with peers of all parties, "women (and men) are first and foremost partisan creatures" (Lawless and Theriault 2016: 17).

Moreover, heightened partisanship has had significant effects on the ability of women to pursue a collective agenda, particularly one committed to acting for women. While CAWP reports detailed the legislative work that went into creating conditions for bipartisan collaboration among women more than two decades ago, similar efforts and successes have proved increasingly difficult as partisan divides among women members have grown (Hawkesworth et al. 2001; Swers 2002, 2013; Dodson 2006; Frederick 2009). As Swers demonstrates in her in-depth analysis of women in the US Senate, "Partisan polarization and the resulting demands for party loyalty in the contemporary Senate affect senators' calculations about whether to emphasize policy preferences based on gender" (2013: 4). Those demands of party loyalty may put even more constraint on women who represent a minority in the majority than on those congresswomen in the less powerful minority party (Swers 2002; Dodson 2006; Volden, Wiseman, and Wittmer 2013). Volden, Wiseman, and Wittmer (2013) find that women in the majority party have become *less* effective in advancing sponsored legislation as Congress has become more polarized, while minority-party women have had more success than minority-party men in keeping their bills alive.

In this study, we examine women members' perceptions of their opportunities to work across party lines, as well as the constraints on their ability to do so, as part of our effort to provide a comprehensive account of how women attempt to have a meaningful impact on public policy and provide effective representation in an era of gridlock and party polarization.

OUR METHODOLOGICAL APPROACH

In this book we illuminate the motivations and priorities of women in the 114th Congress and detail the ways in which they navigated the

partisan, gendered, and racial dynamics of the House and Senate to effectively represent their constituents and influence legislation. To do so,
we rely heavily on in-depth interviews with women representatives and
senators.

Previous research on women in Congress has focused largely on
analyzing secondary indicators of member priorities and positions, such
as roll-call votes, bill sponsorship and co-sponsorship, or floor speeches
(Welch 1985; Dolan 1997; Norton 1999; Levy, Tien, and Aves 2001; Shogan
2001; Swers 2002; Walsh 2002; Schwindt-Bayer and Corbetta 2004;
Gerrity, Osborn, and Mendez 2007; Frederick 2009, 2013, 2015; Osborn
and Mendez 2010; Simon and Palmer 2010; MacDonald and O'Brien
2011; Swers and Kim 2013; Pearson and Dancey 2013; Volden, Wiseman,
and Wittmer 2013, 2016; Dietrich, Hayes, and O'Brien 2017). Also, past
studies have focused on women serving in either the House or the Senate,
but not both.

Few scholars have spoken directly to women members of Congress to
understand their approaches to representation, their policy preferences
and priorities, and/or their experiences within Congress (for exceptions,
see studies based on earlier CAWP research: Dodson et al. 1995;
Hawkesworth et al. 2001; Carroll 2002; Hawkesworth 2003; Dodson
2006). A major departure from past research is that our evidence is based
on the actual first-person voices and perspectives of women members.
Moreover, instead of limiting our analysis of women's influence to a
predetermined set of "women's issues," we let the congresswomen we
interviewed articulate the issues and sites on which they believe they
have the most distinct impact.

While our first-person, interview-based approach provides the most
comprehensive overview to date of how women serving in Congress perceive their roles, contributions, and experiences, we make no judgments
about the accuracy of their perceptions. Although some readers may view
this as a limitation of the approach we have chosen, we maintain that there
is inherent value in understanding how these women see themselves and
assess their impact.

A total of 108 women (20 senators, 84 representatives, and 4 delegates) served in the 114th Congress. We interviewed 83, or 77%, of these women members between September 2015 and April 2017, with all but a few of the interviews completed by the end of August 2016. The interviews ranged between 12 and 77 minutes in length, with the average interview lasting 32 minutes. The vast majority of the semistructured interviews were conducted in person in members' Capitol Hill offices, with a few conducted in other locations or by phone to accommodate members' schedules.[9] All interviews were on the record, but members could choose to go off the record at any point during the interview. Questions focused on representational goals, policy priorities and achievements, and perceptions of gender and race dynamics within the 114th Congress.

Our attention to women serving in both the House and Senate departs from most past research on women and politics. We compare our findings across chambers where possible, although we are constrained by the smaller number of women serving in the Senate than in the House and our lower response rate among Republican women senators than among Democratic women senators.

The information that we gathered from more than 40 hours of interviews is unmatched by that of any recent study of congressional representation—women's or men's. Moreover, the findings presented in this book demonstrate the value of qualitative approaches to understanding important aspects of legislative representation, particularly in a congressional context where polarization and gridlock encourage unorthodox behaviors that fall outside traditional procedural measures of member behavior. Our approach also provides valuable insights into the ways in which congresswomen both experience and engage gender and race, among other identities, in their legislative work. We seek to illustrate how and where categories of identity and experience operate

9. See Appendix A for more details on our methodology, including interview questions, and Appendix B for a complete listing of the congresswomen we interviewed.

simultaneously for women members, complicating prevailing narratives and highlighting the value of challenging single-axis analyses of gender and representation. These categories of identity operate within a congressional institution that is at the same time gendered, raced, and partisan. These dynamics shape both formal and informal rules, norms, structures, and processes, creating diverse conditions for those tasked with navigating them. Our study engages this complexity and—we hope—sets the stage for more fully intersectional analyses of congressional representation.

CHAPTER OVERVIEW

Throughout this book, we analyze women members within a distinctive historical and institutional context, one characterized by slow but steady gender progress and heightened party polarization. Although our work builds upon research that examines whether and where women and men differ in legislative behavior, it focuses on explaining how women in Congress navigate an institution that is gendered, raced, and partisan and why they behave the way they do. Women of the 114th Congress saw unprecedented opportunities but sometimes faced seemingly insurmountable obstacles. They navigated an institution that was simultaneously changing and stagnant. Most important, they engaged and influenced the institution in ways critical to documenting the story of this Congress and contributing to our understanding of women in Congress throughout US history.

In the remaining chapters, we present the unprecedented insights that our interviews provided into women's congressional representation in the modern era. In Chapter 2, we examine how women members of the 114th Congress see themselves as representatives. We explore the range of constituencies and interests they feel a commitment to represent, how life experiences and identities affect their work in Congress, and their commitment to work on behalf of women and other underrepresented groups.

In Chapter 3, we outline the challenges women confront in entering and navigating a male-dominated and majority-White institution but note the ways in which congresswomen are largely undeterred by them. While they share experiences that serve as reminders of the masculine dominance of Congress, they also point to the opportunities their service provides them, including those specific to being women members.

Chapters 4 and 5 focus on congresswomen's perceptions and navigation of partisanship in the 114th Congress. In Chapter 4, we review members' perceptions and evidence of institutional polarization, providing important context for an evaluation of the popular view that women are more likely than men to reach across party lines. We also outline women's strategies for navigating a Congress characterized by party polarization. Chapter 5 examines the relationships that members build, across and within gender groups, that have the potential to foster bipartisanship in legislative behavior and outcomes. We find that most women in Congress believe women are more bipartisan than their male colleagues.

In Chapters 6 and 7, we outline the sites in which women say that their presence in Congress matters. More specifically, in Chapter 6, we evaluate the influence women have on policy agendas and debates, highlighting the issues, perspectives, and voices that would have been missing from the legislative process were it not for the diversity of women serving in the 114th Congress. In Chapter 7, we argue that the significance of women's congressional representation is not limited to legislative accomplishments. Congresswomen share with us the ways in which they disrupt the image of who can and should be in Congress, as well as the ways in which congressional power is exercised.

We conclude by discussing the implications of our findings for both scholars and practitioners, particularly those advocating for greater gender parity in political representation. Our findings contribute to the case for women's political representation, even where they reveal similarities in experience, behavior, and influence with men. This book does not assume any inherent or universal gender difference in the policy priorities, legislative behavior, or institutional engagement of men and women in Congress. Instead, and drawn from first-person perspectives of congresswomen, it highlights sites where gender appears to function in distinct ways for women in the male-dominated institution of Congress. Moreover, it rejects any notion of universality *among* women, emphasizing the importance of understanding that women in Congress are as diverse and complex as their male counterparts.

2

Representation

Representation is the primary responsibility of any member of Congress. First and foremost, voters send officials to Washington to act on their behalf and enact policy that will further their interests.

Political scientists and political theorists have written extensively on the subject of political representation, exploring multiple aspects of the relationship between representatives and those they represent. Perhaps the most well-known and historically enduring theoretical distinction is that between *delegate* and *trustee* conceptions of representation. The delegate conception, as advocated by James Madison among others, requires that representatives follow the preferences of their constituents, while the trustee conception, as espoused most notably by Edmund Burke, dictates that representatives rely on their own judgment regardless of the preferences of constituents (Eulau et al. 1959; Rehfeld 2009).

Hannah Pitkin (1967) advanced the theoretical consideration of political representation by identifying four distinct views of representation—formalistic, descriptive, symbolic, and substantive. Her work has been very influential among scholars of women and politics who have been especially interested in the relationship between descriptive representation, the extent to which a representative resembles or "stands for" those he or she represents, and substantive representation, the extent to which a representative "acts for" the represented. In particular, empirically oriented scholars have been concerned with investigating whether increased descriptive representation of women leads to increased substantive representation of women. Do women representatives not only "stand for" women but also "act for" them? More recent literature has further complicated the way we understand representation, proposing more forms of representation and ways of representing (e.g., Mansbridge 2003; Saward 2006).

This chapter examines the motivations and perceptions of the women who serve in the US House and Senate. Although we did not ask specifically about the forms of representation just referenced, we did want to explore how congresswomen see their roles as political representatives. Whom do they feel a responsibility to represent? And what considerations most strongly influence how they see their representational responsibilities? The choices and activities of women in Congress—the committees on which they serve, the political relationships they form, the legislative priorities they pursue—are all likely to be strongly influenced by their perceptions of their representational responsibilities. And so we begin our analysis of the roles and contributions of women members of Congress with their views of themselves as political representatives.

Every member of Congress understands that his or her primary responsibility is to his or her district as a whole (or state, in the case of senators)— what Richard Fenno (1978) calls the "geographic constituency." After all, representatives must run for reelection every two years and senators every six, and the desire for reelection is a major factor ensuring that members are concerned with satisfying their constituents (Mayhew 1974; Fenno 1978). If too many voters believe that their member of Congress is not adequately representing their interests, that member risks being defeated in the next election and replaced by someone new.

Polls have found that a majority or near majority of voters believe that the US representative from their district is doing a good job, even as their evaluations of the performance of Congress overall have reached record lows. For example, in monthly polls from January 2014 through June 2016, Gallup found that the proportion of the public approving of the way Congress was handling its job ranged between 11 and 20%. In contrast, just a few weeks before the 2014 congressional elections, a much larger proportion, 54%, expressed approval when asked whether they "approve or disapprove of the way the representative from your congressional district is handling his or her job" (Gallup, "Congress and the Public").

This discrepancy between the level of approval for individual members and that for Congress as a whole suggests that most members are indeed attentive to the overall needs and interests of the districts or states they represent. But members also have life experiences, personal preferences, and political commitments that may affect the policies to which they devote their attention. And sometimes these interests take them well beyond the borders of their district or state (Carroll 2002).

The complex interplay of factors affecting representational perceptions and behavior was evident, for example, in our interview with Senator Amy Klobuchar (D-MN). She summed up the mix of concerns that shapes how she sees her role and priorities as a senator as follows: "[T]here are things that come out of my state . . . ; things that I'm interested in as a policy matter; and then . . . sometimes you're just called upon to do something and it's not what you expected you would be doing." She pointed to "steel workers getting laid off" as an example of an issue of concern to her because it directly affects the lives of people in her state. Meanwhile, personal interests led her to get involved with legislation on Cuba and sex trafficking. Senator Klobuchar explained, "I'm leading the embargo bill. Yes, my state has interests, but it is a lot bigger than that. It's a foreign policy issue that I care about." And as for sex trafficking, "we have some of it but it's not like we're the state with the most or something. And that is an issue that really came from my background as a prosecutor and what I've seen and how I feel that if we don't stand up for them [the victims of sex trafficking], no one will." Finally, Klobuchar's priorities as a senator are influenced by a leadership role she has assumed since her election to the Senate. Early in her Senate career, Democratic Majority Leader Harry Reid appointed Klobuchar to co-chair the Canada–United States Interparliamentary Group (Klobuchar 2015: 268), and in this capacity she is "always pushing things with Canada and our relationship." She has taken on this role "because I was given that power. I do have a border with them [Canada], but I don't think I would be doing it otherwise."

The legislative priorities and actions of women serving in the 114th Congress, like those of Senator Klobuchar, were shaped by how they viewed their roles as representatives. And as with Senator Klobuchar, their views of their representational roles were influenced by a number of considerations.

To develop a more comprehensive understanding of how women members of Congress perceived their representational responsibilities, we asked each woman we interviewed whether, in addition to representing her district or state as a whole, she felt a commitment to work in Congress for particular people or interests inside or outside her district. Only a couple of women members suggested that they did not. The answers of the other congresswomen, along with additional information they provided over the course of their interviews, provide a rich and textured portrait of how women serving in the 114th Congress viewed their jobs as elected representatives.

THE ROLE OF GEOGRAPHY IN REPRESENTATION

The longest-serving woman member of the House of Representatives in the 114th Congress, Representative Marcy Kaptur (D-OH), noted, "I always try to make sure that what I do has deep taproots in my district." The comments of many of the congresswomen we interviewed suggest that they share Kaptur's commitment to be ever-attentive to the interests of their geographic district or state. US senators generally have larger and more multifaceted geographic constituencies than do US House members, except in the seven states (Alaska, Delaware, Montana, North Dakota, South Dakota, Vermont, and Wyoming) that have only one US representative. Nevertheless, the women we interviewed from both chambers were similarly and strongly committed to representing their geographic constituencies.

Richard Fenno has observed that "members feel more accountable, and doubtless are more responsive, to some of their constituents than to others" (1978: 234). He has argued that members conceive of their districts as a "nest of concentric circles," consisting of different constituencies, with the *reelection constituency*, composed of those perceived as likely to vote for the representative, and the *primary constituency*, composed of a representative's strongest supporters, nested within the legally bounded *geographic constituency.*

Although members of Congress could be expected to pay closer attention to those narrower reelection and primary constituencies, a few of the women members made a special point of underscoring that they have an obligation to all the constituents in their districts or states, not just to the people who vote for them. As Representative Loretta Sanchez (D-CA) explained, "[T]he people who elect me come first and foremost. And not just the people who elect me, but everybody who lives in my district, whether they vote or not, whether they're capable of voting or not . . . If we were only going for voters, for example, we would never do anything for kids [since] by definition they can't vote." Similarly, Representative Chellie Pingree (D-ME) observed:

[W]hen you get elected to public office, you represent basically everyone who lives or has an interest in your district. It's funny because sometimes I'll run into someone or I'll meet them and they will say, "Well I didn't vote for you, so I'm not sure you want to hear what I have to say." And I'll say, "You know, it sort of doesn't matter if somebody votes for me or they support all my ideas." . . . [I]t's sort of like I love all my children equally.

Nevertheless, many women did single out key interests or groups within their districts to which they devote particular attention in their congressional work. The range of these interests and groups illustrates the diversity of districts the women represented geographically and demographically.

Senator Debbie Stabenow (D-MI), who represents a state bordering four of the Great Lakes, explained, "I am a very passionate longtime leader in Great Lakes issues, for instance. We have 20% of the world's freshwater. . . around our state, and it's really our way of life as well as about our economy. So I am deeply involved in that." Representative Cynthia Lummis (R-WY), the lone representative from her state, also stressed the importance of natural resources. She said of her constituents:

So the issues that they care about are the issues that I work on the most. So that is water [and] land quality and uses. It is forests and their health. It is the opportunity to have access to public lands. The national forests and national parks and BLM [Bureau of Land Management] lands and the way they're managed are important to the people I represent and to me.

First-term representative Elise Stefanik (R-NY) is particularly attentive to agricultural issues. Stefanik observed, "I have a lot of agriculture in my District. So . . . while I'm not on the Agriculture Committee . . . I'm constantly making sure that North Country farmers have a seat at the table when we're discussing agriculture policies." Similarly, Representative Ann Wagner (R-MO), who serves on the Financial Services Committee, is especially concerned with financial services:

St. Louis—and I represent the suburbs of St. Louis—is a big financial service sector . . . They call it the Wall Street of the West . . . [It is] home base to great companies like Wells Fargo, Edward Jones, Stifel Nicolaus, Scottrade, a lot of insurance and banking industries. And all the back channel jobs that come with that—anywhere from 85[,000] to 100,000 jobs that are really in this sector.

In a few cases, traumatic events in their districts have influenced the issues women members see themselves championing. As a congresswoman from the area most affected by the terrorist attack on the World Trade Center on September 9, 2011, Representative Carolyn Maloney (D-NY) noted that the geography of her district has exerted a distinctive and central influence on the way she sees her responsibilities as a representative. As she explained, "Even though almost every single state . . . and [so many] congressional districts sent people to 9/11, it is primarily this [the New York City] area." She continued:

We lost 3,000 people on 9/11. We've lost many more since because they worked in this environment with deadly toxins . . . , and they are sick and dying. And so I do a lot of work through my committees, but my signature bill probably was the James Zadroga 9/11 Health and Compensation Bill, which will bring a billion dollars to the city of New York and New Jersey and Connecticut.

Similarly, Representative Elizabeth Esty (D-CT) represents the district where Sandy Hook Elementary School, the scene of horrific gun violence in 2012, is located. The shooting there led her to be a strong advocate for gun control, "a role I wish I didn't have but I do. And however long it takes on that issue, I will be fighting for that, whether I'm in Congress or not, because I feel strongly about it."

Several of the women members with a strong military presence in their districts emphasized their commitment to represent active military members, military families, and/or veterans. For example, Representative Renee Ellmers (R-NC) explained, "I represent Fort Bragg, so national defense, national security . . . issues with our military, military families, and our veterans are very, very important." Similarly, Representative Gwen Graham (D-FL) noted, "My very first piece of legislation was the Veterans, Education, Training Act to help veterans as they transition from active duty status into veteran status with all the bureaucracy." She explained:

> We have a significant military presence in north Florida and . . . the first campaign event I went to as a newly announced candidate was . . . a very large opportunity for homeless veterans in north Florida to come together at the fairgrounds . . . [where] they're provided all types of services. And I was really taken aback by how many homeless veterans there were. And so I developed a particular commitment to helping in that area.

Representative Susan Davis (D-CA) reported that she "was very instrumental in working on the repeal of 'Don't Ask, Don't Tell,' because in San Diego that mattered to people. I have so many stories of people who were so marginalized in the service. And that wasn't right. And so I think that it really does make a big difference where you come from and your perspective."

A number of women members pointed to racial and ethnic groups within their districts or states whom they feel a special responsibility to represent. Of course, many African American and Latina congresswomen serve in majority-minority or other districts with sizable Black or Latino populations and, not surprisingly, representing those groups is an important component of how they see their jobs as representatives. As an example, Representative Ileana Ros-Lehtinen (R-FL), herself a Cuban immigrant, observed that the ethnic diversity in her district affects her constituent service as well as the policy stances she espouses. She explained, "I represent a district that is majority Hispanic . . . [C]onstituent service work is very important to me because a lot of these folks . . . come from Colombia, . . . Nicaragua, Venezuela, Brazil and we do a lot of immigration constituent work." But she also feels a responsibility to speak out on matters in their home countries, even when they are not directly related to congressional action. Ros-Lehtinen noted, "Sometimes there is a big disconnect between what my district constituents are involved in, interested in, and what is going on here in Congress. For example, I represent a lot of Colombian Americans, and I spoke today on the floor about the peace treaty that the Colombian government has with the FARC [the oldest and largest rebel group in Colombia], [making clear] that I'm against the peace treaty."

Similarly, Representative Loretta Sanchez (D-CA), who is herself Latina, emphasized her commitment to representing Latinos. But Sanchez, like several other congresswomen, expressed a commitment to work on behalf of a racial or ethnic group of which she herself was not a member. In addition to Latinos, Sanchez pointed to "the Vietnamese population at large. I have the largest Vietnamese population outside of Vietnam in the world . . . and . . . I am their Vietnamese congresswoman in the Congress." Likewise, Representative Judy Chu (D-CA) stressed her sense of responsibility to represent not only Asian Americans but all the diverse groups within her district. She explained:

Well, my greatest priority is representing my district, and my district is very diverse. I'm so proud of that because we have a large

population of Caucasians, Latinos, Asians, and we have a significant African American population. So it gives me the opportunity
to work on all those issues. For instance, with both the Latino and
the Asian population I've worked on immigration, and in fact my
greatest goal in coming to Congress in 2009 was to bring about comprehensive immigration reform . . . And I've been very, very active
on civil rights issues, in voting rights. I know how important that is
to everybody, but especially the African American population.

Non-Hispanic White women whose districts include ethnically diverse
populations also expressed their commitment to represent specific ethnic
groups. Representative Dina Titus (D-NV) observed that she has "a very
ethnically diverse district, so I'm very much involved in the immigration
issues . . . I feel a real obligation to help people who are here as immigrants."
Representative Debbie Dingell (D-MI) was quick to note, "I've got one
of the largest Arab American communities in the country." As a result,
she feels a commitment to represent their interests in the work she does.
Similarly, Senator Heidi Heitkamp (D-ND) finds it important to represent
the Native American community. She explained, "I've been very involved,
in part because North Dakota has one of the highest percentages of Native
Americans. And I've spent a lot of time working in Indian country, both in
public life and private life, [and consequently] feel a lot of sense of urgency
to address a lot of those issues."

A concern with representing specific constituencies within their districts
or states may often, or even usually, be the driving force behind the legislative priorities and actions of women in Congress. However, the representation of these district interests may have repercussions far beyond the
geographic areas these women represent. In this sense congresswomen
sometimes engage in and contribute to what Robert Weissberg (1978) has
termed "collective representation," acting in the interests of voters beyond
the boundaries of the representative's geographic district with whom
the elected official has no electoral connection. Unlike dyadic representation, illustrated by the examples above, in which congresswomen look
out for the interests of constituents who reside in their districts, collective

representation is concerned with how well Congress as an institution represents the entire American public. By acting on behalf of voters outside as well as inside their districts or states, women members contribute to the representation not only of their own electoral constituencies but also of the citizenry of the United States more broadly.

Representative Marcy Kaptur (D-OH) described this phenomenon of simultaneously representing and serving voters both inside and outside her district. She explained that her district constitutes a "lens" through which she approaches policy, but that the effects of those policies are often felt beyond the borders of her district. Kaptur illustrated this point with examples related to solar energy, agriculture, foreign affairs, and the establishment of the World War II Museum on the National Mall in Washington, DC. She explained the role that her district played in motivating her commitment to establishing the museum as follows:

> I've done a lot of work to serve the nation through the lens of my district. You look at the World War II Memorial that took us 17 years; that was our bill. And now it's the most popular memorial in Washington, with over 43 million visitors. But that came from knowing people in my district, from understanding their sacrifice, my own personal interest in history, but a recognition that something was really missing.

Similarly, Representative Martha Roby (R-AL) described how the work she does to meet the needs of the constituents who elected her also has implications well beyond her geographic district. She explained:

> I sit on the VA [Veterans' Affairs] committee, so working towards making sure that the VA is really meeting the needs of our veterans, not only in our district but across our country, is a big priority for me. Immigration reform is something else that is extremely important to my district, but I think very important for the country and the economic stability of our country . . . I also have . . . agriculture and forestry as the number one industry in our state, and so whereas

I've worked very hard to ensure that the farmers in Alabama's second district have in place good farm policy and a safety net that makes good fiscal, conservative sense, I know that the work that I do on behalf of them also has an impact across the country as well. So yes . . . this is a representative government and I'm here to work on behalf of the people that I represent, but clearly the work that I do on specific issues has . . . far more of a reach across the country.

Senator Kirsten Gillibrand (D-NY) described how issues that are brought to her attention by constituents in New York often lead to legislative initiatives that could affect voters across the country. She explained, "So sometimes an issue will help people everywhere, but I might get to know about it because New Yorkers brought it to my attention, and it usually breaks my heart and I have to fix it. I have to fix that problem. So a lot of my issues come through New Yorkers, but they are national issues."

THE ROLE OF PERSONAL EXPERIENCE AND IDENTITY IN REPRESENTATION

In addition to the important influence that factors related to their geographic districts have on how women in Congress see their jobs as representatives, personal experience and identity also affect how congresswomen view their representational responsibilities (see Brown 2014). Representative Cathy McMorris Rodgers (R-WA) told us, "I find that representatives all are a product of our own experiences, too . . . [T]hat does influence [us] at times because our experiences often drive our passions." In McMorris Rodgers's case, she has "a child with special needs. And that has . . . not only introduced me to the disabilities community, but . . . I want to make sure that I'm giving . . . those issues a priority in Congress."

Like McMorris Rodgers, a number of congresswomen pointed to their families and/or their experiences growing up as important factors influencing their work in Congress. Representative Niki Tsongas (D-CT) explained:

Well, I certainly feel a commitment to working on behalf of the people who serve in the military. It's probably born more of the fact that I grew up in the air force. My father was a survivor of Pearl Harbor. And so I spent a lot of time in an environment of those who were committed to serving their country.

Similarly, Representative Rosa DeLauro (D-CT) pointed to her family background as one of the reasons for her strong interest in fair wages for working-class people: "[L]ook, I'm from a blue-collar working family. My mother worked in the old sweatshops. My father was an insurance agent. So . . . the wage issue just kind of permeates all the economics." Maxine Waters (D-CA) also described how her experiences growing up influenced her interests:

And so, if I'm working on an issue, as we had to work starting in 2008, where the predatory lending was so pronounced and people were losing their homes and all these foreclosures were taking place across the nation, of course I identified with that. I come from a community, growing up, where I saw people who were evicted from places, who lost their homes, and so even though this was a more sophisticated way of doing it, through your banking institutions, of course I identified with that.

Personal medical crises have led some women members to give priority to certain health issues and to representing those who suffer from those conditions. Representative Debbie Wasserman-Schultz (D-FL) acknowledged, "I'm a breast cancer survivor . . . I've subsequently had . . . a great relationship and affiliation and affinity towards breast cancer organizations." Representative Rosa DeLauro (D-CT) talked about being a survivor of ovarian cancer and how that experience influenced her initial committee preferences: "I first wanted to be on the Energy and Commerce Committee because that's where they were doing health. But I couldn't get there. But then I got to Appropriations." Through her work in Congress on the Appropriations Committee and elsewhere, DeLauro found a way to "focus on women's health issues, which I have spent a lot of time on over the last 25 years."

Professional and occupational experiences also helped to shape congresswomen's views about whom they represent and how they represent them. Before entering Congress, Representative Debbie Dingell (D-MI) spent three decades working for the General Motors (GM) Corporation, where she was president of the GM Foundation and a senior executive responsible for public affairs. Her professional background clearly influences how she sees her job as a congresswoman: "I'm proud to come from a manufacturing background, so I think I have a responsibility to be a voice for manufacturing."

Similarly, the professional experiences of Representative Martha McSally (R-AZ), a retired air force colonel who was the first woman to command a US combat aviation unit, strongly affect how she sees her representational responsibilities. McSally told us:

I feel that I have two main roles here. One is to be a strong advocate for my district and fight for what matters to them, but also be a strong voice for our military, for national security, for taking care of veterans. It is a part of my background, it comes with the obligation, with the experience and the expertise that I have, and it's obviously also a passion of mine. We have to make sure we keep our country safe, that we give our troops everything they need in order to do that, and that we take care of them once they are no longer serving.

Like Representative McSally, another veteran, Representative Tulsi Gabbard (D-HI), reported that her priorities as a legislator have been heavily influenced by her military experience:

You know, one of the main reasons that I ran for Congress was that I was a veteran. I served two Middle East deployments, and I saw how few people in Congress had ever worn the uniform before and how few people understood from a firsthand experience what the consequences are to the very important decisions that Congress does make—and even that the president makes—with regard to how they are impacting our military, our veterans, their families, . . . and our country as a whole . . . [S]eeing and experiencing firsthand every day . . . the human cost of war, I felt it was important to do my best to try to run for Congress to bring voice to my brothers and sisters in uniform, to those who have served, to our veterans who come home and still face a tremendous number of challenges.

Several of the women who are attorneys were influenced by experiences in their legal careers before their election to Congress. Senator Claire McCaskill (D-MO) described how her professional experience as a prosecutor and an auditor influences her congressional work:

I am really fortunate in that I came to this office from an auditor's office, and before that [I was] a prosecutor. So I enjoy investigations that lead to effective oversight because an auditor's job is an oversight job and a prosecutor's job is about developing the facts to support a certain action. And so an oversight role in the Senate is very similar to kind of a hybrid between a prosecutor and an auditor. So I am very comfortable in that space; I enjoy that space.

Many of the women came to Congress after serving in other political positions, and their work in those positions often came to influence how they saw their roles in Congress. For example, Representative Kay Granger's (R-TX) strong interest in national security issues had its origins in her focus on crime when she served as a mayor. She explained, "[W]hen I came to Congress my issue was always security, what we do to keep the nation safe. I was a mayor, and crime was a big issue when I became mayor of my city, so that's what I ran on and that's what I spent most of my time [on]." Representative Susan Brooks (R-IN) described how her experiences as a criminal defense attorney and a public official worked together to create within her a strong interest in and commitment to dealing with substance abuse issues. She explained:

I have been involved my entire career in many ways with the criminal justice system, and once arriving here have found an opportunity to get really involved in substance abuse issues and mental health issues. And so I've been trying to introduce some legislation but am also trying to speak about it as much as I can . . . [I am] a former criminal defense attorney, and then I was the deputy mayor in Indianapolis, where I worked with the police department, and then I was US attorney in the Bush administration. And all of those times during my career I've seen substance abuse and addiction, whether it is alcohol or drugs, has just a devastating impact on individuals and on families and communities.

Adult life experiences outside the workplace matter as well. Representative Barbara Lee (D-CA) described how "being on welfare in the past" influenced her perspective and work in Congress. She explained, "I lived on food stamps and public assistance, single mother and all that stuff, which . . . is kind of normal for a lot of women living in this country . . . And so I bring, like other Black women bring and other women of color bring, kind of whatever they went through and the barriers they faced, [and I'm] trying to knock down some of those to make things better for everybody."

Other congresswomen of color also described how their identity and experiences as women of color influence the way they see themselves as representatives, echoing evidence from past research on minority legislators (e.g., Swain 1995; Gill 1997; Casellas 2011; Brown 2014). Delegate Stacey Plaskett (D-VI) suggested, "And, you know, it goes without saying—well, maybe it doesn't go without saying—but as someone of African descent, the issues that are really relevant to African Americans are things that are really important to me as well." Representative Grace Meng (D-NY) noted, "Being an Asian American, so either Asian American or a woman of color, those are also interest areas . . . [where] I feel that I have a responsibility to speak." Representative Linda Sánchez (D-CA), who was chair of the Congressional Hispanic Caucus (CHC) in the 114th Congress, echoed these sentiments: "Because I come from [an] immigrant family and my parents are Mexican, I certainly . . . feel a sense of responsibility of being a voice on behalf of the Hispanic community."

Senator Tammy Baldwin (D-WI), the first openly gay or lesbian person elected to the US Senate, noted that her identity has influenced not only her legislative work, but also the dynamic surrounding discussions of LGBT issues. She observed:

> But certainly in the Senate, when you're a first, you change the dy-
> namic. So one of the ways I put it rhetorically is: when you're not in
> the room, people are having a conversation about you. And when
> you're in the room, they're having a conversation with you.

She described how she brings a perspective that was previously lacking:

> So in all of history prior to there being an out gay or lesbian person
> in the Senate, when they either discussed advancing civil rights for
> the LGBT community or . . . how to prevent the advancement, . . . all
> of those discussions have occurred in rooms without voice from
> the LGBT community participating. And now they're happening in
> rooms where I'm present and can represent a perspective.

Some legislators find that their personal experiences or identity corre-spond closely with those of their constituents, so bringing their experiences to bear and representing their geographic constituents are one and the same activity. Experiences or identities are shared with significant blocs of voters within districts, thereby reinforcing the commitment to work on behalf of these constituencies. Perhaps this is most evident in the case of racial and ethnic identities. Representative Terri Sewell (D-AL) was raised in Selma, Alabama, in the majority-Black district she now represents. She described herself as "a proud product of this district" with an "incredible sense of need to give back to a community that really nurtured me and told me that I could be somebody." She explained, "I don't apologize for being a Black woman. I see it as a badge of honor that I am who I am. And who I am is a very complicated mixture of small-town America from rural

Alabama, growing up . . . cognizant of the fight for civil rights and voting rights because you can't grow up in Selma and not understand that."

This correspondence between personal experience and the interests of the geographic constituency is evident among nonminority legislators as well as legislators of color and among Republicans as well as Democrats. For example, Representative Ann Wagner (R-MO) stressed that she cares "a lot about defense" in part because "I am the proud mother of a West Point grad and army captain." But she also has "a big Boeing facility" and a "big VA hospital" in her district that have led her to emphasize military-related interests and priorities as a member of Congress.

While the experiences and identities of women members of Congress sometimes correspond closely with those of their geographic constituents, in other cases personal experiences and identities lead them to be "surrogate representatives" responsive to groups that live well beyond the borders of their districts and states. As Jane Mansbridge has explained, surrogate representation is most commonly based on a shared ideological perspective or group identity. Moreover, Mansbridge has argued, "That sense of surrogate responsibility becomes even stronger when the surrogate representative shares experiences with surrogate constituents in a way that the majority of the legislature does not" or "when the legislature includes few, or disproportionately few, representatives of the group in question" (2003: 523). Several women members described how aspects of their identities or their experiences created a bond with voters beyond their district boundaries and led them to feel a responsibility to act as surrogate representatives.

Mansbridge has argued that surrogate representatives do not have to be "descriptive representatives" who share the demographic characteristics of those they represent. But, she has observed, "it is in this surrogate process that descriptive representation often plays its most useful role, allowing representatives who are themselves members of a subordinate group to circumvent the strong barriers to communication between dominant and subordinate groups" (1999: 642). Thus, perhaps not surprisingly, women of color were particularly likely to see themselves as surrogate representatives of people who shared their racial and ethnic identities. For example, Representative Loretta Sanchez (D-CA) observed, "There are so few Latinos . . . still in the Congress . . . [relative to the number of] Latinos across the nation. If they don't have someone in their area, . . . they can reach out to us and . . . ask us to work on issues for them."

Similarly, as the only openly gay person in the US Senate, Senator Tammy Baldwin (D-WI) serves as a surrogate representative of members of the LGBT community across the country. Even more broadly, Baldwin, who had a long history of working on progressive causes prior to her election to Congress, is viewed by rights activists from across the country as someone who will champion their issues. She noted:

And so while I think I view the bulk of my responsibilities as being representative of the people of the state of Wisconsin, there are any number of issues that I've worked on that have had that far-reaching impact. And some of those, well, most of them predate my election to the Senate and reflect perhaps my activism early on . . . [A] lot of it is in the civil rights arena. So LGBT rights, women's rights, certainly a fair amount of work in racial equality, as an example.

On the more conservative side of the political spectrum, Representative Vicky Hartzler (R-MO) sees herself as someone who has a shared perspective with and represents the interests of pro-life voters across the county. As she explained, "And certainly my views on life and the respect for life extend beyond just parochial issues in my own district, although my district is very pro-life, so I think I reflect those values."

Other women members described how they sometimes act as surrogate representatives on issues where they have expertise or are institutionally positioned to hear from people outside their district. For example, Representative Chellie Pingree (D-ME), who serves on the subcommittee of the House Appropriations Committee that deals with agricultural issues, explained, "[W]e work on a lot of agricultural and food-related issues. So it's not uncommon that we would hear from somebody anywhere in the country on that particular topic . . . [I]t's very common that we will meet with somebody on any related issue if it has something to do with informing us or being a part of committee work I do."

And while most congresswomen spoke about their work representing citizens within the United States, their actions as surrogate representatives took a few of them beyond the borders of the country. Representative Eddie Bernice Johnson (D-TX), for example, reported:

> But I've always been very strong on diversity. And I've kept in touch with the people from all over Asia, really all over the world . . . I've learned so much, and it has really increased my involvement internationally . . . And that's one of the things that has encouraged me to start my extracurricular program, which is a World of Women for World Peace, where I worked around the world on that.

THE SUBSTANTIVE REPRESENTATION OF WOMEN

Much of the literature on women serving in elected office has focused on the relationship between descriptive and substantive representation of women (Reingold 2000; Carroll 2001; Swers 2002, 2013; Dodson 2006). By virtue of their inclusion in the social category "women," women members of Congress descriptively represent, or "stand for," women in the general population. But do they also feel a commitment to representing women substantively? Do they not only "stand for" but also see themselves as "acting for" women (Pitkin 1967; Phillips 1995)?

We did not directly ask the women we interviewed whether they feel a responsibility to represent the interests of women in their work in Congress. But their interviews reflect a widespread commitment to doing so. Of course, consistent with the findings of past research (Carroll 2002), partisan as well as individual differences are apparent in the specifics of what that commitment means.

A handful of women on both sides of the aisle rejected the idea that they have a particular responsibility to represent women. Representative Vicky Hartzler (R-MO) explained that she is "more concerned about advancing issues of my district, my priorities and things" and that "philosophically

I don't think there are women's issues." She continued, "I don't have those same goals to advance women's issues. I want to advance conservative solutions that our country needs . . . whether they are women's ideas or the men's ideas." On the Democratic side of the aisle, Louise Slaughter (D-NY) noted, "I feel a responsibility to all my constituents—man, woman, child, all of them. There are some issues that women live that only we know, and those are certainly part of an agenda as a woman that I know about. But no, I don't compartmentalize myself."

But during their interviews, most of the women in Congress expressed a commitment to represent women in their legislative work (often in conjunction with children and families) and/or the importance of having their lived experiences as women represented in legislative deliberation and decision-making. Some of the congresswomen, especially those with longer tenures in public life, talked about the role that congresswomen have played historically in expanding the policy agenda because of their commitment to representing women. For example, Representative Rosa DeLauro (D-CT), when asked about the difference the presence of women has made in Congress, observed:

It's been remarkable. I mean historically remarkable . . . [T]he press asks us all the time, "Isn't this a male-run operation?" Yeah, well, hell, we're an institution that runs by numbers. You have to have votes, and there's just not enough of us here, we need to have more people here . . . But women have changed the agenda and focus, which is what I think is critical.

In her colorful way, DeLauro (D-CT), who first entered the House of Representatives in 1991, pointed to women's health as an example:

So Nita Lowey, myself, and Nancy [Pelosi] sat on Appropriations. We were the first women on the Democratic side to sit there and force the issue on women's health issues. Forced the issue. You can see the three of us up there. They used to call us the "DeLoSi's" [because of] what we were plotting. It was DeLauro, Pelosi, and Lowey. And we went in and, you know, stormed the Bastille with the chairman of the Appropriations Committee at the time—a Democrat, Neal Smith—[and] told him about what we needed to have for women's health.

Representative Jackie Speier (D-CA), who spent 18 years in her state legislature before coming to Congress in 2008, discussed her own rationale for working to expand the policy agenda to include women's issues:

When I got elected to the state legislature, my campaign consultant said to me at the time, you have to broaden your area of interest beyond women. And I thought about it, . . . but in the end I realized if I didn't take on the issues that were important to women, who was going to? So it [women's issues] has been a strong component of my legislative agenda, really since the very beginning.

Similarly, Representative Alma Adams (D-NC), who served in her state legislature before coming to Congress, commented on women's role in agenda-setting:

I just want to reiterate that women need to be here, and they need to be here because everything impacts us and our families and our communities. And if we're not here, then the issues that need to be talked about the most won't be talked about. They won't be addressed. You know, they'll never get to the table. So we need to be . . . in the room, at the table, feet planted firmly under the table, so that we in fact have the kind of voice that we need to have.

While some emphasized women's role in agenda-setting as one aspect of how women members of Congress have represented women, others, such as Representative Linda Sánchez (D-CA), talked about how they employ gender as a lens that they bring to bear on various issues, not just issues that might commonly be considered women's issues. Sánchez explained, "[B]ecause I am a woman I do think that I look . . . at legislation . . . and policy through the prism of 'How does this impact women?'" Similarly,

Representative Elise Stefanik (R-NY) expressed her belief that "women bring a different perspective on every single issue. So I'm a believer that all issues are women's issues, and they affect women in some ways differently." These women believe that applying a gendered lens results in public policy outcomes that better serve the public as a whole. Senator Patty Murray (D-WA), for example, suggested, "I think having women at the table, whether you are in a corporate boardroom or you're in politics or you are . . . anywhere, is really important because then whatever you do, whatever you accomplish, works for everybody." While Murray emphasized the improvement in policy that can result, women's involvement can also help block legislation that might be harmful for some women. Representative Yvette Clarke (D-NY), specifically discussing reproductive rights from her pro-choice perspective, observed, "You know, if it weren't for women on Capitol Hill fighting back each and every day, giving voice to women in their ability to think for themselves, to act for themselves, to govern themselves, bad things could happen."

While a number of congresswomen identified women as a specific group that they represented in their legislative work, another bloc of congresswomen talked about representing some combination of women, children, and families as interwoven pieces of the same fabric. Representative Anna Eshoo (D-CA) reported that she felt a responsibility to represent "certainly women and children, because I'm a woman and I have children. I brought children into this world." Similarly, Representative Doris Matsui (D-HI) suggested, "Looking back on what I'm doing here, I think women and children . . . have been of particular interest to me." Senator Barbara Boxer (D-CA) explained that she and the other women "carry with us the needs of women and their families. And of course, as you fight to protect women and children in your state, you're also protecting the nation."

Numerous women pointed to their societal roles—as mothers, grandmothers, daughters, and caregivers—and their shared life experiences, often in those roles, as sources of their ability to represent women and bring distinctive gendered perspectives to bear on their congressional work. Senator Heidi Heitkamp (D-ND) observed:

We're moms. I think that's a huge thing that we have in common . . . [A]nd we're daughters. So many women, at least at my age, are dealing with elderly parents and see the challenges. And these are experiences that we have that are different from the male members. I think there is . . . a sense of greater responsibility for the family that women have.

Representative Lois Capps (D-CA) explained, "Well, I am a mom and a grandmother, and so I care about these issues as well, and particularly as a school nurse I care a lot about kids . . . And so there is a built-in agenda for . . . what I bring as a woman . . . We all bring our experiences." Representative Martha Roby (R-AL) observed, "For us to have a seat at the table and be able to share our experience as wives and mothers is important." Representative Kristi Noem (R-SD) suggested:

I'm a mom, and the majority of voters in the country are women . . . I just think we bring a completely different perspective to the conversation. Most of the voters in this country are women. So they deserve to be represented and have people there that think like they do.

Representative Nita Lowey (D-NY) also expressed the view that many women share some common issues stemming from their experiences as women and that these affect their work in Congress:

Women come to Congress bringing with them their life experience. Some of us are married, some are divorced, some are single, some have children, some don't have children. But in general, although we've had different life experiences, I do think that for me, as a mother of three and a grandmother of eight, I bring my personal experiences to the work I do. And I have greater understanding of what some of these struggling women go through . . . although I was very fortunate. I didn't run for Congress until I was 50, but I was working for part of the time I was raising children. And I . . . felt

guilty whether I was home . . . [or] whether I worked. I [just] felt
guilty. So I think women do share important perspectives whether
they work at home, whether they work for nonprofits, whether they
were getting paid. The same struggles were shared by most women.

Representative Ann McLane Kuster (D-NH) explained that "family-
work balance . . . providing opportunity, being able to care for their
families" is "part of my own personal story being a working mom, and
it's part of what I care about going forward." She continued, "[H]aving
working mothers, having grandmothers, having people involved
in the process who have experienced gender discrimination, wage
discrimination—that gives the whole Congress a much broader perspective. And it's very important." Representative Katherine Clark (D-
MA) described how she is "in that sandwich generation, and I relate to
it." Acknowledging her many advantages, she nevertheless explained
how the pressures she feels from the responsibilities of her gendered
roles as mother and caregiver for her parents give her a perspective that
helps her be a better legislator:

> I have a lot of resources . . . that other people don't have. You know,
> I have a good-paying job . . . I have a husband who has a job. So that
> gives us a huge leg up on a lot of people. I have a schedule that, while
> insanely busy, is also flexible; if I need to be home with a child or with
> my parents, I can do that. And that isn't something that everybody
> has. But . . . knowing those pressures and how real they are . . . helps
> us be. . . better in the way we set policy and the way we think about
> our economy and . . . the way we provide healthcare and how we plan
> for the future, how we access education, what we are researching, the
> importance of federal dollars to that, and how it affects our budget
> ultimately. All those pieces, you know, I pull in my driveway and it's
> all right there. My parents live next door, so it's all right there and
> I think that's an important perspective that would be very different
> from one my brother has.

Many women talked about the responsibility they felt to represent women in the context of a specific issue or policy area. As chair of the Senate Aging Committee, Susan Collins (R-ME) explained that she has "a special interest and a special desire to try to help our nation's elderly, which are disproportionately women." Similarly, Senator Mazie Hirono (D-HI) expressed her commitment to "making sure that Social Security remains strong, knowing full well that the fact that women do not get paid the same as men . . . has a huge impact cumulatively on their Social Security payments." Representative Elise Stefanik (R-NY) described how she has "really focused on my work on the House Armed Services Committee since I represent Fort Drum, home of the Tenth Mountain Division, the most deployed unit in the US Army. And that includes military spouses. That includes women in the military."

Women of color, especially African American women, often spoke about their commitment to represent women in conjunction with the commitment they felt to represent people of color. For these women members of Congress, the two commitments often went hand in hand. For example, when asked about whom she felt a responsibility to represent, Representative Robin Kelly (D-IL) responded, "[D]efinitely my district, but also, of course, African Americans and women." Similarly, Representative Marcia Fudge (D-OH) replied, "[M]y priorities are people who live in high-poverty areas, minorities, and women. Obviously I represent all of the people of my district, but my particular areas of interest are the poor, minorities, and women." Representative Joyce Beatty (D-OH) suggested, "[B]ecause I am female and African American, I know that I have a laser eye on gravitating to women's issues, issues for minorities, [so] that I can make sure that they are included more." Delegate Eleanor Holmes Norton (D-DC) explained:

I'm concerned that women be able to have abortions anywhere in the world. I'm concerned with HIV, not only in my district but throughout the world, and the way it disproportionately affects women. So I have my interest in women's issues—not only women in the United States, but women worldwide. I'm a member of the Congressional Black Caucus, [and] I have a special interest in what's happening to Africans in particular.

Representative Donna Edwards (D-MD) also talked about the commitment she felt and the important role she played in making sure that minority women at the intersection of the categories of race and gender were not overlooked. She reported:

I'd say that in representing my district, I really reflect the needs and concerns of some broader populations. And so, for example, the work that I do more broadly here in Congress around issues that people call women's issues, although I don't like to think of them that way, obviously has a direct impact on my district, but [also] has a broader impact across the country. And so I think one of the elements that I brought to the discussion around equal pay for equal work, for example, was to always put that in terms of what those overall numbers mean for Black women, for Latinas. Because I think just articulating the difference between saying a general number like 78 cents on the dollar [for women overall compared with White men] and saying 64 cents [for Black women] or 49 cents for Latinas helped my district relate to an issue that was thought of as a broader women's concern, but not really a concern for women of color. And I think that helped our [Democratic] caucus to understand that as well.

Indeed, the 114th Congress saw the creation of a new group aimed at ensuring that attention would be placed on the needs of women and girls at the intersection of gender and racial categories who are often rendered invisible. The Congressional Caucus on Black Women and Girls was created in 2016 by three Black women in Congress: Representatives Bonnie Watson Coleman (D-NJ), Robin Kelly (D-IL), and Yvette D. Clarke (D-NY).

THE SYMBOLIC REPRESENTATION OF WOMEN

Although particularly concerned with the substantive representation of women, political scientists have also recognized the potential importance of women's symbolic representation, described by Jennifer L. Lawless as "the attitudinal and behavioral effects that women's presence in positions of political power might confer to women citizens" (2004: 810). The results of studies on women voters in districts with women candidates or representatives have been mixed, with some finding evidence that the presence of women candidates or incumbents enhances political engagement, knowledge, and interest (e.g., Koch 1997; Burns, Schlozman, and Verba 2001; Atkeson 2003; Lawless 2004; Schwindt-Bayer and Mishler 2005; Campbell and Wolbrecht 2006; Dolan 2006; Atkeson and Carillo 2007; Reingold and Harrell 2010; Fridkin and Kenney 2014; Wolbrecht and Campbell 2017). Nevertheless, the congresswomen in our study were very optimistic about the impact they can have on women and girls. They seemed keenly aware that their visibility as officeholders makes them role models and offers them opportunities to inspire other women to become involved politically and perhaps even to follow in their footsteps.[1]

Senator Jeanne Shaheen (D-NH) shared the following anecdote:

> After I got elected governor in New Hampshire, the newspaper in the state capital, the *Concord Monitor*, did a lovely cartoon and it was me with a pickax standing next to a pile of shattered glass, and the point was that the glass ceiling had been broken. I think that's true, and it's certainly true for a lot of women in this country, but it's not true for every woman. I think one of the things that motivates me, and I know motivates a lot of women in the Senate, is wanting to see that glass ceiling broken for every woman . . . so that everybody has access to the same opportunities as the men in this country.

1. We elaborate on these opportunities to disrupt the public's image and expectations about congressional leadership and to inspire other women in Chapter 7.

The congresswomen we interviewed tended to be aware of the role they could play, whether through their presence or actions or both, in motivating others to get involved, thereby helping to shatter the multitude of glass ceilings that continue to restrict women's political opportunities.

Representative Susan Davis (D-CA) observed, "You can't be what you can't see." Congresswomen are among the few female political leaders who can be seen at the national level, and as such they have a potential impact on the political aspirations of women and girls throughout the country. Representative Susan Brooks (R-IN) explained, "We have . . . an opportunity to try to be role models for women and men in our states and in the country and [to] try and change the mindset about women and girls' thinking about running for office."

Richard Fenno, in his in-depth study of Black representatives and their constituents, suggested that symbolic connections were even more important for African Americans than for Whites (2003). And they certainly were an important focus for the women of color in our study. Representative Joyce Beatty (D-OH) pointed to the unique opportunity she and other women of color in Congress have to influence the aspirations of young women in their racial and ethnic groups. Beatty described the importance of students seeing in her a member of Congress they could relate to, adding:

> Then when they turn on the TV and they see a Robin Kelly from the same district and state as the president of the United States, or they see a person from New York who sits on Energy and Commerce that is under 50 years of age and is an African American female, or when they see somebody from the Virgin Islands that grew up from the islands and came here and went to an Ivy League law school and private boarding schools, they go, "Wow. I, too, can be that."

However, Beatty also took care to explain that her influence as a role model was not limited to her racial and ethnic group:

Yes, we make a difference, [but] not only for our communities...I have young White girls—10, 13, 18, 20, and 40 years old—that wait hours without an appointment to say, "I just want to come in and talk to her for a moment or get a picture with her because I saw her on CSPAN or CNN or MSNBC." ... Sure, it makes a difference. Sure, it is influential. Sure, it has impact.

Women members of Congress often spoke passionately about their efforts to reach out and encourage other women to become involved in politics. Although they lead very busy lives, they frequently take advantage of or create opportunities to speak with groups of girls and women and urge them to become more politically engaged. Representative Cheri Bustos (D-IL), for example, explained:

[M]y passion is having women and people of color run for office. And the major reason is both groups are so underrepresented still in elected office and public service. And I happen to think that if we do better in those areas, we are going to be a better country ... For those of us who have been fortunate enough to achieve some level of success in our careers, we better darn well help other women because we've got a long, long way to go . . . So I think it's part of my life's mission to help women succeed and be in positions to help make a difference in our state, our country, and our world.

Similarly, Senator Kirsten Gillibrand (D-NY) feels such a strong commitment to increasing women's political involvement that she initiated a campaign called Off the Sidelines (http://offthesidelines.org/) in 2012 to encourage women and girls to make their voices heard on issues of concern to them. She told us:

I spend a lot of time recruiting candidates, helping candidates to be successful, giving them guidance, giving them advice, engaging women all across the country to care about politics, to vote, to be advocates for the issues they care about . . . [M]y tag line is "Always

be heard." . . . Be heard on the issues you care about . . . [W]omen's
voices really are important.

And Representative Jackie Walorski (R-IN) reminded us, "I think there
should be more [women] on both sides [of the aisle] . . . [E]very chance
I have, whether I'm speaking to girls in high school or in civic groups,
speaking to women, moms, I'm always talking about [the need for more
women to get involved].

REPRESENTING THE VOICELESS

Many congresswomen feel a strong responsibility to represent women
both substantively and symbolically, but women are not the only underrepresented segments of the population for whom congresswomen
feel such a commitment. The growing body of scholarship on women of
color legislators has demonstrated that these officeholders devote consid-
erable attention to policies affecting minority communities and women
of color in those communities (Barrett 1995; Fraga et al. 2006; Bedolla,
Tate, and Wong 2014; Brown 2014; Hardy-Fanta et al. 2016). However, less
attention has been paid to congresswomen's representation of other here-
tofore underrepresented groups. One of the patterns that emerged in our
interviews was a desire on the part of many of the women in Congress
to be, as Senator Kirsten Gillibrand (D-NY) termed it, "a voice for the
voiceless"—those whose interests have been overlooked, marginalized,
and/or underserved in the halls of Congress.

Senator Gillibrand elaborated on her own commitment:

Well, I really want to be a voice for the voiceless and for people who
have no real . . . power in Washington— . . . the people who don't
have fancy lobbyists, people who don't have huge special interests
for their agenda, . . . women and children, and children who are
ill, . . . LGBT rights. Those are all things I tend to gravitate toward
because they don't have as many champions.

Senator Patty Murray (D-WA) voiced similar sentiments while describing how she became involved in electoral politics:

> In general I feel that it's really important to be a voice for people who don't feel anybody is listening to them . . . [W]hat . . . started me in politics to begin with is when I had a state legislator tell me I couldn't make a difference because I was just a mom in tennis shoes. I thought, "Who are you to say that to me? Moms in tennis shoes have just as much right to be heard." So I'm always super sensitive to people who feel their voices aren't heard or aren't important because they are, and I want to speak out for them.

Representative Kathleen Rice (D-NY) described how she felt a commitment to act on behalf of "the marginalized":

> I spent my entire career as a prosecutor because I always wanted to be a voice for those who didn't have one, those people who were marginalized—whether it is a young African American kid who is struggling in school because he's in a poor-performing school because of the zip code he was born in, or a single mother who is struggling to keep a roof over her head and is being fleeced by a bank that's charging her a too-high interest rate because she's a vulnerable individual . . . There are so many marginalized people, not just in my district, but across the country. So that is a big focus of mine.

Some women members talked specifically about their desire to represent people and groups who do not have lobbyists in Washington watching out for their interests. For example, when asked whom she feels a commitment to represent or work on behalf of, Senator Claire McCaskill (D-MO) replied:

> Everybody who can't afford to hire a lobbyist . . . [E]very day when I'm confronted with an issue to decide on, I try to think through in my mind, "Okay what would the single mother living in Arnold,

Missouri with three kids who makes $27,000 a year, how will this
help her or hurt her?" So I really try to do that filter every time.
There are a whole lot of things that don't get enough oxygen out
here, and almost invariably they are people or issues that don't have
lobbyists.

Similarly, Representative Gwen Moore (D-WI) told us, "I have an
organizing principle that I'm here because the people that I represent don't
have well-paid lobbyists to represent their interests in particular." Noting
that many of those who aren't represented need "educational opportunity,
job opportunities, . . . social support in the midst of high unemployment,"
she explained, "I'm very, very proud to fight for food stamps and social
services to meet the needs of people when they are down and out."

This desire to represent underrepresented segments of the population was more frequently articulated by Democrats, but some
Republican women expressed such a commitment as well. For example,
Representative Ann Wagner (R-MO) explained that she has a "mission
statement" for her and her staff and that "we hang it everywhere in
our offices." She continued, "So our mission statement . . . . centers
around . . . serving a cause greater than oneself . . . It talks about giving
voice to the voiceless, and how important that is, and how we have to
remember that's why we're put here in this legislative role." Her congressional campaign website echoed this commitment: "Ann has pledged to
serve a cause greater than oneself by standing on common sense conservative principles, confronting injustice and serving as a voice for the most
vulnerable in our society. From protecting the unborn to standing up
for our military men and women to making things just a little easier for
that single mother of two in Ballwin, she has undertaken an aggressive
legislative agenda during her time in Congress" (see https://annwagner.
com/issue-accomplishments/).

Some of the women talked about their commitment to working on behalf of a specific underrepresented group or constituency. Of these groups,
perhaps children were most frequently referenced. In fact, Delegate Stacey
Plaskett (D-VI) said, "I don't know any woman in Congress who is not

fighting for children." One example of a woman who fights for children is Representative Katherine Clark (D-MA), who elaborated on the responsibility she feels:

> I really feel that we talk a great game about kids and doing work for children in the United States, but in the end they don't vote, and a lot of our policies just leave them out. So I feel a particular need . . . [to work on] issues around income inequality and how do we bolster our public schools and early education and healthcare for kids . . . It always comes back to kids, and especially kids who are low income, and just making sure that we keep having opportunities for every kid.

A couple of the congresswomen who are pro-life took their concern for children one step further and explained that they felt a commitment to represent the interests of the unborn. Representative Martha Roby (R-AL), for example, told us, "[D]efending the unborn is a tremendous privilege, and it's one that I will not stop, and I will not apologize for."

As another example of commitments to working on behalf of specific underrepresented groups, a few of the congresswomen talked about the responsibility they feel to citizens who face particular kinds of health challenges. Representative Debbie Wasserman-Schultz (D-FL) talked about the impact she has had as a breast cancer survivor. She explained, "I can't tell you how many times young women, older women, the husbands of or family members of women [who had breast cancer] have come up to me and said I made a difference in their lives because I shared my story. Just the fact that I was public after I went through my experience [was important to them]." Likewise, Representative Michelle Lujan Grisham (D-NM) had spent most of her pre-Congress career working on behalf of "disabled adults and senior citizens and retirees" and said she "came to Congress really to work on healthcare." She noted that she feels "especially responsible to make a difference for those folks who aren't in positions to really make decisions for themselves because we create such terrible barriers to independence."

CONCLUSION

The women who served in the 114th Congress represented a wide array of geographic districts and states, as well as interests within those districts that they felt committed to serving. They also brought a range of life experiences and identities to their work as representatives. But while their districts and their life experiences varied, what these women shared—and what we heard in interview after interview—was a strong passion for the jobs they do and the people they represent. These women believe that their work makes a difference in people's lives and that their presence in the institution of Congress matters. Most of them also shared a commitment to make the lives of women (and often other underrepresented groups) better and to use their positions as congresswomen to encourage other women and girls to become more politically engaged. The women's shared passion for and commitment to the work they do, along with the mix of district and personal interests that they represent, are factors that helped shape their roles and actions in the 114th Congress. Later chapters in this book will examine more closely the efforts of congresswomen to influence public policy and legislative politics—efforts that were motivated in large part by how these women perceived their representational responsibilities and their jobs as elected representatives. However, we first examine another factor that influenced their roles and actions: the institutional barriers and opportunities they confronted as women members of Congress. This is the subject to which we turn in the next chapter.

3

Obstacles and Opportunities

The representational styles and priorities of women members of Congress are at least partly rooted in their shared experiences as women—whether inside or outside of political institutions. Not all of those experiences are positive. Women members confront challenges that their male colleagues do not, reminding us that the ties that bind women are sometimes rooted in shared struggles to navigate spaces and norms that were established by and for men. Representative Dina Titus (D-NV) told us, "I think [women] have in common the fact that they have to overcome the obstacle of being a woman, whether they're a Democrat or a Republican. There are obstacles that they all face, and that gives them a common bond." Representative Cathy McMorris Rodgers (R-WA) echoed that sentiment, observing, "There is a bond among the women members, just because we have in common the fact that we are serving in Congress and wrestling with the challenges that we do have in common."

In this chapter, we examine the extent to which being a woman poses obstacles for women members of Congress. More specifically, what are the challenges, if any, that women members of Congress share? And how do they overcome them? We also discuss the opportunities that gender affords women members of Congress, demonstrating the ways in which women take advantage of being a woman in a male-dominated institution.

The findings presented in this chapter come primarily from responses to two questions we posed to women members. First, "Do you think women members face any unique challenges or opportunities within Congress because they are women?" And second, "Clearly there are differences, but do you think women in Congress have anything in common?"

We found that the women members in our study consider the most explicit and significant gender-related problems to be those that affect their entry into Congress. Fewer women identify challenges distinctive to women within the institution today, noting the evolution of gender dynamics and improvements in the status of women over time. Still, navigating Congress as a woman is not devoid of hurdles rooted in gender stereotypes and gender disparities in numbers and power. In some cases, these hurdles vary by chamber, party, and the member's race or ethnicity. However, women members have developed strategies for clearing these hurdles and even capitalizing on the potential advantages of their gender. Finally, in their collective affirmation of the need for more women in Congress, the women members we interviewed expressed their desire for an institution with fewer gender-based hurdles.

OBSTACLES TO ENTRY

When asked about the challenges they face as women and what women members have in common, multiple female members emphasized that the obstacles to entry into Congress are more significant than any gender bias they confront once they are inside.[1] We found that the bonds they share as women are forged in part by the shared struggle to launch, wage, and win a campaign within a political system that remains characterized by an imbalance in gender power. Representative Brenda Lawrence (D-MI) summarized this view: "Being here in Congress is not as hard as it was to get here."

Gender differences in supportive campaign infrastructures and the standards by which candidates are evaluated were among the top challenges

---

1. Although our questions focused on their experiences (challenges or opportunities) once in Congress, at least 22 congresswomen of the 83 we interviewed identified campaigning as a challenge for women in office.

women identified in their paths to political office. Representative Kathleen Rice (D-NY) noted this commonality among women members: "We know the struggle of actually trying to put together a winning campaign—to put together a financial infrastructure and a political infrastructure that is not already premade for us like it is for men." Women members emphasized the financial costs of campaigns as a particular challenge. The challenge of funding campaigns was emphasized by Democrats and Republicans and women members across races and ethnicities, though House members were more likely to raise this issue during our interviews.

While scholarly literature shows that women candidates raise as much money as their male counterparts in comparable general election races (Uhlaner and Schlozman 1986; Wilhite and Theilmann 1986; Burrell 1994, 2008, 2014; Fox 2010), some research shows that they receive smaller individual contributions and, thus, expend greater time and effort to match men's fundraising totals (Dabelko and Herrnson 1997; Baker 2006; Crespin and Deitz 2010). Many women also find it necessary to fundraise outside of traditional networks (Fox 1997; Jenkins 2007). In other words, gender parity in political fundraising totals is not an indicator of gender neutrality in the process of raising campaign money.

That is certainly the view of the congresswomen we interviewed. Representative Lois Capps (D-CA) expressed this frustration, telling us, "It is much harder for women to raise money than men. We don't have the same natural circles." She added, "You can do it, but you have to be twice as good and work twice as hard." The views of these congresswomen are consistent with those of women state legislators, who also see fundraising as harder for women (Jenkins 2007; Carroll and Sanbonmatsu 2013). Women of color may experience the greatest hurdles in establishing the financial infrastructure necessary to compete in political campaigns, as shown by research demonstrating racial differences in donation sources and levels (Theilmann and Wilhite 1989; Singh 1998), as well as perceptions among minority women legislators that fundraising is particularly difficult for them (Carroll and Sanbonmatsu 2013).

The challenge of raising money is not only a hurdle to waging a successful campaign, women members told us, but also a deterrent to running in the first place. For those potential candidates who do not come to politics with access to moneyed networks, confronting the "rich man's club," as Representative Robin Kelly (D-IL) characterized it, is both unattractive and daunting. And money does not decline in importance once members are elected. An ability to raise significant amounts of money is a quality sought in party leaders, compounding the effects of gender disparities in the fundraising process. Representative Brenda Lawrence (D-MI) explained that this may be particularly problematic for Black women members' institutional advancement: "I think Black women can get votes, but to be able to be in leadership and do everything, you have to raise money. Women inherently have a harder time raising money." Representative Donna Edwards (D-MD), who served as co-chair of the House Democrats' Steering and Policy Committee, echoed these sentiments, noting that raising substantially less money has been a barrier to leadership for members of color overall. She explained that she herself ascended to a leadership post "precisely because I put my nose to the grindstone for the last six years, raising money for other candidates, traveling to districts, playing leadership roles at the DCCC," adding, "those . . . are things that mostly Black members had not done." Thus, having to raise sufficient money is not only a barrier to getting to Congress, but also a challenge for women who seek to stay in Congress and is even more of a challenge for those who wish to advance to leadership positions within their respective party caucuses. While fundraising is just one aspect of the perpetual campaign, the statements of congresswomen that we have highlighted here serve as reminders that—even once in office—women members are always officeholders *and* candidates, and thus face the challenges of both roles simultaneously.

The costs of campaigning are not only financial. Some women emphasized gender differences in how candidates are treated and evaluated as an additional obstacle to entering congressional office. Women members identified the heightened scrutiny of their personal lives, consistent with research that has found greater attention paid to women candidates' family members, marital status, and personal histories (Aday and Devitt 2001; Bystrom, Robertson, and Banwart 2001; Bystrom et al. 2004; Heldman, Carroll, and Olson 2005; Dunaway et al. 2013; Miller and Peake 2013; for an exception, see Hayes and Lawless 2015). Even the mere prospect of an invasive campaign has been shown to deter women from considering a run for political office (Lawless and Fox 2010; Shames 2017). As Representative Suzanne Bonamici (D-OR) observed, women considering a congressional bid frequently ask themselves, "Why would I put my family through that?" Her senior colleague, Representative Jan Schakowsky (D-IL), agreed that women's personal lives are scrutinized to a greater degree than men's, adding, "I think women are more reluctant to have their lives examined up and down, and in and out . . . Women are more inclined to say, 'Who needs it?!'"

For the women who have made it to Congress, enduring this heightened scrutiny is often accompanied by an understanding that they will be held to higher standards than their male counterparts on the campaign trail. Senator Debbie Stabenow (D-MI) observed that "we vote for a lot of male candidates that are not perfect," despite the expectation of perfection in women who run for office. Tessa Ditonto, Allison Hamilton, and David Redlawsk (2014) offer some support for Stabenow's claim, finding that voters seek greater competence-related information for women candidates than they do for men.[2] Meeting those higher standards is sometimes difficult, forcing women to "fight hard" to earn political power, according to Representative Grace Napolitano (D-CA). She adds that women, especially minority women, have "to be strong and vocal and loud to be taken seriously" on the campaign trail and in the roles that lead them to Congress. Scholars have also found that women candidates come to campaigns with more qualifications than their male counterparts (Pearson and McGhee 2013), an advantage that appears to combat gender-based doubts at the ballot box (Fulton 2012), especially when emphasized on the campaign trail (Mo 2015). But even before becoming candidates, women have long

2. Carew (2012) finds some evidence that Black women candidates are evaluated more harshly than their opponents with respect to their policy competency outside of issues most explicitly characterized as race or gender issues, and Cargile (2016) offers evidence that non-Latinos are more skeptical of Latina candidates' competency than are Latino voters.

had to prove themselves worthy of running for congressional seats. As House Democratic Leader Nancy Pelosi (CA) told us about her first bid for Congress in 1987, "[The guys] would say things like, 'It's not your turn.' I said, 'How can it be my turn? You established this line a long time ago. We've been waiting over 200 years. It is our turn.'"

The women we spoke with overcame these obstacles to entry, as well as additional structural and cultural hurdles confronting women candidates on the campaign trail.[3] According to some, their campaign success proved their seriousness as officeholders. Representative Jackie Walorski (R-IN) explained that the process of getting to Congress proves that candidates have what it takes to be successful legislators. She argued, "If you can come through that and you have proven yourself to people that believe in you, [if you have proven] that you are the best person to fight for them, I think that's the key." Representative Niki Tsongas (D-MA) similarly claimed that women have "earned the right" to be in Congress after going through "the fire of a campaign," a fire that may burn somewhat differently for the women who run. Once members are sworn in, Representative Eddie Bernice Johnson (D-TX) explained, "[t]here's not a question of whether or

3. Dittmar (2015) details the ways in which campaigns are gendered institutions, presenting different electoral realities to and shaping the strategies and tactics of the women and men who run. The hurdles confronting women on the campaign trail are both structural and cultural. Single-member districts, party gatekeepers, the strength of incumbency, and the financial demands of candidacy have all been shown to be distinctly challenging for women candidates in the United States (Carroll 1994; Darcy, Welch, and Clark 1994; Dabelko and Herrnson 1997; Fox 1997; King 2002; Baker 2006; Sanbonmatsu 2006; Palmer and Simon 2008, 2012; Trounstine and Valdini 2008; Crespin and Deitz 2010; Kanthak and Krause 2012). But the gender–power imbalance in campaigns is also maintained by gender stereotypes that continue to shape voter evaluations of women and men candidates' character traits and issue expertise (Fridkin, Kenney, and Woodall 2009; Banwart 2010; Dolan 2010, 2014; Koenig et al. 2011; Schneider and Bos 2014; Pew Research Center 2015). While some scholarship has questioned the influence of gender stereotypes in candidate evaluation (Brooks 2013) or their impact on electoral outcomes (Dolan 2014) today, Mo demonstrates that "gender attitudes in the electoral process remain consequential," even as they become more implicit than explicit (2015: 360). For example, Ditonto (2017) finds an indirect effect of gender stereotypes on evaluations of candidate competency. Moreover, expectations and experiences of gender-stereotypical terrain continue to influence how candidates and campaign practitioners perceive and wage political campaigns (Fox 1997; Bystrom et al. 2004; Panagopoulos 2004; Banwart and McKinney 2005; Dolan 2005; Schneider 2007; Dittmar 2015).

not somebody is qualified to be here." In addition to proving that women are equally capable of congressional service, some women members argued that overcoming campaign obstacles also makes women tougher and more prepared to take on challenges, including those related to gender, once they enter office.

NAVIGATING A GENDERED INSTITUTION

Although many of the women we interviewed perceive being a woman in Congress as easier than being a woman candidate, are obstacles associated with their gender evident once they are sworn into congressional office? At least nine women members responded with a clear no when we asked whether women faced gender-specific barriers or challenges in Congress. Delegate Eleanor Holmes Norton (D-DC) told us, "I could not think of one," and Representative Diana DeGette (D-CO) explained, "I've had a very successful time in Congress and I haven't really had anybody hold me back because of my gender." When asked about gender-based challenges, Representative Ileana Ros-Lehtinen (R-FL), the most senior GOP woman in the House, responded, "I don't see it, I don't feel it, I don't sense it," adding, "Things have changed a lot."

In characterizing the institutional environment, multiple senior women members, like Ros-Lehtinen, noted that it is easier being a congresswoman today than it was when they first entered the House or Senate. They shared stories of overt gender bias that women faced more than two decades ago. Representative Nita Lowey (D-NY), who entered Congress in 1989 with Ros-Lehtinen, recounted that in 1973 Armed Services Committee chair F. Edward Hébert (D-LA) forced Representative Pat Schroeder (D-CO) to literally share a chair with Representative Ron Dellums (D-CA), a Black congressman, at the committee's organizational meeting because he was incensed that a young woman sat on his committee.[4] Two decades later, Representative Lucille Roybal-Allard (D-CA), mistaken for a staff person,

4. See http://history.house.gov/People/Listing/S/SCHROEDER,-Patricia-Scott-(S000142)/

was stopped by chamber security and told she would have to wait outside. Similarly, coming out of her orientation in 2001, Representative Susan Davis's (D-CA) husband, who had joined her, was assumed by members of the press to be the new member of Congress.

Senator Dianne Feinstein (D-CA), one of only four women senators when she entered office in the early 1990s, recalled how she and her female colleagues were ridiculed for wearing colorful jackets on the Senate floor and were assumed to be conspiring against the men when they spoke to each other. House Democratic Leader Nancy Pelosi (CA) shared a similar observation:

> When we first came [the men] thought it was pat, pat, pat we have some women here. Then when our numbers grew and they would see us, I'd say, "Let's just go on and talk and they will get scared." [*Chuckling*] Not scared, but you know, "What are they doing now?" And they were always like, "What are you doing now?" And then there was a certain number and . . . they were a little apprehensive about it. I don't want to say threatening to them, but it was like, "Wow. What is going on here?" Some real changes.

In the House, Representative Marcy Kaptur (D-OH), who took office in 1983, described the disregard for women's voices during her first years in office. She said that when women would go to the floor to speak, "there was all this din in the chamber," adding, "It took almost eight years for anyone to really start listening to me."

These stories, recalled by women whom we questioned specifically about the challenges they face in Congress, are consistent with others that women members of Congress—both past and present—have shared publicly about the gendered treatment they received when they were even fewer in number and less powerful than they are today.[5] But many of the same women celebrated women's progress to date in acquiring congressional power and

---

5. See Dodson et al. (1995), Foerstel and Foerstel (1996), and Hawkesworth et al. (2001) for interviews with congresswomen that detail these instances of gender bias.

eliminating the most overt gender biases. Changes over time enabled Senator Shelley Moore Capito (R-WV), who entered the House in 2001, to report in a 2015 interview that gender biases were gone from Congress.[6]

The women Senators with whom we talked seemed most optimistic about this positive change, in part because of the power they hold in Congress's upper chamber. Senator Claire McCaskill (D-MO), who has documented the sexist treatment she experienced while in state government, told us, "I've never felt sexism since I've come to the Senate. I really haven't." Senator Heidi Heitkamp (D-ND) explained that being a senator has spared her from some of the biases she experienced earlier in her public service, "partly because you are at a level where [people] know they are dealing with a United States senator." Male senators recognize that women have the same power men have, according to Senator Barbara Boxer (D-CA). She talked about how the power of a single senator to hold up legislation is an institutional rule that levels the playing field for all members, women as well as men. As a result, she elaborated, "if you have a man who is prejudiced against women and comes over and says something stupid . . . you could hold up every single bill that guy ever put in." She added, "So go over and insult someone . . . at your own peril," concluding, "[H]e's not going to do it." Individual members of the House do not share the same power to hold up the legislative process,[7] creating conditions where bad interpersonal behavior may have fewer legislative consequences.

Representative Marcy Kaptur (D-OH), who was at the time of our interviews the longest-serving woman in the House, assured us that women are faring better in the lower chamber as well. She poignantly noted, "Margaret Chase Smith once said to me the progress is slow but it's steady. And I would have to say I repeat those words because it's been,

---

6. In an interview with *Cosmopolitan* magazine, Capito said, "I think whatever gender biases there might have been are gone" (Filipovic 2015).

7. Individual senators can place a hold on a bill or measure before it reaches the floor for consideration. The hold, which is communicated to the members' floor leader, is effectively a warning that the member may filibuster the measure if it is brought to floor debate. The power of the hold, reliant on the Senate rules' unique allowance of the filibuster, has no match in House legislative procedure.

I think, faster than I think she anticipated, but it's been steady ... It's a new day. There is an acceptance of woman members." Nancy Pelosi (D-CA), Minority Leader—and former Speaker—told us, "Once a woman has had the gavel, it's all different and changed."

Despite the reduction in the most overt gender biases over time, Pelosi and some of other women we interviewed emphasized that women still face some gender-related challenges in navigating the institution of Congress. Representative Maxine Waters (D-CA), who was first elected to Congress in 1990, told us that women's progress is tempered. She observed that while "[it] may not be as obvious as it used to be ... there are challenges" confronting women members of Congress. Senator Dianne Feinstein (D-CA) agreed: "It's very hard still to be a woman in this arena." House Democratic Leader Pelosi (CA) reported, "This [job] is not for the faint of heart, and you really have to be ready to make the fight. It's worth it. It's necessary for our country. But it is hard." Among the remaining challenges, according to women members, are the need to work harder to prove they belong and have a voice in what remain male-dominated spaces, the different demands and/or scrutiny they face in juggling work and family, and—most overtly—the gender disparities in congressional membership and positions of party and institutional leadership.

Scholars such as Wendy Smooth (2001, 2008) and Mary Hawkesworth (2003) make clear that Congress is not only gendered but also raced, creating distinctive conditions for its members. Consistent with the findings of this research, Representative Bonnie Watson Coleman (D-NJ), who is Black, told us that "women of color have unique challenges everywhere they go and under any circumstance." Discussing Congress specifically, she elaborated, "Racism is the most prevalent and pernicious and consistent hate in this country. So any time, any institution that we are engaged in, coming into that institution ... and happening to be African American, that's the first thing that you encounter." Studies of race and ethnicity in the US Congress, alongside the gender literature, illustrate the challenges that minority legislators, male and female alike, face in gaining and exercising influence (Singh 1998; Tate 2003, 2014; Casellas 2011; Tyson 2016). Brown and Gershon emphasize, however, that assuming for minority women that the interaction of race and gender acts only as a hindrance and is never advantageous is problematic (2016: 3).

In the remainder of this chapter, we investigate the ways in which challenges and opportunities are identified and experienced differently— or similarly—among congresswomen who navigate their work across lines of race and ethnicity, party, and position. Both within and across categories, women remain what Nirmal Puwar (2004) calls "space invaders" in the nation's federal legislature, marked as visible and apart from the norm in ways that affect their experiences and engagement with constituents and colleagues.

Women (Need to) Work Harder to Prove They Belong

Senator Barbara Mikulski (D-MD) has described how the "whole architecture" of the Senate was designed for men (Filipovic 2015). When she became a senator, women did not even have access to a bathroom near the Senate floor. Until recently, women were barred from swimming in the chamber's pool because some male members preferred to swim in the nude. And women members—with the help of Senator Chuck Schumer—challenged a rule that prevented members from exposing bare arms while on the Senate floor. Women in the House have faced similar structural challenges, celebrating the opening of their own bathroom in 2013.

But the biased infrastructure of congressional chambers is not limited to women-unfriendly rules or spaces. The dominance of men and masculinity in Congress pervades public expectations of who belongs, creating additional work for women members to prove themselves capable of congressional service. Senator Susan Collins (R-ME) put this explicitly with regard to women's entry into the Senate:

My experience has been, and sadly I think this is still true today, that when a woman is elected to the Senate, she still has to prove that she belongs there, whereas when a man is elected to the Senate, it's assumed that he belongs here. I will say once you pass that first test . . . then you're a member of the club. But I think there still is a barrier that men don't face, and I think that's true of Democratic women as well as Republican women.

Her colleague, Senator Amy Klobuchar (D-MN), summarized the doubts women like her confront: "It's people sort of thinking you can't govern or be in charge, even though you can."

This skepticism is not limited to senators, as women remain apart from the norm in both congressional chambers. Representative Kathleen Rice (D-NY) echoed her Senate colleagues' understanding of the dynamics at play, telling us, "People are not used to seeing women in these positions. So we have to work twice as hard to prove ourselves." Nirmal Puwar describes this phenomenon as "disorientation," characterized by "an element of surprise associated with seeing people who are assumed to belong elsewhere" (2004: 71). More than just unfamiliarity, Representative Marsha Blackburn (R-TN) described how Republican women face more explicit opposition to women in political leadership roles among some of the men in her party's ranks. Blackburn's observation aligns with research that has revealed partisan differences in voters' perceptions of women's capacity to meet the trait and issue competency expectations of elected office (Sanbonmatsu and Dolan 2009; Dolan 2010; Pew Research Center 2015; Dolan and Lynch 2016). Additional research indicates that Republican voters are less likely than Democrats to express a preference for women candidates or, more generally, support greater gender parity in government (Sanbonmatsu 2003; King and Matland 2003; Dolan and Sanbonmatsu 2009; PerryUndem 2017; Dolan and Hansen 2018). Blackburn told us, "Now, when it does come to inside of our party and inside conservative ranks there, I think it should be noted that some conservative men do not . . . view women as full and equal partners in the workplace. And I know for some men, that is never going to change." Her work, then, encompasses doing her part "to change their attitude . . . by doing a very good job" as a US representative, a task not similarly required of the men with whom she serves.

The standards by which members are deemed to be doing a good job may be different for women than they are for men. Senator Dianne Feinstein (D-CA) showed us a framed drawing that was gifted to her in 1992 by the mayor of Ottawa. The caption read, "Whatever women do they must do twice as well as a man to be thought of as half as good—luckily this is not difficult." Though she received the drawing decades ago, she believes its message still applies to women in power today. "I think women work harder than men," she explained. "We don't want to be wrong. We want to know the answer." Inherent in Feinstein's observation is a perception that the penalties for *not* knowing the answer are greater for women, who have to work harder to prove that they belong in an institution that has for so long been dominated by men. In her work on women in Parliament in the United Kingdom, Puwar refers to this as the "burden of doubt" that "natural" occupants of these spaces place on women and non-Whites; "they are not automatically expected to embody the relevant competencies," she writes, adding that they may experience "super surveillance" in which "their every gesture, movement and utterance is observed since they are viewed rather suspiciously" (2004: 73). Consistent with Puwar's observation that "minor mistakes are more likely to be noticed and amplified" for women legislators (2004: 73), Representative Lucille Roybal-Allard (D-CA) told us, "We're still evaluated or looked at in a much more critical way than our male counterparts," adding, "I think if a woman makes a mistake or says something [wrong], she is judged more harshly." Feinstein and Roybal-Allard were not alone in this perception, as multiple members pointed to the need for women to prove themselves as credible and competent members of Congress. Representative Rosa DeLauro (D-CT) said, "Women still have to prove their competency . . . You need to know more. You can't just answer the first question."

Some women, like Representative Martha McSally (R-AZ) and Senator Susan Collins (R-ME), believe that establishing credibility early can remove doubts about women's capacity to lead. But for others, like DeLauro and Roybal-Allard, this heightened scrutiny feels incessant. DeLauro, who has served 13 terms in the House, noted that women have to continue to prove their competency "no matter how many times that you demonstrate

[it]," and Roybal-Allard saw no end in sight for this gender disparity: "I think that constantly women have to keep proving themselves, and I don't know when that will end."

Whether the challenge is persistent or impermanent, tasking women with proving themselves to the public and to their peers as capable members of Congress creates additional work not shared by their male counterparts. Part of that work includes dismantling an institutional infrastructure built for men so that women are taken seriously as equally likely—and credible—leaders, as we discuss more in Chapter 7.

Women Fight to Have a Voice in a Boys' Club

Being taken seriously requires that women members' voices be heard on all issues and in all congressional spaces, which is not always easy according to the women we interviewed. Representative Grace Napolitano (D-CA) emphasized the need for women to break through the "old boys' system": "You kind of have to speak out. I'm here, I have a voice. [You have] to know when, where, and how to interject yourself to be able to be heard and understood." Sometimes that requires walking a "fine line," as Representative Cynthia Lummis (R-WY) told us, "between being viewed as without passion for a subject or being overly emotional about a subject."

That double bind has long confronted women in politics, whether on the campaign trail or in office, and is rooted in the misalignment of stereotypes and expectations we hold of officeholders and gender (Mandel 1981; Jamieson 1995; Eagly and Carli 2007; see also Schneider and Bos 2014). Perhaps revealing one effect of these expectations, Karpowitz and Mendelberg (2014) find that women speak less than their male counterparts in deliberative bodies, including school boards, in which they are underrepresented. They also find that women, when underrepresented, speak more in deliberative settings where decisions require unanimity, not a simple majority. This latter finding may help to explain why the House members we spoke with were more likely than their Senate colleagues to identify "being heard" as a challenge; while the Senate does not require unanimity, it is preferred and encouraged via institutional rules that require supermajorities and allow individual senators to hold up legislative progress. This may foster a more opportune environment for women to speak out.

Even when women do speak out, however, they are not always heard. Some women expressed frustration at being ignored, only to have a male colleague repeat and receive credit for an idea or point they previously raised. Representative Cathy McMorris Rodgers (R-WA) noted her own experiences of being overlooked, adding, "I'm always trying to figure out how to present in a way that will be heard." Breaking through ensures that women claim and receive credit for their contributions to congressional debates and achievements. And being heard ensures that women's perspectives and expertise are included in discussions across all policy issues on the congressional agenda.

Too often, multiple women members told us, women are looked to for expertise, opinion, or counsel on gender-stereotypical issues but are left out of debates on issues that are deemed the territory of men. Representative Kathleen Rice (D-NY) identified being "painted into a corner" of caring only about "women's issues" as the biggest challenge for women members. Challenging those assumptions of gender-specific areas of expertise or "appropriate" sites for policy engagement has been work that women members have done for decades. Representative Kay Granger (R-TX) recalled the responsibility she felt in the 1990s to push back on House Speaker Newt Gingrich (R-GA) on this issue:

> He called and he said, "Kay, we have a woman's issue coming up on the floor that we'd like you to address." And I said, "Oh? Is it health-care or education? Which one is it?" And he said, "I knew you'd say that." So I thought it was, sort of, my job to say we're [everywhere]— labor issues are ours, financial issues are ours.

She noted that progress has been made in recent years, crediting women with "being bold" and carving places for themselves in spaces where women's voices have not always been heard.

Granger has carved out such a place in the areas of global security and national defense, serving as the chair of the State and Foreign Operations Subcommittee and vice chair of the Defense Subcommittee on Appropriations. She points to newer women members like Martha McSally (R-AZ) who have established themselves as clear experts in this field as well. Nevertheless, establishing expertise on defense or security issues often requires more work for women than for men, Representative Kathleen Rice (D-NY) told us. She asked, "Given my position on the Homeland Security Committee, do I have to maybe work twice as hard to be heard and to be considered a credible voice on an issue that women have not really ever weighed in on before because they weren't in a position to?" Yes, she—a former district attorney—implied.

It is not only on security or defense issues where women's expertise is sometimes underrepresented, undervalued, or overlooked. Agriculture is another policy arena where women's voices have not always been valued. Representative Chellie Pingree (D-ME) described feeling discounted in her post on the Appropriations Subcommittee on Agriculture: "I'm sure there are many times when I raise my hand to speak on the Agriculture committee and take a particular point of view [that is] not always in sync with conventional agriculture [that] people are kind of like, 'What does she know about it?'" Attributing some of that skepticism to gendered expectations, she added, "Maybe they wouldn't feel that way if I was a male." Senator Debbie Stabenow (D-MI) has spoken publicly about being underestimated as chair of the Senate Agriculture Committee in the 113th Congress, where she pushed through the reauthorization and expansion of the Farm Bill.[8] She succeeded in passing the bill, and her female counterparts have made their voices heard on a wide range of policies not typically deemed "women's issues," combatting limitations on where and when women's contributions are valued.

8. She told *Cosmopolitan*, "I was sitting like this with someone, who at the end of the conversation reached across and patted my arm and said, 'Well, you know, this is going to be really tough, but I know you'll do the best you can,'" observing, "I doubt if that was said to the last chair of the Ag committee who wrote the Farm Bill" (Filipovic 2015).

Representative Donna Edwards (D-MD) raised a somewhat different challenge confronting some women of color. Despite representing one of the wealthiest districts in Maryland, her involvement in the Congressional Black Caucus has led her to advocate for policies that are not necessarily of greatest concern to her geographic constituents, sometimes taking energy and attention away from the issues key to her district agenda. "We haven't figured out a way to challenge those other members [in] districts which are equally, if not more, poor than some [to advocate for these issues]," she told us. She explained, "I shouldn't have to be the one who goes to the floor to talk about food stamps . . . I shouldn't have to be the one all the time to defend affirmative action." Edwards noted that in addition to placing an extra burden on women of color, putting Black women into this "cookie cutter box" presents a hurdle to attaining party leadership or higher office.

Finally, some conservative women and women of color identified distinctive challenges of being heard in political and policy debates. Representative Marsha Blackburn (R-TN) argued that challenges to Republican women came less from their party than from a media biased in "the way they talk to us and about us and exclude [us]." She added, "I find it really quite interesting that conservative women can be accomplished, polished, and they are pushed aside [by media] . . . [T]hey're not celebrated in the manner that liberal women are." Representative Virginia Foxx (R-NC) cites this as a more systemic bias in media against the Republican Party, arguing that the party's historic and current involvement in contributing to women's empowerment "has been negated . . . by the media."

Some Black women members expressed similar concerns about being heard in party and race-specific spaces. Representative Karen Bass (D-CA) observed that women members of the Congressional Black Caucus (CBC) "don't automatically think that the White women in the [Democratic] caucus will fight for their interest" in terms of issues and overall inclusion. When women of color *are* heard, they may be subject to greater backlash or scrutiny for speaking up. Representative Barbara Lee (D-CA) observed within her own party, "Sometimes some of the guys try to take on women of color when they wouldn't take on their own peers." But when this has happened, the women have not been deterred, she assured us. "It was wrong, and we beat it back."

Representative Bass (D-CA) joked, "The men couldn't silence the women if they wanted to." Even within the CBC, though, one member told us that she felt "men's concerns" are often positioned "at a higher order." Together, these experiences are evidence of the intersectional challenges women confront across congressional spaces. As Representative Alma Adams (D-NC) said when asked about challenges distinct to women of color, "[W]e have two things that we are battling, the color of our skin and the fact that we're women." These dynamics are at play across the multiple challenges that women members identified in our interviews with them, including posing hurdles to women's voices being heard, valued, and acted upon.

Women Are Evaluated on Style over Substance

Being taken seriously also requires that women be evaluated on substance over style, a challenge they still face on the campaign trail and once in Congress. Senator Kirsten Gillibrand (D-NY), who has famously written about male members' comments on her weight, told us, "Women are often judged on their appearance," adding, "They are often judged on nonsubstantive issues." Representative Renee Ellmers (R-NC) explained, "[Congressmen] put the suit on . . . and get in front of a microphone and debate an issue. When we do it, it's, 'Wow, what's that all about? She's got nice shoes on.'" Senator Tammy Baldwin (D-WI) added, "They still are more judgmental about women's appearance than male appearance," noting that these comments "are still . . . in abundant supply." That means that women often spend more time thinking about how they look and what they wear. Despite feeling no more challenged by her gender than her male colleagues in Congress, Representative Gwen Graham (D-FL) lamented, "I would say my biggest challenge of the day is just figuring out what to wear."

The media reinforce this focus, according to multiple members we interviewed, who derided media coverage of women's looks.[9] Representative Elise Stefanik (R-NY) identified differences in how the media treat women versus men in public service, telling us, "There are challenges in terms of your appearance, what you're wearing, whereas men don't often face that [type of coverage] as much." Representative Dina Titus (D-NV) characterized media scrutiny of women's looks as "Look at her hair, her earrings are too long or too short, skirt is too long or too short." Titus added, "They're not talking about a man's tie like that." Representative Anna Eshoo (D-CA) noted that this challenge limits not only to how but where women are covered. She noted, "[M]ore often you see our pictures and stories about us in the style sections rather than in the business sections," discounting women's policy expertise.[10] While multiple women noted this challenge, they described it more as an annoyance than a barrier to doing their jobs. Gillibrand explained, "I think [it's] no different than any workplace," and described it as a challenge "you have to just be able to navigate."

Women Juggle Demands of Work and Family

Congress is not just "any workplace," however, and the challenges members face in navigating the often conflicting demands of work and family seem to weigh especially heavily on women members, especially those with

9. About two decades ago, Niven and Zilber (2001) found that the views of congressional press secretaries were similar to those of the women we interviewed, arguing that the press defined women members of the US House by their gender.

10. Existing research on media coverage of women officeholders, not candidates, is limited but not inconsistent with congresswomen's concerns about whether their substantive work will break through. A recent analysis of male and female senators found that women senators receive less coverage than their male counterparts and that the messages they seek to communicate to voters are more often distorted by the press (Fridkin and Kenney 2014). Gershon (2012) finds differences in congresswomen's media coverage by race and ethnicity, with Black and Latina women candidates receiving less coverage than White women and Latinas' coverage being more negative and race-focused than coverage of their White female counterparts.

young children.[11] In addition to influencing their willingness to run for office in the first place, women's responsibilities at home create different conditions for and reactions to their service. As a result, today, as in the past, most women in Congress do not have young children at home.[12] But a notable few do.

Older women members, most of whom did not enter Congress until their children were grown, felt that the challenge of balancing work and family was even more acute when they were first elected. Senator Dianne Feinstein (D-CA) noted, "I see women, younger, able to raise children and do this. I would never have been able to do that." Representative Nita Lowey (D-NY) agreed that "it's very different" from when she was elected in 1989. Their reflections were mixed with both envy and awe. Representative Maxine Waters (D-CA) praised one young mother's capacity to take on multiple challenges as an "example of the will that exists in women."

While the perceptions among long-serving women were that women members of Congress today are better able to "have it all" than were previous generations, women of a variety of ages cautioned that they still may struggle in ways that their male colleagues do not to have it all at once. Representative Ann McLane Kuster (D-NH) observed, "My women colleagues with young children pay a hefty price." That price was described in different ways by the mothers of young children with whom we spoke. Some confronted judgment over their priorities and criticism that they were incapable of meeting the demands of both motherhood

11. This challenge is not unique to the US Congress. A 2010 report by the Inter-Parliamentary Union relied upon survey data from 123 parliamentarians from 50 different countries, in addition to supplementary interviews, and cited balancing work and family as the greatest challenge highlighted by survey respondents, with women parliamentarians challenged most by persistent gender role expectations in the home (Palmieri 2010). This is consistent with country- and government-specific studies conducted in the United Kingdom (McKay 2011; Charles 2014; Allen, Cutts, and Winn 2016), Germany (McKay 2011), and Australia (Crawford and Pini 2011) that rely upon direct reporting from members about the challenges they face in serving.

12. Just 16 of the 108 women in the 114th Congress, including delegates, had children who were in high school or younger.

and congressional service. Delegate Stacey Plaskett (D-VI), a mother of five, said she has fielded questions about who is taking care of her children while she is in Washington, while her male colleagues are rarely asked that question. Representative Grace Meng (D-NY) described the bias she has faced when bringing her young sons to events with her:

> People will say to me, "Oh, we didn't vote for you to be a babysitter," where I don't sense [that] the same thing is said to men. They think it's very noble for a father to bring his own child out, whereas for us, it's like, "What are you doing?"

Though Meng and others recognize and reject the bias in comments like these, facing criticism of their parenting can compound the guilt women may already feel about being away from their families. Delegate Plaskett (D-VI) expressed the guilt she was feeling the day we interviewed her, knowing that her son had a high school application essay to write and she could not be home to help him. She believes that women members struggle with this guilt more than men, but added:

> I think that the fear is that if you discuss it too openly, people will say, "Well, what the hell are you doing here, then?"—that if you have these problems, that means . . . you shouldn't do the job.

Minimizing guilt means that some women choose time with their families over networking or events in Washington, DC. Representative Meng (D-NY) said, "I try to spend virtually all my free time with my kids. And so, sure I might miss out intentionally on some events or activities, but it's because I choose to be with my children." Representative Martha Roby (R-AL), a mother of two school-aged children, talked about the dearth of time to be social—a challenge to forming relationships across the aisle—as a result of women wanting to get their jobs done and "then getting back home to our husband and children."

But sometimes the shared experience of parenting young children while in office creates opportunities for relationship-building. It was

Representative Cathy McMorris Rodgers (R-WA), the first woman to give birth to two children while serving in Congress, who encouraged Representative Martha Roby (R-AL) to run, assuring her she could handle the demands of work and family (Trinko 2013). In our interview with her, Rodgers noted that two Democratic women—Representative Debbie Wasserman Schultz (D-FL) and Representative Carolyn Maloney (D-NY)—hosted a baby shower for her, evidence that the commonality of motherhood can traverse partisanship. Schultz, who also entered Congress when her kids were school-aged, emphasized the importance of women's willingness—and capacity—to run for office with young kids. "I have had a much longer ramp in the arc of my career to more carefully make decisions, to balance my life, and consider possibilities as they came up because I started so early," she observed.

Women members forge bonds not only as mothers, but also as caregivers. As Representative Kay Granger (R-TX) claimed of women, "We're still the caretakers . . . we're taking care of our children, taking care of parents," creating a "harder tug and pull" than that faced by their male colleagues. Representative Ann McLane Kuster (D-NH) agreed: "I have many more female colleagues worried about caring for their spouses who are ill, their parents who are aging. I rarely had that conversation with my male colleagues." While these responsibilities represent challenges to women members who work to juggle multiple demands on their time and energy, they have also motivated and informed their policy advocacy. Many congresswomen are concerned with addressing work–family balance, elder care, and access to resources to ease the struggles that so many women—in and out of Congress—disproportionately face.

Women Remain Underrepresented

Perhaps increasing women's presence and power in Congress will normalize perceptions of members as individuals who lead both public and private lives. The members we interviewed pointed to women's underrepresentation as a primary challenge for all women across chamber, party, and race. Numbers matter, according to women members, and not just for the sake of fairness. The level and location of women's representation shape the influence women can and do have on policymaking, as well as the symbolic effects on women who may consider throwing their hats into the ring as candidates.

Despite the growth in members' diversity, neither chamber reflects the diversity of the US population. Representative Lois Capps (D-CA) observed, "[W]hen you are in the visitor's gallery on the floor of the House when everybody is there for a vote, the predominance of White males is still so strong." Her observation is backed by the numbers; of 435 House members in the 114th Congress, more than two-thirds were White men. Of the 100 senators, 74% were White men (Manning 2016). Women's underrepresentation was—and continues to be—particularly acute in the Republican Conference, where Representative Jackie Walorski (R-IN) described women members as a "tiny group." In the 114th Congress, Republican women were just 9.3% of their party caucus and only 5.2% of all members of Congress. The longer-serving members we interviewed, including Capps and Granger, noted their disappointment that the numbers of women have not changed drastically since they entered office. Similarly, other members expressed frustration that their numbers fare poorly in comparison with the rest of the world.[13]

Coming chapters will outline the myriad ways in which women believe their presence mattered to policy processes and outcomes. But women members also posit that the *lack* of women in Congress makes a difference in the allocation and exercise of power and influence. First, as Representative Elizabeth Esty (D-CT) observed:

Representative democracy is supposed to be responsive to and reflective of the needs of the entire populous. And so if you are getting this tiny slice, you're not going to be able to be as responsive and as attuned to different approaches.

13. As of May 2018, the United States ranked 103rd out of 193 countries in terms of the percentage of women serving in the national legislature (Inter-Parliamentary Union 2018).

Responsiveness is at least partly determined by who has and who does not have power, and power, particularly in the House, is determined by numbers. Representative Dianna DeGette (D-CO) argued, "I don't think that we have enough women members for it to really change the narrative." Representative Donna Edwards (D-MD) agreed, arguing, "[W]hen [women] are really part of the discussion and the decision-making, our voices are distinct . . . But we're just not to scale . . . There's just not enough of us, period."

Representative Susan Brooks (R-IN) made the case that developing greater "strength in numbers" would ensure that women "become an even stronger factor in how the House runs." That sentiment was shared by multiple women, particularly Republican women who face the greatest levels of gender disparity in their caucus. That disparity has a number of effects on members' behavior. First, without strength in numbers, Republican women take more risk in standing against their party. Democratic Representative Carolyn Maloney (D-NY) illuminated this reality when crediting Representative Marsha Blackburn (R-TN) with "going out on a limb" to back legislation creating a National Women's History Museum. Maloney explained, "When we think about it, it doesn't look like a profile in courage because it's such an easy thing for a member of the Democratic Party to support. But it was very difficult to be a Republican and support it." Other Democratic women opined that Republican women might be more reluctant to work with them, fearful of being labeled too moderate.

Multiple women members mentioned the need to reach representational milestones, calling directly for a "critical mass" of women in Congress overall or within their parties. While the recent literature on critical mass has cast doubts on whether there is an ideal level of representation that would allow for women's influence or effectiveness to be fully evident (see "Do Women Represent Women?" 2006), some congresswomen endorse the idea that reaching a minimum proportion of institutional membership—whether 25, 30, or 40%—will result in a Congress that is more responsive to women's experiences and perspectives in both policy and practice.

Representative Martha McSally (R-AZ) talked about the need for women to be at least one-quarter of the House Republican Conference. "From my experiences in the military, generally speaking, you are treated as an exception and a token sociologically until you have about 25% [representation]," she observed. "That's when . . . you actually become . . . part of what defines the organization and [are] helping to lead the organization." She noted that while GOP women have had a strong voice, "On the Republican side, we've got a long way to go to get to that 25%."

The leadership to which McSally alludes is of particular importance for women's congressional representation. The impact of increasing women's representation is limited if that representation does not extend across committees, caucuses, and positions of institutional and party power. Reflective of women members' disappointment with slow progress and concern over being niched into "women's issues" spaces, Representative Ileana Ros-Lehtinen (R-FL) emphasized the importance of adding more women's voices across all committees. She noted, "I'm saddened that when I got here I was the only Republican woman on the Foreign Affairs Committee, and now 26 years later I'm still the only Republican woman on the Foreign Affairs Committee." Ensuring that women are well represented across committees also increases the chances that they can advance into leadership positions on these committees.

But those chances are also shaped by committee leadership selection procedures that differ by party. For Democrats, greater reliance on seniority has created opportunities for women to "work their way up the ladder" to earn positional power, according to Representative Debbie Wasserman Schultz (D-FL). While House Democrats still vote on who chairs committees, Caucus rules dictate that the Steering Committee—which makes the selections to be ratified by the full Caucus—consider "merit, length of service on the committee and degree of commitment to the Democratic agenda of the nominee, and the diversity of the Caucus" (qtd. in Schneider 2006: 3). In the Senate, seniority has also been the top determinant in selecting committee chairs. Senator Amy Klobuchar (D-MN) praised the transparency of a seniority system, noting the challenges for women in more informal groupings or allocation of power.

Senior Republican women in today's Congress may confront greater challenges due to Speaker Newt Gingrich's 1995 break from seniority-based selection of committee leaders. At that time, Republicans not only changed Conference rules to allow members to vote by secret ballot for a committee chair without privileging senior members, but also imposed a six-year term limit on chairpersons (or ranking members, when in the minority). That term limit was notable for one Republican woman in the 114th Congress; Representative Ileana Ros-Lehtinen (R-FL), who ranked tenth in seniority among all Republicans in the 114th Congress, served as chair of the House Foreign Affairs Committee for only two years (2011–13) before her six years of leadership (including her time as ranking member of the full committee) expired. Ros-Lehtinen's situation was unique, however, because just three women ranked among the 50 most senior Republicans in the 114th Congress.[14] The sole Republican woman committee chair in the 114th Congress, Representative Candice Miller (R-MI), ranked 52nd in seniority among Republicans.

Today, the process of acquiring committee leadership posts is more competitive for Republicans, moving beyond established service as a criterion for appointment and being influenced by factors like party loyalty, personal relationships, and ideological alignment (see Schneider 2016).[15] Arguably, it is *both* the dearth of senior Republican women and the competitive process of attaining a committee leadership position that led to the very notable gender disparity in committee chairs in the 114th Congress. Although Republican women chaired multiple subcommittees, only one Republican woman served as a committee chair in the House. Similarly, just one Republican woman chaired a Senate standing committee in the 114th Congress. In contrast, Democratic women, who made up about

14. Representative Kay Granger (R-TX) ranked 24th and Representative Marsha Blackburn (R-TN) ranked 42nd in Republican House member seniority in the 114th Congress. The full list is available at https://pressgallery.house.gov/member-data/seniority.

15. Seniority seems to remain the most determinative factor in the acquisition of committee leadership positions among Republicans in the Senate, more so than in the House, but Senate Republicans are beholden to Conference rules on term limits in leadership posts (podesta. com).

one-third of their party's caucus, were ranking members on 7 of 20 House and 5 of 16 Senate standing committees.[16]

Representative Susan Brooks (R-IN) told us that there are not enough women chairing House committees and explained why that matters: committee and subcommittee chairs determine which legislation is debated, which earns hearings, and which ultimately moves forward in the legislative process. Democratic women added that the dearth of Republican women in committee leadership roles makes bipartisan female collaboration less likely, since the Democratic women gain more from lobbying powerful Republican male members who have greater positional power on the issues they seek to address.

Party leadership positions are also extremely, and increasingly, influential in setting legislative agendas and allocating institutional power to members. Here, both perceptions and realities of the status of women vary by party. Democratic women we interviewed pointed to the Republican Party's dearth of women in party leadership, perceiving the task of influencing party business as more daunting for their female counterparts across the aisle than for themselves in the Democratic Caucus. Two women cited the Republican leadership race in the fall of 2015 as evidence that Republican women have a steeper hill to climb in attaining top party posts. They both expressed a desire to see Representative Cathy McMorris Rodgers (R-WA) advance in party leadership, along with their disappointment that she dropped out of the leadership race soon after it began. One argued, "Obviously she wasn't supported," and the other assumed "that the boys would not allow it." However, Republican women, including Rodgers, did not confirm these claims. Instead, Rodgers noted the challenge of numbers and seniority in positioning women for party leadership. Representative Virginia Foxx (R-NC), who serves as Republican Conference secretary, mentioned that the gender disparity might also be

16. Democratic women senators served as ranking members on three additional Senate committees in the 114th Congress: the Select Committees on Ethics (Barbara Boxer, CA [co-chair]), Intelligence (Dianne Feinstein, CA), and Aging (Claire McCaskill, MO). Senator Amy Klobuchar (MN) and Representative Carolyn Maloney (NY) served as the ranking Senate and House Democrats on the Joint Economic Committee.

explained by differences in men's and women's decision-making calculus when it comes to running for leadership positions.

Contrary to the less positive characterization by Democratic women, Republican women such as Representative Martha McSally (R-AZ) noted the women they *do* have in leadership posts as evidence of power, progress, and influence in their party. Representatives Cathy McMorris Rodgers, Lynn Jenkins, and Virginia Foxx occupied three of eight Republican non-committee leadership posts in the House as Republican Conference chair, vice chair, and secretary in the 114th Congress.

In addition to these posts, Representative Brooks pointed out that women occupy leadership positions on subcommittees and special committees, which are often overlooked. For example, Representative Vicki Hartzler (R-MO) chaired the Oversight and Investigations Subcommittee of the Armed Services Committee, Representative Jackie Walorski (R-IN) chaired the Agriculture Committee's Subcommittee on Nutrition, and Representative Marsha Blackburn (R-TN) chaired the Energy and Commerce Committee's highly publicized Select Investigative Panel on Infant Lives in the 114th Congress. Brooks argued, "I've been really pleased at the opportunities presented to the women, [but] there just aren't enough of us." Even where Republican women do not hold formal leadership positions, they have influence, argued Representative Ros-Lehtinen (R-FL). She told us, "I think most women would say in the GOP that they have the ear of the leadership, that the leadership is interested in what we have to say," adding, "That's quite different than long ago."

Democratic women painted an even more optimistic picture of their influence in their party, pointing to the selection of a woman leader—Nancy Pelosi (D-CA)—as evidence, according to some, that they are on equal footing with men when it comes to power in their caucus. Representative Lucille Roybal-Allard (D-CA) argued that Pelosi's leadership has shown that women are both willing and able to succeed in congressional leadership roles, and Representative Maxine Waters (D-CA) called her "the poster woman for supreme leadership." Waters added that Democratic women's leadership goes beyond (or below) Pelosi, listing the women in ranking member positions across committees and subcommittees. Both Representatives Lois Frankel (D-FL) and Jan Schakowsky (D-IL) went so far as to describe a "good old girls' network" in the House Democratic Caucus as evidence that Democratic women are faring quite well. The Democratic women in the Senate also held positions of significant influence in the 114th Congress, serving as ranking members on 8 of 20 standing and special committees, including Appropriations, Intelligence, and the Committee on Health, Education, Labor, and Pensions.[17]

Both House and Senate Democratic women point to the policy impact of having women in positions of power within their party. Although women have expanded their presence in the Democratic Caucus and leadership, some women members noted that the Democrats still have work to do when it comes to gender equality in access, power, and influence. Representative Anna Eshoo (D-CA) described "the lack of deep and broad respect for women in leadership positions" in Congress, despite women's success. Eshoo challenged the Democratic Caucus's norm of privileging seniority in committee chair selection when she contested Representative Frank Pallone (D-NJ) for the ranking member post on the House Energy and Commerce Committee in the 113th Congress. Despite Eshoo's being backed by House Democratic Leader Nancy Pelosi (CA), Pallone—the most senior member of the committee—was selected by the majority of his peers. Eshoo's colleague, Loretta Sanchez, also lost a leadership race for chair of the Armed Services Committee in 2010 to Representative Adam Smith (D-WA). Sanchez told us, "[I had] more experience, I had shown up the whole time . . . I had done more for people to get elected in our caucus, etc., and they chose a man." Interestingly, the Caucus did not select the most senior Democrat on the committee, Representative Silvestre Reyes (D-TX), bucking the norm of privileging seniority in selecting committee chairs. Sanchez would have been the first woman, and the first Latina, to chair the Armed Services Committee.

17. Appropriations (Mikulski), HELP (Murray), Intelligence (Feinstein), Agriculture (Stabenow), Environment and Public Works (Boxer), Energy and Natural Resources (Cantwell), Ethics (Boxer), and Joint Economic (Klobuchar).

The Democrats' seniority system has worked to minority women's advantage when it comes to committee leadership, however. Elected primarily from majority-minority districts that are safely Democratic, women of color have been reelected at high rates and have accumulated significant seniority across House committees. In the 114th Congress, five of seven women ranking members of House committees were women of color, representing one-quarter of all top Democratic committee spots. They included three Black women (Maxine Waters, Financial Services; Eddie Bernice Johnson, Science, Space, and Technology; and Corrine Brown, Veterans' Affairs)[18] and two Latinas (Nydia Velázquez, Small Business; and Linda Sánchez, Ethics). This success reflects previous findings on the success of Black women Democrats in gaining committee and subcommittee leadership roles in Congress (Tate 2003; Rocca et al. 2011). That work raises an important point about *which* committees are led by minority members, necessitating attention to the substantive focus and overall prestige and power of the committees on which minority women lead (e.g., Tate 2003; Rocca et al. 2011). These findings align with comments by multiple members of the 114th Congress who noted that women of color may confront some distinct barriers to committee power and influence, whether because leadership seeks to spread the still relatively few women of color across committees (sometimes overriding their committee preferences) or because they are still not represented in the top Democratic Party Caucus leadership posts.

Notably, just two women of color held party leadership posts in the 114th Congress; Representative Terri Sewell (D-AL) served on the minority whip team, and Representative Donna Edwards (D-MD) served as co-chair of the Steering and Policy Committee.[19] Beyond the number of elected women in these posts, Representative Karen Bass (D-CA) noted

18. Representative Corrine Brown (D-FL) stepped down as ranking member of the House Committee on Veterans' Affairs in July 2016 after being indicted on 24 counts related to conspiracy and fraud in the operation of a charity founded by her chief of staff and used to fund the congresswoman's personal expenses. In May 2017, she was convicted on 18 criminal counts, including mail and wire fraud and filing false tax returns.

19. This is based on Minority Whip Steny Hoyer's March 2015 naming of his 114th Congress Whip Team. See https://www.democraticwhip.gov/content/hoyer-announces-castro-joining-democratic-whip-team-114th-congress.

the lack of diversity at the Democratic Party headquarters, reflecting that there is still a problem with full inclusion into party power.[20] Moreover, she argued that, within the Democratic Party Caucus, "the challenges ... [are] more about race than [they are] about gender."

While the level of women's institutional power may vary depending on how and where it is measured, the most persistent observation across all the women we interviewed was that there are still not enough women either in Congress at large or in leadership positions to have their voices sufficiently heard and their impact fully registered. Moreover, women's underrepresentation contributes to or enhances the other challenges cited by congresswomen. Not until significantly more women enter and acquire power in Congress will they have the ability to seriously weaken men's dominance or dismantle the historically masculinized infrastructure that works to women's disadvantage. As the highest-ranking woman in the House—Nancy Pelosi (D-CA)—told us after noting the import of her winning a "seat at the table" of congressional power, "We want more. We want more."

STRATEGIES FOR CONFRONTING CHALLENGES

Women in Congress are aware that they are members of a male-dominated club, and their discussions of the challenges they face reflect that continued imbalance of gender power. However, as our interviews suggest, the hurdles women must overcome once in office seem to be less severe than those they cleared on the campaign trail. Moreover, women members are quick to note that they do not allow obstacles of underrepresentation, unequal power, or institutional bias to get in their way. Instead, they push through, harness power in the numbers they do have, and strategically navigate congressional institutions to maximize their political influence.

20. This interview was completed before Donna Brazile became the interim chair of the Democratic National Committee (DNC) in late July 2016. In 2017, two minority men—Tom Perez and Keith Ellison—were selected as chair and deputy chair of the DNC.

Clearing hurdles of gender bias is not something new for women who have reached this level of political leadership. As Representative Marcia Fudge (D-OH) told us, "You've got to remember most of us have been doing things that are difficult for a long time before we got here . . . Most of us have worked in very male-dominated fields for a very long time." As a result, taking on gender-based challenges in Congress "really isn't much different." About four-fifths of women in the 114th Congress served in previous political offices, whether at the local or state level, before coming to Congress. Many of the women without political backgrounds were leaders in business or law. Four women in the 114th Congress come from the highly masculinized profession of military service. As Martha McSally (R-AZ), a veteran and US representative, observed, "[I've been in this] environment my entire life." She explained, "I think [being in Congress] felt to me similar to being in the military, to come here and be in a male-dominated organization, but I know how to . . . survive and thrive in that."

Sometimes surviving and thriving entails ignoring biases that can hold women back. Senator Jeanne Shaheen (D-NH) explained, "[M]y approach has been to say, 'This is what I'm trying to do' . . . and just keep at it and ignore those forces that may be trying to prevent me from doing that because I'm a woman, because I'm a Democrat." Addressing the harsh criticisms that officeholders sometimes confront, Representative Jan Schakowsky (D-IL) emphasized the need to "get over it" in order to move on. In other cases, however, powering through requires speaking up. Representative Barbara Lee (D-CA), who talked about the ways in which women of color "beat back" unfair scrutiny, elaborated, "I think women of color will call it like it is, really fast, if they are being messed over in the process . . . You know it when you're being jerked around on something . . . and you're not going to tolerate it. That's just our history."

Powering through or standing up to gender-based obstacles may be easier with help, some women members told us. In various ways, women members have created a "sisterhood in the brotherhood," as Senator Amy Klobuchar (D-MN) has called it, to maximize their power and influence, and create a united front when and where it is possible. That sisterhood has been evident in dinners for women senators, which

Senator Barbara Mikulski (D-MD) organized for many years. She told us that the bipartisan dinners originated with the idea that "when we spoke together in a united way, we would be a force." It is also reflected in the objectives of the Republican Women's Policy Committee (RWPC), which was launched in 2012. Representative Renee Ellmers (R-NC), the committee's chair, described the impetus for organizing as women in the Republican Conference: "We understand that there is power in numbers. And that we can empower each other and help promote each other." Coming together can also catch the attention of party leaders, according to Representative Ileana Ros-Lehtinen (R-FL), who told us, "Now that we have a structured group, we have the ear of leadership." The "sisterhoods" created among women members can also serve as a support system that helps others forging similar paths feel less alone. Representative Eddie Bernice Johnson (D-TX) described the attachment that she feels with her Black women colleagues in Congress and noted, "We look out for each other."

Finally, the women who serve must be strategic in order to attain and assert power in a male-dominated institution. As for any officeholder, identifying opportunities for influence is key, but women must also recognize where they confront distinct realities and limitations in order to make the most of those opportunities. Representative Martha McSally (R-AZ) detailed the way in which she positioned herself as a credible expert on national security issues by thinking strategically about where and when she chose to speak out and what she chose to say. Building her credibility over time, she noted, was key to ensuring that she was looked to by party leaders when events required her expertise. While establishing that credibility may require more effort for women than for men, according to some women members, many have cleared these hurdles to enhance their influence on policy. Some women have even used being underestimated to their strategic advantage. Representative Michelle Lujan Grisham (D-NM) elaborated, "I think too often, particularly in this institution, women are underestimated . . . That can play to [our] strength because they are not fighting against you because they don't think you can do it." She concluded, "It's another opportunity."

TAKING ADVANTAGE OF OPPORTUNITIES

Grisham's observation reflects the reality that being a woman in Congress can bring both challenges *and* opportunities. For some women, the opportunities appear greater than the challenges. Representative Marcy Kaptur (D-OH) called women's representation "the new normal" in Congress. Senator Debbie Stabenow (D-MI) implied that the normalization of women's presence is also occurring in campaigns, so much so that being a woman candidate can be advantageous. Stabenow explained:

It is an exciting time for women, and when I first got into elected office it was not viewed as a plus to be a woman. There were many more barriers, many more negative critiques, a lot of very sexist questions. Now it is viewed as a plus when you are running for office, it is viewed as an advantage to be a woman.

Representative Dina Titus (D-NV) was more specific, noting that "women are now being seen as better candidates and are being sought for that reason." While she was careful to reiterate that the challenges are significant, she explained of women candidates:

They work hard. They now are better able to raise money than they used to be. They're not as likely to get caught up in a scandal. And sometimes they're more relatable on the issues that are . . . economic issues in terms of kitchen table.

These insights provide an important reminder that congresswomen do not see the obstacles of being a woman, especially in campaigns, as operating independently of gender-based opportunities.

One of the opportunities cited by the congresswomen in our study is simply the ability to use the power granted to them for good purposes. Representative Gwen Graham (D-FL) said, "I find . . . that we have so many opportunities to make a positive difference and it should not be seen as a negative being a woman; it should be seen as a positive." Women have found various ways and sites in which to make a positive difference, supporting Graham's claim that the benefits of congresswomen's service outweighs the challenges they face.

In discussing women's underrepresentation as both a challenge and an opportunity, Representative Cynthia Lummis (R-WY) told us:

> [Being in a male-dominated institution is] an opportunity because there are times when the importance of women expressing [their] opinion on an issue [is great] . . . It is important to have those voices represented. So that's where the opportunities lie. And in some ways it's reversed sides of the same sword.

Representative Susan Brooks (R-IN) explained, "I actually have found there to be more opportunities than challenges, and I do believe that is because the leadership in both parties recognizes that we need more women in Congress." Relatedly, multiple women members discussed the opportunities afforded them because there were so few of them. Specifically, they noted instances where party leaders looked to them to speak on issues, serve on committees, or participate in congressional travel domestically or abroad in order to present a better gender balance to the public. For example, Representative Kathleen Rice (D-NY) shared her experience of being the only woman on a CODEL—a trip abroad by a congressional delegation—focused on homeland security.[21] She emphasized the motivation of organizers to protect America's reputation by ensuring gender diversity among the delegation, telling us, "There is that desire, I believe, to have diversity—whether it is domestically or when you're traveling abroad" to show "we're not back in the Stone Ages."

Parties may also seek to put women forward in congressional debates to protect their public reputation. When we asked specifically about this, Representative Virginia Foxx (R-NC) agreed, "[T]he party wants to

---

21. We use the term "congressional delegation" to refer to joint travel by a select group of members from multiple states and/or parties for congressional outreach, observation, or investigation.

present an image that is accurate, which is that women are involved and that women are a part of the process." Delegate Eleanor Holmes Norton (D-DC) said the same about her own party, arguing, "If anything, the party is looking for opportunities to make sure women get opportunities because it's very sensitive on women's issues and women's leadership issues." Representative Cynthia Lummis (R-WY) observed that having women spokespeople might be especially important to parties on "women's issues" like abortion. "Otherwise, it looks like they're gender-insensitive," she noted, adding of Republican men, "And I don't really believe they are."

Outside of opportunities given to women to ensure that their party looks inclusive on certain issues, some women members noted that being women affords them access to and insight into issues that their male colleagues may not share. For example, Representative Susan Davis (D-CA) highlighted the opportunity women have to "engage in a different way," as they did upon traveling to Afghanistan to work on women's empowerment there. She explained, "We've had doors open to us there that we wouldn't have had otherwise." Representative Karen Bass (D-CA) described another type of access she has been granted as a woman member of Congress. Discussing her work on child welfare issues, she noted that she sits in on committee hearings related to foster care, even when she is not a member of the committee of jurisdiction. Bass explained that men's deference to her has worked to her advantage, observing, "[T]hey're not really going to do anything to me because they don't know what to do." Whether having doors opened for them or opening doors for themselves that may otherwise seem closed, women members shared multiple examples of how being a woman member in a male-dominated institution actually works to their advantage.

However, that does not stop them all from advocating an end to men's dominance in Congress. When we asked about opportunities distinct to women in Congress, the most common response was related to women members' capacity to inspire and encourage more women to run for elected office. Even more than being role models, as detailed in Chapter 7, multiple women members emphasized the power they have as officeholders to encourage more women to run. Representative Cathy McMorris Rodgers

(R-WA) told us, "I have felt I need to make it a great priority to encourage other women that I believe should consider running for Congress to do so." Representative Suzan DelBene (D-WA) said that Rodgers was not alone: "I think all women have in mind how we help other women going forward." That is not only something women told us they feel they *need* to do, but also something they feel they are provided the opportunity to do because of their own political accomplishments.

CONCLUSION

While much scholarship has noted that legislative institutions in the United States, including Congress, are gendered, few studies have been able to illuminate the complexity of gender dynamics in institutional "processes, practices, images, ideologies, and distributions of power" (Acker 1992: 567). Doing so requires insights into both formal and informal processes and practices that create "distinctively gendered cultures" through which individuals' experiences vary by both sex and gender (Lovenduski 1998: 348). In this chapter, we provide insights into the gendered culture of the House and Senate by speaking directly to women members of the 114th Congress about how they experience the institution *as women*. When asked explicitly about gender-specific challenges, the women we interviewed identified much progress and—for some—an institution free of gender bias. But others claimed the playing field was not entirely level between men and women in Congress, noting persistent gender differences in presence, power, and perceptions that women are just as capable as their male counterparts. Understanding the ways in which Congress is gendered may also require recognition of the gender dynamics evident in the journey to get there. Many women reported that the gender-based challenges they faced in campaigning for Congress were more significant than any they faced once elected. Importantly, our interview evidence indicates that the gendered experiences that women share on the campaign trail may very well shape how they approach life as women in Congress.

The evidence of these challenges in campaigning and serving, and insights into how women overcome them, demonstrate that Congress is not only a gendered institution but also an institution in which race and ethnicity intersect with gender to present distinctive realities for women of color. Moreover, the "obstacles of being women," as described by Representative Titus (D-NV) at the start of this chapter, both heighten and are complicated by the hurdles of partisanship, demonstrating that finding ties that bind women together may be even more difficult in a polarized Congress. Structural differences between the House and Senate also influence congresswomen's experiences, with women in the Senate more emphatic about the power they can exercise in a smaller, supermajoritarian chamber.

Where women members are most united is in their belief that they need more women in the halls of Congress. They identify underrepresentation as one of the most significant challenges facing women in Congress today, and many pledged their commitment to inspire and recruit more women to run and to support them once they do. Sharing their stories and strategies for being effective in spite of institutional challenges is key to making good on that commitment. We delve more deeply into one of those institutional challenges—partisan polarization—in our next chapter.

4

Navigating Partisan Polarization

Partisan polarization has become a defining feature of American politics. Representative Zoe Lofgren (D-CA) commented that polarization "has been a major impediment," adding, "It's very frustrating." And polarization extends across issues; as Senator Tammy Baldwin (D-WI) explained, "It used to be that there was a whole bunch of issues that were out there that just weren't partisan." But this is no longer the case.

Voters are increasingly separated by partisan loyalties, with even social networks implicated in the partisan divide. Democrats and Republicans in Congress have grown farther apart with respect to ideology, largely driven by the Republicans' shift rightward (McCarthy, Poole, and Rosenthal 2006). Occupying a middle ground in Congress, and especially in the House, is precarious. The closeness of recent national elections has intensified the influence of parties within Congress; both Democrats and Republicans have ever-greater incentives to deny the opposing party a policy victory (Lee 2016). Indeed, congressional scholars Thomas E. Mann and Norman J. Ornstein (2006) have dubbed Congress "the broken branch," as both comity and transparency have eroded on Capitol Hill.

The women in Congress we interviewed largely confirmed that today's legislators face significant challenges due to the rise in partisanship. Not surprisingly, their responses depended on their status as majority- or minority-party members. The Republican women, as members of the majority, were less troubled by polarization than their Democratic women colleagues; they did, however, regret the gridlock, which they felt was caused by a president (Barack Obama) from the opposing party. Democratic women, and especially House Democratic women, expressed frustration over their ideological disagreements with Republicans. In this chapter, the evidence gleaned from our interviews illuminates the difficult partisan climate that contemporary legislators face as they pursue their goals—regardless of gender. This evidence is only part of the story, however, and we will turn to women's bipartisan activities and relationships in subsequent chapters.

CONTEMPORARY POLARIZATION

Congressional reforms of the 1970s, tied to changes in floor and voting procedures, consolidated and strengthened the power of party leaders and helped to enforce and promote greater party cohesion—a pattern that continues today (Rohde 1991; Han and Brady 2007; Hetherington 2009; Sinclair 2012; Pearson 2015). Lee aptly concludes, "These institutional changes emerged out of increased party conflict but also created feedback loops that have deepened and perpetuated it" (2015: 258). Theriault (2008) affirms that the increasing homogeneity of party caucuses allowed for the aggrandizement of power by party leaders, yielding further party discipline. Sinclair (2012) uses the term "unorthodox lawmaking" to describe the phenomenon of contemporary lawmaking that no longer resembles an expected, textbook process.

Less formal institutional changes have also contributed to a decline in bipartisanship. Members spend less time in Washington, DC, than at previous points in the 20th century, and bipartisan co-delegations to domestic and international sites for congressional outreach, observation, or investigation are increasingly rare (Hetherington 2009: 426; Alduncin et al. 2014). These changes in member relationships may be more exemplary of exogenous political changes than institutional modifications of rules or access. Redistricting has led to less electoral competition within districts and, thus, less concern among members about taking more extreme positions (Hetherington 2009). The characteristics of congressional districts have changed in other ways as well, including growing gaps in income inequality and partisan realignment in southern states in the latter half of the 20th century (McCarty, Poole, and Rosenthal 2006; Han and Brady 2007; Hetherington 2009).

Broader demographic changes and pressure by interest groups and other organizations also influence members and have contributed to party distinctiveness and polarization (Brewer, Mariani, and Stonecash 2002; McCarty, Poole, and Rosenthal 2006). Finally, increased polarization, or at least greater "party sorting," in the electorate contributes to polarization at the elite level (Fiorina and Levendusky 2006; Hetherington 2009). The Pew Research Center (2014) reports that the percentage of Americans who held ideologically consistent positions on major issues doubled between 1994 and 2014 (cited in Lee 2015: 264). In a 2016 report, Pew highlights the increased animosity between parties' public members as a key marker of persistent polarization.

Serving in Congress in this environment is not easy. Indeed, Representative Tom Cole (R-OK) explained to a reporter, "We're seeing the political equivalent of segregation going on in the country"—a partisan "segregation" that makes relationships across the aisle difficult and ultimately punishes members for finding ways to compromise (Warren 2014).

As Mann and Ornstein (2006) observe, personal relationships among individual members of Congress have suffered as partisanship has increased, procedural norms have eroded, deliberation has been curtailed, and the minority party is increasingly sidelined. The larger context of interest group and donor polarization means that even gestures of bipartisanship by members may be received negatively and become fodder for criticism from within a legislator's partisan camp—criticism that is then amplified by the 24-hour news cycle and social media environment. In their view, those entering Congress today have different expectations and perceptions of their constituencies than past generations and seem less dedicated to Congress as an institution (Mann and Ornstein 2006).

An important research finding indicates that the consequences of party polarization are more evident in the ability to move legislation than in the ideological leanings of legislative outcomes (Brady, Ferejohn, and Harbridge 2008; Hetherington 2009). As Binder writes, "Polarized parties—coupled with bicameral hurdles to compromise—undermine [legislative capacity]" (2014: 5). She finds persistent evidence of congressional "stalemate" on key policy issues from the 106th (1999–2001) to the 112th (2011–13) Congress, detailing a pattern whereby "[w]hen elections yield more polarized parties and chambers, bargaining is more difficult and compromise is more often out of reach" (Binder 2014: 16; see also Binder 2003).

WOMEN'S PERCEPTIONS OF PARTISAN POLARIZATION

Republican Women

What about women in Congress? How do they perceive the institution and the role of partisanship? Do their perspectives align with those of outside observers?

As members of the majority party in both chambers, the Republican women we interviewed were much less troubled by polarization than the Democratic women. We asked women in Congress, "How has the current environment of party polarization affected your ability to pursue your goals?" Republican women agreed that polarization exists, and as Representative Kristi Noem (R-SD) commented, "You know, it's been a little bit tough." But mentions of polarization, personal experiences with excessive partisanship, or concern about partisanship were simply less evident in our interviews with Republican women.

The severity of the perceived problems wrought by the growth in interparty differences within Congress was most commonly articulated by more senior women, by women serving in the House, and by Democratic women. Thus, dissatisfaction varied in largely predictable ways across our interviews according to party and chamber. Interestingly, Republican women were less likely to match the seniority of the Democratic women and thus may have been less likely to remember a more bipartisan time.

While polarization and minority status have largely disempowered House Democrats, such is not the case for House Republicans with their commanding majority. Republican women members did, however, note the ideological gap between the Democratic and Republican Parties with respect to divided government and the constraints House Republicans encounter in seeking to reach agreement with the Senate.

Some Republican congresswomen expressed their disagreements with the agenda of the Obama administration and the failure of the Senate to act on bills the House had approved. Representative Marsha Blackburn (R-TN), for example, was disappointed that bills from her chamber were not getting a hearing in the Senate: "The bills are sitting over in the Senate. I think we've got about 300 bills sitting over there right now." Likewise, Representative Vicky Hartzler (R-MO) observed that "in the House we've been able to get things passed that reflect my priorities, but due to the rules and the lack of the numbers and partisanship in the Senate, those have gotten blocked."

Divided government also meant that Republican women in the House saw Democratic control of the executive branch as a more pressing problem than partisan disagreement within the chamber. As Representative Ileana Ros-Lehtinen (R-FL) observed, "I would say that most of my battles in terms of foreign policy are against the Obama policies, and not necessarily against the policies of the US House of Representatives or the Democrats."

Democratic Women

The congresswomen who spoke the most passionately about the harms of polarization tended to be liberal Democrats. These women, who are the most ideologically dissimilar from the average House Republican, saw pressing problems—district, national, and global—in need of congressional action. Representative Anna Eshoo (D-CA) observed, "The majority really rules in the House. And so, if the majority, whatever party it is, is not functioning, then action for the country stops. It's very serious."

It is worth remembering that at the time of our interviews, Republicans held majorities in both chambers. But outside observers of Congress have blamed leaders of both major parties for exploiting their influence when in the majority (Mann and Ornstein 2006). Thus, concerns about polarization, while most frequently articulated by the Democratic women we interviewed, probably would have taken a more Republican flavor had we conducted this study during a period when Democrats controlled both chambers of Congress.

It was not just their minority status that House Democratic women lamented in our interviews. They noted the ideological distance between the two parties and the wide gulf that separates legislators—particularly House members—on such issues as civil rights, women's rights, and social welfare. These are issues at the heart of the policy agenda for many Democratic women, and especially Black women. The two parties switched places on racial issues over the course of the twentieth century, and the Democratic Party became known as the party of civil rights (Carmines and Stimson 1989).

Representative Maxine Waters (D-CA), who is Black, struck a defensive posture similar to that of other House Democratic women:

> This polarization is about a Republican Party versus a Democratic Party. A Republican Party that is influenced greatly now by the Tea Party members. And they don't believe in government as we know it. They believe that government must be substantially dismantled or downsized, particularly as it relates to public policy that deals with poor people. That deals with children. That deals with civil rights. That deals with women. I mean they are very much organized around undoing . . . many of the public policy achievements that . . . happened throughout the Congress of the United States for many years . . . This is about a Republican Party that is set in its ideology, and they're not moving.

Compared with their female House counterparts, Senate Democratic women were usually less likely to express such feelings of marginalization.

After all, institutional differences between the two chambers are real, and the Senate affords the minority a far greater role in policymaking than the House. Senator Heidi Heitkamp (D-ND) set the contrast: "[E]ven when we are able to do things in the Senate in a bipartisan way, whether it was immigration reform last Congress or No Child Left Behind reform this Congress, we always run into that brick wall of ideological purity over in the House."

Polarization is felt in both the House and Senate, but the role of parties and the nature of polarization are not the same across the two chambers (Mann and Ornstein 2006; Sinclair 2006; Monroe, Roberts, and Rohde 2008; Lee 2009). In part by design, the minority party has always retained more influence in the Senate than in the House. As Binder observes, all individual senators are empowered by Senate rules; today's senators, including those of the minority party, have rights similar to those they have enjoyed throughout US history (1997: 41). Norms of courtesy, respect, and reciprocity have long characterized relationships among the senators (Baker 1980; Sinclair 1989). And Baker notes that despite partisan voting on the floor, bipartisan relationships are still evident in the Senate today, including "cordial and cooperative relationships" among senators otherwise divergent in their ideological outlook (2015: 13).

Longer-serving Democratic women senators, such as Senator Barbara Boxer (D-CA), were more conscious of changes in the way partisanship has altered the legislative process over time:

Just to do something that used to be pretty routine like a transportation program, the highway trust fund, has become an obstacle course, to be honest, and I get it done . . . have gotten it done and also water infrastructure, flood control, safe drinking water, we get it done, but it is such a Herculean effort, and it is because there are people here now who don't believe in government, who don't want to do anything, who feel the state should do everything except the military.

Boxer's comments about gridlock echoed that of Democratic House women who yearn for a larger government role in solving problems.

Other Democratic women noted the difficulty of working in Congress when even facts can be in dispute, as Representative Jan Schakowsky (D-IL) observed: "For years I've said, talked about parallel universes, but I don't believe it's ever been more true than it is right now. That we see things so entirely differently that [there's a] whole different set of facts and truths over there."

More senior House Democratic women were especially cognizant of changes in the institution and seemed disheartened when we asked them to reflect on what had changed over time in Congress. They recalled their personal contributions to landmark legislation in years past, expressing pride in their experiences and accomplishments in the majority party.

An over time perspective led some members to pinpoint the institutional sites in which increased polarization affected them the most directly. For example, polarization can sour relationships with committee members, as Representative Eddie Bernice Johnson (D-TX) observed about her work on the Science, Space, and Technology Committee over the past two terms. She explained, "It's been very difficult to try to do anything to work that out. Now I have worked under probably five Republican chairs of that committee. And two Democrats. And this is the worst experience I've had since I've been in Congress."

Relationships have arguably deteriorated on the House Appropriations Committee as well. Representative Nita Lowey (D-NY), who is the ranking Democrat on the committee, observed, "I have always worked across the aisle and in fact as an appropriator, now a ranking top Democrat, we always used to say, 'There are Democrats and Republicans, and [then there are] appropriators.' But that's not the case anymore."

Some scholars have pointed to the election of more ideological members to Congress as one source of partisan polarization (Carmines and Stimson 1989; McCarty, Poole, and Rosenthal 2006; Theriault 2008). But both the electoral and institutional contexts that members of Congress face have been transformed. Even when individual members have stayed the same, the possibilities for cooperation may have changed. For example, Representative Lois Capps (D-CA) noted that her relationship with Republican colleague and fellow Californian Mary Bono had eroded over the years. The two worked together on heart disease legislation aimed at women, including provisions that were passed in the Affordable Care Act. But polarization intervened, and Capps noted that "there came a time when the Congress became increasingly partisan [so] that there was real pressure on [Bono] not to work across the aisle."

Thus, it is not only the replacement of members that has altered legislative life. Instead, congresswomen understand the real consequences they face from their leadership. In the past, securing funding for women's health and including women in government-funded health research united Republican and Democratic women (Schroeder and Snowe 1994). Bipartisan efforts had far fewer negative consequences than they do today.

In the next chapter, we will see that most of the women members we interviewed believe that women in Congress are more bipartisan than men. However, a few of the Democratic congresswomen we interviewed saw polarization as gender-neutral, including Representative Zoe Lofgren (D-CA), who observed, "When you say this, you run the risk of sounding like you're a partisan. But the Republican Party has gone off the deep end. And it's including the female members of the party."

We did not query congresswomen about their beliefs on the origins of polarization in Congress. But some of the women legislators saw larger national forces hindering bipartisanship. They pointed to the gerrymandering of congressional districts, making for more homogeneous and ideological districts, and the growing influence of ideological interest groups. Representative Marcy Kaptur (D-OH) observed, "It's very hard to get cooperation when there's acid in the pool. And that acid is unrepresentative government really because of the gerrymandering."

Even when their Republican colleagues might have a personal interest in an issue or a genuine desire to work across party lines, Democratic congresswomen said that bipartisanship does not always prevail in the end because members are constrained electorally. Colleagues of the other party may even convey a sense of regret. Representative Roybal-Allard (D-CA) explained, "And so you will get members who want to work and to compromise but say, 'I can't because I ran on this platform and if I go back home I could lose the election because I would be seen as caving in.'"

Similarly, some Republican members fear that bipartisan collaboration might generate a primary challenge. Representative Jackie Speier (D-CA) claimed, "It's all about the risk of having a boatload of money dropped into a primary against them that prevents them from doing what is right."

From these House Democratic women's perspectives, the rise of conservative interest groups and conservative members is exacerbated by the size of the Republican majority. For example, Representative Brenda Lawrence (D-MI) described her view of how marginalized the Democratic Party has become in her chamber:

> I have met my colleagues on the other side of the aisle, great people, individuals, love their family, love their country, but it's something about once it gets to that leadership piece, we'll just go under this umbrella and vote against things that we've talked about and I know they believe and support. I don't get that . . . "Oh, I can't do that," you know—the party . . . I firmly believe in this two-party system . . . I'm an African American in the United States and at one time I was considered property, at one time I wasn't allowed to vote, but a two-party system [ground] out a Constitution and amendments that give rights and freedoms . . . I know that there is a grind between the two philosophies that produce some amazing freedoms and democracies and policies, but I don't see us grinding . . . I don't think you should ever have a supermajority like we have here.

One member, Representative Debbie Wasserman Schultz (D-FL), noted that congressional staffers can be an impediment as well: "[O]ftentimes, there are staff who stand in the way and who make presumptions about the member on our side of the aisle that, you know, they don't want to work, or they don't want their boss working with us."

We should note, however, that some of the congresswomen we interviewed believed that the extent of partisan conflict among members is often exaggerated. Representative Virginia Foxx (R-NC) told us, "There is polarization, but it is misunderstood that we get along personally very well. I suspect you've heard that from other people. There isn't animosity between and among individual members." Similarly, Delegate Eleanor Holmes Norton (D-DC) explained that policy disagreements can co-exist with friendships: "[There are] terrific friendships. People don't carry off the floor what they see on C-SPAN, they do not carry that with them . . . These are grownup people here." Indeed, Representative Gwen Graham (D-FL) observed that her friendships and relationships within Congress have survived despite explicit instructions to the contrary from party leaders:

> I think because I was one of only two Democrats to defeat a sitting Republican incumbent in 2014, my election was very high profile and therefore the party apparatus . . . and this is not exclusive to Democrats or Republicans, but the National Republican Congressional Campaign Committee has said to members in Congress, "Don't help Gwen." You know, "Don't work with Gwen, because we don't want her to be able to point to achievements and being effective." But I give great credit to my friends and colleagues who have not allowed that to stand in the way of working together with me.

PARTISAN ISSUE DIFFERENCES

At its heart, partisan polarization is about policy disagreement. And strong policy differences were certainly apparent in most of our interviews with women in Congress. Several of our interview questions concerned some of the most salient debates taking place in the 114th Congress.[1] Republican and Democratic women positioned themselves very differently in these

1. We tailored one or two policy questions in each interview to the particular member of Congress, depending on her policy priorities and the salience of those issues in the 114th Congress. We sought women's perspectives on the major legislation facing the 114th, including abortion and Planned Parenthood, criminal justice reform, education, gun control, human trafficking, immigration reform, opioids, and addressing sexual assault on campuses and in the military. The women we interviewed also shared their policy activities and positions in response to our open-ended questions about their representational goals and current priorities.

debates, often expressing their views and characterizing those of their partisan opponents with great passion. While we would not necessarily anticipate that women would speak with one voice on partisan issues (Swers 2013; Harbridge 2015), it is worth highlighting some of the partisan differences that emerged in the course of our interviews.

Immigration is a good example. Democrats and Republicans have failed to find a path forward on the issue. During the 114th Congress, the Supreme Court's willingness to review President Obama's executive orders about delayed action for certain groups of undocumented individuals led to distinctive congressional stances, and Democrats and Republicans weighed in with briefs for and against Obama's policies in *United States v. Texas*.[2] The 2016 presidential election and Donald Trump's intense anti-immigrant rhetoric underscored the Republican Party's position against reforms that would ease restraints on immigration. When Speaker John Boehner (R-OH) resigned his post unexpectedly in 2015, opposition to immigration reform appeared to be a litmus test in the selection of his successor.

In contrast, the Democratic Party continues to champion immigration reform, even if certain issue areas, such as deportation, separated congressional Democrats from the Obama administration. While reform was not on the agenda of the 114th Congress, a host of issues related to immigration such as sanctuary cities, the increased number of unaccompanied minors at the border, and border security attracted attention.

Still, some areas of agreement between the two parties on immigration can be detected. After all, the Senate passed comprehensive immigration reform in the 113th Congress when the Democrats held the majority. Polls reveal majority public support for aspects of immigration reform proposals, and according to some observers, there may be greater House Republican support for reform than is often assumed. Thus, while the issue is certainly partisan, Republicans are somewhat divided internally on the issue.

---

2. The Supreme Court's 4–4 ruling on the case in June 2016 effectively blocked implementation of President Obama's "Deferred Action for Parents of Americans and Lawful Permanent Residents," or DAPA, program.

We posed a question to several of the congresswomen we interviewed about whether any bipartisanship exists among women legislators on immigration-related issues. . A typical response was that of Representative Ileana Ros-Lehtinen (R-FL), who commented, "I would say not as much, no. That is more driven by party lines than anything." Asked the same question about whether women in Congress had worked together on immigration across party lines, Representative Zoe Lofgren (D-CA) responded, "We haven't seen the Republican women step forward and help in any way."

It is not just immigration. Among the most contentious issues of the 114th Congress were policies related to abortion and federal funding for Planned Parenthood. And a partisan gulf among women was quite clear in our interviews in these areas.

Representative Carolyn Maloney (D-NY) explained that she was the first to use the slogan the "War against Women," designed to call attention to Republican efforts to curtail women's reproductive choices. Another of our interview subjects, Representative Marsha Blackburn (R-TN), had been chosen to chair the House Select Investigative Panel on Infant Lives, tasked with investigating tissue procurement and abortion provider business practices in the wake of controversy around Planned Parenthood. Congressional hearings about Planned Parenthood in response to se-cretly recorded, and later proved to be doctored, videotapes concerning fetal tissue research provided some of the most dramatic, and partisan, moments of the entire 114th Congress.[3] Representative Blackburn noted that her selection as committee chair was "a distinct honor."

Our interviews with women legislators often delved into these partisan differences over abortion among women. Representative Bonnie Watson Coleman (D-NJ) stated, for example:

It's rare now that Republicans and Democrats come together. But it's also a polarization that exists within women. So we can't depend

3. On December 30, 2016, the panel issued a final report targeting Planned Parenthood and denouncing the value of fetal tissue research. The report offered no evidence that abortion providers profit from fetal tissue research, which was what spurred the creation of the panel.

upon women in the Republican Conference to support fundamental issues of a woman's right to choose. We can't expect them to work with us on what we consider to be a war on women and negatively impacting access to healthcare.

Republican control of the House and Senate had put the Democratic Party on the defensive with respect to abortion-related provisions that are regularly attached to a wide variety of bills (Ainsworth and Hall 2011). As a result, Democratic women believed they must be vigilant throughout the legislative process. As Senator Patty Murray (D-WA) observed, "Every time they bring up legislation to take away a woman's right to choose, I'm out there blocking it."

In sharp contrast, Republican women spoke passionately about their pro-life views and advocacy against Planned Parenthood funding. Our interview with Representative Martha Roby (R-AL) is a good example:

> My colleagues on the other side of the aisle continue to make this . . . or try to coin this in terms of women's health. Abortion is a terrible thing, it's very ugly. It not only kills the baby but it has tremendously harmful . . . has very harmful effects on the woman who made that decision. So if it's about women's health, we have rural health centers all over the country that do provide the type of care that my Democratic colleagues are defending Planned Parenthood on, and they outnumber Planned Parenthood clinics . . . 20 to 1.

When abortion first emerged as a national policy issue, it was not partisan (Adams 1997; Sanbonmatsu 2002). There was no clear pattern between the parties in Congress. But as pro-life and pro-choice interest groups aligned with the Republican and Democratic Parties respectively, abortion would come to differentiate the party's agendas and be viewed as a litmus test for candidates up and down the ballot (Freeman 1987; Wolbrecht 2000).

Republican women who have entered Congress in recent years have been more conservative than their predecessors, consistent with the increasing polarization between the two parties and the election of more pro-life women; but not all Republican women in Congress are interested in serving as their party's spokeswomen on this topic (Swers 2002, 2013). In contrast, studies show that Democratic women are usually the most vocal advocates for reproductive rights in both the Senate and the House (Dodson 2006; Swers 2013).

Related to these highly partisan policy disagreements on women's reproductive rights is the gradual decline in the ability of the Congressional Caucus for Women's Issues (CCWI) to unite women of both parties behind a legislative agenda. Founded in 1977, the caucus successfully involved women from both parties in efforts to further the status of women (Gertzog 2004); the caucus is credited both with helping to pass landmark legislation and achieving more modest gains. For most of its history, women in the caucus have agreed to disagree on abortion (Gertzog 2004; Dodson 2006). Among its many accomplishments, the CCWI helped to extend the ratification deadline for the Equal Rights Amendment (ERA), promote economic equity for women, pass family leave at the federal level, and secure equal treatment for women's health issues and research. In the 103rd Congress, 66 CCWI bills were enacted, setting a record (Dodson 2006). At that time, almost all women in the House were members of the caucus.

But in 1995, when Republicans took over the House, the leadership ended official recognition of legislative service organizations, including the CCWI, which severely weakened the caucus (Gertzog 2004). The CCWI, like other caucuses, had enjoyed resources, office space, staff members, and other benefits that accompanied official recognition. The CCWI continues to function as a congressional membership organization, but the loss of recognition as well as the election of more conservative Republican women and increased polarization between the two parties has reduced its significance (Gertzog 2004). In some of our interviews, it was apparent that the decline of the CCWI was exemplary of the dramatic partisan changes women members in the House experienced. Representative Eddie Bernice Johnson (D-TX), who was serving in her 12th term at the time of our interview, observed:

> Many of the issues . . . we try to work through [in] the women's
> caucus across party lines will go just so far. Now there are a number
> of—I'm a nurse by profession— . . . a number of nurses who have
> joined the Republican side. But I've not been able to develop much of
> an exchange of ideas. They seem to really want to walk pretty much
> [in] lockstep with their party.

Serving in the same occupation can sometimes bring women in Congress
together. Yet even commonality arising from a shared, female-dominated
occupation is not always a sufficient basis upon which to forge a bipartisan
policy agenda.

Other, expected partisan disagreements came to the surface in our
interviews. Some of the Democratic women we interviewed spoke
proudly of passage during the 111th Congress of the Affordable Care
Act (ACA)—President Obama's landmark healthcare legislation that
was enacted without a single Republican vote. In contrast, opposition
to the ACA has been a source of great partisan interest and enthusiasm
among Republicans, inspiring at least one of the Republican women we
interviewed, Representative Renee Ellmers (R-NC), to seek office.

In the years after passage of the ACA, including the 114th Congress,
Republican party leaders took dozens of votes to repeal Obama's signature
policy accomplishment, making opposition to the legislation their central
campaign issue. Women legislators on both sides of the aisle, including
then–Speaker of the House Nancy Pelosi, have played key roles working
for and against the legislation (Jacobs and Skocpol 2010).

The subject of guns is increasingly dividing the two parties as well,
with the Democratic Party more supportive of gun control efforts, and
the Republican Party largely opposed (Cook and Goss 2014). Many
Democratic women we interviewed spoke very critically of the Republican
Party's stance on guns, including Representative Robin Kelly (D-IL), who
stated: "[T]he NRA and the Republicans are hand in hand now and they
have made me, you know, the enemy."

Meanwhile, Representative Tulsi Gabbard (D-HI) noted the problems
partisanship poses for a host of issues, including gun control:

The hyperpartisanship is something that not only affects things that I would like to see enacted, but really affects the overall productivity of Congress in a very negative way. You know, too often important issues to the American people, not to one party or another, are politicized and turned into these issue footballs that are lobbed back and forth with the objective of seeing who can score the winning touchdown for their party rather than saying, "How do we actually sit down and work this out so that we can score a win for the American people?"

After a mass shooting in Orlando, Florida, in June 2016, Senator Chris Murphy (D-CT) led a nearly 15-hour filibuster by Senate Democrats to demand a vote on gun control legislation. As Murphy requested, votes were held the next week on two Democrat-backed, gun-related amendments to the fiscal 2017 Commerce, Justice, Science spending bill, but both were rejected along mostly party lines.[4] One week later, in one of the most dramatic moments of the 114th Congress, House Democrats seized control of the floor and staged a sit-in that lasted for more than 24 hours to protest the lack of congressional activity on gun violence. One of the leaders of that protest was a Democratic woman, Representative Katherine Clark (MA), who has made gun safety one of her signature issues. In contrast, Republicans decried the sit-in, and some members, including Representative Diane Black (R-TN), took to CNN and other media outlets to criticize their Democratic colleagues. Black, for whom protecting gun rights is a central campaign issue, objected to the sit-in on procedural grounds. House Speaker Paul Ryan (R-WI) agreed, calling the sit-in a "publicity stunt." Despite turning to unorthodox methods to combat the

4. Senator Dianne Feinstein's (D-CA) measure to let the attorney general deny firearms and explosives to any suspected terrorists fell on a 47–53 vote; one Democrat, Senator Heidi Heitkamp (ND), voted against the measure, and two Republicans, Senators Kelly Ayotte (NH) and Mark Kirk (IL), voted for it. The second amendment, sponsored by Senators Chris Murphy (D-CT), Cory Booker (D-NJ), and Charles Schumer (D-NY), would have expanded background checks for anyone trying to purchase a firearm, not just at stores but also at gun shows and online. That measure fell 44–56; three Democrats—Heitkamp, Senators Joseph Manchin (WV) and Jon Tester (MT)—opposed it, and just one Republican—Kirk (IL)—voted for it.

gridlock they perceived, Democrats had little success in overcoming the strong partisan unity and strict procedural rules of the House. No legislation was passed directly addressing gun violence in the 114th Congress.

DEMOCRATIC WOMEN'S STRATEGIES FOR NAVIGATING POLARIZATION AND MINORITY-PARTY STATUS

Because they are in the minority in both chambers, polarization arguably poses a greater set of challenges for Democratic women than Republican women as they pursue their policy goals. Some of the congresswomen we interviewed shared their insights and described their strategies for being effective legislators within the current environment. The interaction of minority-party status with partisan polarization has led some Democratic women in the House, in particular, to be both creative and persistent and to pursue multiple avenues of advocacy in the face of gridlock.

Not surprisingly, Democratic women often see their role as one of blocking the Republican majority, as is typical of the minority party (Jones 1970; Connelly and Pitney 1994; Green 2015). As Representative Dina Titus (D-NV) observed, "We have to play a good defense as well as an offense." Representative Doris Matsui (D-CA), who also spoke about her party's blocking strategy, noted that they are playing a "long game" and argued that Democrats know they will need to "fight another day."

As some of the Democratic women in Congress noted, party cohesion is critical in the face of their wide seat disadvantage. In our interviews, House Democratic Leader Nancy Pelosi (CA) was credited with holding House Democrats together to block Republican proposals. And as Representative Yvette Clarke (D-NY) explained, unity within subgroups of Democrats, such as the Congressional Black Caucus (CBC), was also useful in helping hold the Democratic Caucus together. She argued that the CBC might "see that something is coming down the pike that across the board will have an adverse impact for our constituents, and for the nation by extension, and you know we will hold together as a voting bloc."

What Senator Claire McCaskill (D-MO) spoke of as "oversight" is another way that members can exert influence in what is often a dysfunctional environment. She explained:

> I'm lucky that I really enjoy oversight, and oversight around here is like shooting fish in a barrel . . . So I have found a lot of satisfaction in just oversight . . . I have always seen my job as try[ing] to make government work better and smarter for the great people who are paying for it every day.

Some women members of Congress gave specific examples of interventions they have waged on important matters for their districts. Gridlock can lead legislators to look for strategies for influence beyond passing legislation. For example, some of the women we interviewed, such as Representative Chellie Pingree (D-VT), focus on the executive branch and the arena of rule-making:

> You know, we keep running the Department of Agriculture, the Department of Interior, or the VA, and in a tricky environment like this I think the way that, you know, we continue to feel productive and useful to our constituents is by making sure we keep a lot of our focus on those things where the progress isn't going to stop.

Likewise, Representative Marcy Kaptur (D-OH) explained how she tackled an environmental challenge affecting her district, noting that it isn't only at the level of the federal government that women can make a difference: "If I have an objective I will find a way to meet it . . . We work collaboratively on many levels to try to accomplish a given goal that matters to the district and hopefully to the country."

The Democratic women we interviewed also spoke of the need to think beyond the halls of Congress to make progress. Representative Jan Schakowsky (D-IL), for one, pursues her legislative goals outside as well as inside the institution, describing her involvement with groups outside Congress advocating for the minimum wage—advocacy that can affect the congressional agenda. As she noted, "I think a lot of those growing movements are helping to shape the environment in important ways." Most of the evidence concerning partisan polarization that emerged from the interviews had a negative cast, as women members noted the lack of progress and challenges that stand in the way. Interestingly, however, one of our interviews provided a more positive perspective. For Representative Gwen Moore (D-WI), disagreements within the Republican Conference provide openings for influence:

> The other side of it is that the fact that Republicans have been so dysfunctional . . . [has] created tremendous opportunities for people like me. Because when they can't get something like the Export-Import Bank, for example, out of the committee because of their chairman's ideological views, you know, then they have to sneak, tiptoe behind and come up with a strategy, and they look for people, they know that I'm there. I'm floating around looking for a chance to help get it over the finish line because it's important work. I'm looking forward to that on some of these other social issues.

Of course, the most direct way for Democrats to gain more control over the legislative agenda would be to flip control of the House and Senate. Indeed, Democratic women such as Representative Rosa DeLauro (D-CT) emphasized the need to change the national conversation to demonstrate the importance of Democratic issues and help elect a unified Democratic government. Likewise, Representative Bonnie Watson Coleman's (D-NJ) response was simple. When asked how she wanted to accomplish her most important goal for the 114th Congress, which is equality, she replied that she would be "fighting very hard for a Democratic majority."

At the same time, even Representative DeLauro said she was working to find ways to make a difference within the context of a Republican-controlled House, explaining, "But you have to play hardball to get things done here . . . You gotta work the system as it is . . . You gotta find out what that person cares about, what they're interested in, and make the case, you know." This pragmatic outlook helps women surmount polarization, as we will see in greater detail in the next chapter.

CONCLUSION

That partisanship has been on the rise in Congress is not in doubt. Women in Congress with more seniority were especially cognizant of how the institution had changed with time. Our interviews, and particularly those with longer-serving members, confirmed the existence of discontent and perceived dysfunction. Democratic women—particularly in the House— lamented their minority-party status and, relatedly, their lack of influence in an especially polarized environment. The gridlock and challenges created by divided government affected women across party lines and chambers, however. To some extent, women's strategies in this environment are what one could anticipate as legislators continue to find ways to tackle the issues of greatest importance by partnering with activists and groups outside of Congress or seeking engagement with the executive branch. And even though Republican women did not always articulate this view in their interviews with us, Democratic women sometimes noted that their Republican colleagues would be more inclined to find bipartisan solutions were it not for the constant threat of a primary challenge from the right.

Despite the many obstacles created by a partisan environment, our interviews revealed that women in Congress do often work across party lines and even Democratic House women find ways to influence policy. Oftentimes, this work is with other women. This is the subject of the next chapter.

5

Congresswomen's Work across Party Lines

Strong institutional and electoral forces and vast policy differences work against bipartisanship on Capitol Hill. Yet we will see in this chapter that women in Congress regularly work with members of the other party. They do so with male and female colleagues across a host of issues, including issues of special concern to women as a group. Virtually all of our interviews provided specific examples of this bipartisan work. The extent of these bipartisan efforts is somewhat surprising, given that existing accounts emphasize gridlock and the absence of comity between the two parties in Congress.

We also find, notably, that the majority of the women members in our study believe that women in Congress are more likely than men to work in a bipartisan fashion. As one example, Senator Tammy Baldwin (D-WI) responded to our question "Do you think the women in this Congress are more or less likely than the men to work together across party lines?" with a simple response: "More! And I put an exclamation point after that." This sentiment was widespread. No differences were apparent to us on the basis of legislators' race/ethnicity or chamber. And both Democrats and Republicans viewed women as more bipartisan than men.

In this chapter we probe congresswomen's reported reasons for engaging in bipartisanship. Their hypotheses were several, but the most common reason they offered was the existence of personal relationships.

These relationships and networks emerge out of expected sites such as committees where members of both parties serve together and interact regularly. It is important to note, though, that they also develop through single-sex settings such as women-only dinners and the congresswomen's softball team.

Women's collaborative leadership style is conducive to working across the aisle, according to some members. Others perceived that women's bipartisan proclivity arises from their minority status within the institution. Overall, the interviews provide a window into life in Congress and reveal a more complex relationship between gender and partisanship within Congress than is often portrayed.

PARTY, GENDER, AND LEGISLATIVE BEHAVIOR

Past work on gender and political parties has generally conceptualized party as a constraint on the ability of women to work within legislative institutions collectively as women (Sanbonmatsu 2008). Certainly, the current environment of what has been termed hyperpartisanship has implications for all members of Congress—male and female alike—as we saw in the preceding chapter.

A standard approach in studies of gender and legislative behavior is to control for political party in a quantitative analysis, essentially pitting the explanatory power of gender against that of party (Sanbonmatsu 2008). Scholars of women in Congress often do so in order to test the hypothesis that women legislators are more likely than their male colleagues to represent women as a group on what could be considered women's rights or traditional women's issues, although studies have extended beyond issues with a disproportionate impact on women (Carroll 2001; Rosenthal 2002; Dodson 2006).

Scholars often uncover an independent effect for gender on measures of legislative behavior such as bill sponsorship, once party and other control variables are taken into account (Swers 2002, 2013; but see Lawless and Theriault 2016). These effects are most commonly seen early in the policymaking process, at the bill introduction stage, and are least commonly visible at the end of the process, at the voting stage (Swers 2002; Lawless and Theriault 2016).

And one must consider majority-party status when evaluating how gender interacts with legislative behavior (Dodson 2006; Swers 2002, 2013). In particular, Republican women are less likely to work with Democratic women on women's rights when Republicans are in the majority. On the other hand, Volden, Wiseman, and Wittmer (2013) show that women in the House fare better than their male colleagues in advancing their bills through the legislative process when they are in the minority. Volden, Wiseman, and Wittmer (2013) speculate that women's propensity for consensus-building is at work, though only under certain conditions.

As we saw in the last chapter, the current context of ideological polarization and partisan mistrust increasingly separates Democrats and Republicans into competing camps. The presence of moderates in Congress, either male or female, has diminished over time (Frederick 2009; Thomsen 2015). Whereas moderate Republican women crossed party lines to vote in support of women's rights legislation in the past, party polarization and greater party discipline mean that moderates have been replaced by more conservative members and that leaders are more likely to demand party unity (Swers 2002).

Past research has not focused on how women in Congress perceive their female colleagues' bipartisan orientations. While women senators' contribution to ending the 2013 government shutdown attracted widespread popular attention and projected an image of women's bipartisan camaraderie, scholars have yet to provide an in-depth analysis of how women within both the House and Senate view bipartisan collaboration.

WOMEN'S BIPARTISAN ACTIVITIES

We asked women legislators, "Do you think the women in this Congress are more or less likely than the men to work together across party lines?" It was the belief of most of the congresswomen we interviewed that women are more likely than men to collaborate with members of the other party, and the coming pages provide an analysis of that perspective. Our question did not specify a particular type of bipartisan activity. The women's responses included assessments of legislators' bipartisan policy efforts, personal relationships across the aisle, and work style. In some cases, women spoke about more than one of these forms of bipartisanship.

But not all of the women we interviewed perceived women to be disproportionately bipartisan. We first consider this minority view, which we found among both Democratic and Republican women and some women in both chambers.

Some of the women we interviewed, such as Representative Jackie Speier (D-CA), stressed that bipartisan inclinations depend on the individual rather than gender: "I think there are examples of men and women on both sides of the aisle who are willing to work across party lines. So I don't know that's gender-based." Likewise, Representative Carolyn Maloney (D-NY) noted, "I think there are a lot of like-minded men who care deeply about our issues . . . I work with women and men, and I think it's basically finding someone who will work and not just put their name on it." She also acknowledged the necessity, as a member of the minority party, of bipartisan efforts. She explained, "You have to work with the other side of the aisle or you don't get anything done." Some Democratic senators shared this view that bipartisanship depends more on the individual than on gender, including Senator Dianne Feinstein (D-CA), who elaborated, "I think the ability to work across the aisle is not determined by sex. It may be determined by your background, what kind of offices you had, how you got things done in the past, whether you're bound to everything the party says or you realize that you have to come together."

Some Democratic women argued that their female Republican colleagues were too partisan. Representative Maxine Waters (D-CA), for one, argued that Republican women follow the lead of their party—"following the company line"—rather than partnering with Democratic women: "I don't see any great coming together of issues from women on both sides of the aisle. No, I don't see that." Likewise, Representative Nita

Lowey (D-NY) observed, "On appropriations in general, the women vote the way the Republican leader suggests they vote."

Other interviews focused on numbers and internal party dynamics. Some Democratic House women placed their Republican women colleagues within the context of the Republican Conference. Delegate Eleanor Holmes Norton (D-DC) observed, for example:

> Most of the issues I work with the other side on are issues where there are not a lot of women; they don't have many women. The committee chairs . . . I work with are men. So I can't say that there is a woman that kind of stands out as a person. They also don't have a lot of power. I don't know how many chairs they have, one, two. So you wouldn't go to them unless they could strike a deal, assuming they do so. I don't see that the women here are any women I would find unpleasant to work with at all. I just don't—they don't stand out as being more willing to work with—across the aisle.

When asked if women are more likely to work with members of the other party, Representative Karen Bass (D-CA) answered, "No, I actually find it a little less [easy to work with the women]. I find it easier to work with the men. And I attribute that to fear on the women's part. This is just a subjective analysis, okay. But there are so few Republican women that I've had a much easier time [with men]." Republican women's minority status in Congress—as just 9% of the House Republican Conference—and their status as the majority party can intensify pressure for party loyalty (Swers 2002).

Delegate Stacey Plaskett (D-Virgin Islands) also interpreted our question about women's greater bipartisanship as one of whether Democratic women were more likely to work with Republican women than with Republican men, noting that there are simply fewer opportunities for interaction with Republican women. But she also echoed the notion of constraint, saying, "I think that the ones that are over there more often than not have to walk an even finer line of conservatism than the men do. And so there is less likelihood for us to find agreement on issues."

And regardless of women's "personal cooperation" on the annual Congressional Women's Softball Game, which we describe later,
Representative Dina Titus (D-NV) did not see many openings for policy
cooperation, noting, "I hate to say this, but I don't. I think that right now
divisions are so hard." Her sentiment echoes what we described in the
preceding chapter.

Believing that partisanship characterizes both women and men in
Congress did not preclude other women legislators from sharing concrete details of their own bipartisan activities and friendships, however.
For example, Representative Nita Lowey (D-NY), who works closely with
Representative Kay Granger (R-MO) on the State and Foreign Operations
Appropriations Subcommittee, said that the two women actually "like
each other": "I know what she believes in, she knows what I believe in,
and she said, 'Nita, I just can't do this.' And I say, 'Okay I get it; I'm going
to fight you all the way on it.' But we have a mutual respect and we are very
fond of each other." Indeed, virtually all of our interviews included specific
examples of bipartisan legislative activities and/or relationships.

Bipartisan Relationships among Women

The majority view, however, was that women in Congress are more bipartisan than their male colleagues. Some of the legislators we interviewed
initially hesitated to make generalizations about gender differences but
expressed support for this view nevertheless. Other responses were less
tentative; some women asserted yes immediately in response to our
question. We were also able to ask almost all of the women we interviewed
to tell us about their bipartisan activities, and in many cases their activities
with other women in Congress were the first ones they described.

The belief that women are more bipartisan than men in Congress could
be found in both parties and both chambers and across racial/ethnic groups.
Representative Ileana Ros-Lehtinen (R-FL), for example, saw a tendency
for women to work across party lines with other women. She explained, "I
would say that the women in the House interact in more favorable, more

harmonious ways than our male counterparts or opposing [men] . . . of different parties." Likewise, when asked whether women in Congress are more bipartisan than men, Senator Barbara Boxer (D-CA) observed:

> I think the proof is already out there that we do [work across party lines]. Because if you look at the most successful legislators the last couple of years, they are women. It's Dianne Feinstein on cyber security, it's Debbie Stabenow on an [agriculture] bill, it's myself on a transportation bill and a water bill, it's Patty Murray on a budget deal, and I can go on. It is Maria Cantwell on passing legislation for the Export-Import Bank.

Women's work encompasses relationships with women and men across the aisle. But, interestingly, we found that these bipartisan relationships have often been forged in single-sex spaces—single-sex spaces that were usually formed in response to women's minority status within the institution. As Senator Mazie Hirono (D-HI) noted, women are more likely to work together across party lines "because we talk to each other and get together more than the men do."

The Senate dinners initiated in 1993 by Senator Barbara Mikulski (D-MD), the first Democratic woman senator elected in her own right and the longest-serving woman senator of the 114th Congress, continue today. These dinners still serve their original purpose, which is to bring women together periodically across party lines; they're informal social gatherings not intended for policy discussions. All of the women senators participate in the dinners, which Senator Claire McCaskill (D-MO) referred to as "a little island of civility and support and friendship." McCaskill noted, "We spend less time talking about business and more time talking about children, and grandchildren, and feet that hurt, and, you know, stuff like that."

One might wonder how dinners lacking a policy focus can affect policy. But the women senators pointed to indirect effects on lawmaking. Senator Jeanne Shaheen (D-NH) noted that dining together builds trust and a "special bond":

Whatever happens at the dinners stays at the dinners, that's Senator Mikulski's rules. But it has allowed the women in the Senate to get together and to know each other better in a way that is really helpful because we learn to trust each other; we learn . . . that when we have an issue, we can count on our colleagues to support us.

According to Shaheen, women have been less affected by the rise in partisanship within the chamber and the ways that fundraising demands can curtail time spent in Washington and limit senators' ability to develop personal relationships. She noted, "[W]e do socialize, we do get together, we are getting to know each other in a way that is helpful when you're going to make policy because you know being able to find compromise is also about being able to trust each other."

Women senators—a total of twenty at the time of our study—are greatly outnumbered by men, which can make gender a potential basis for solidarity in the chamber regardless of party affiliation. As Senator Amy Klobuchar (D-MN) remarked, "We're still a minority, and so you better stick together, and I'd say the big thing in a power environment is that our power comes from sticking together—and again it's not always all 20 of us."

Trust and personal relationships among women legislators do not mean they hold identical positions on issues, however. Susan Collins (R-ME), well known as one of the only remaining Republican moderates in the Senate, made plain that the women senators are not of one mind with respect to public policy or ideology:

I think women tend to be more collaborative, but I want to dispel the notion that somehow we think alike or that we share the same political views; just as the men in the Senate span the ideological spectrum, so do the women. But I do believe the style of the women senators is more collaborative. I give a lot of credit to Barbara Mikulski for that and the work that she's done to bring the women together informally in dinners that we hold about once every six weeks. That has allowed us to forge bonds and to work together on some issues. For example,

I introduced a bill to congratulate the first two women to pass the Army Ranger course, and virtually all of my female colleagues co-sponsored that resolution.

Women serving in the House do not have an equivalent dinner gathering. The role of parties in the Senate differs from that in the House in important ways due to the Senate's smaller size and distinctive rules, and no doubt this facilitates the women senators' dinners. Of course, there are far more women serving in the House than in the Senate. A dinner gathering of all women would be a much more challenging endeavor, and a less intimate one; in the 114th Congress, a total of 88 women served in the House, including 4 women delegates.

And yet women from the sophomore class, who first entered the House in 2013, shared with us that they dine together. Representative Susan Brooks (R-IN) noted that these dinners provide a way for these women to overcome the typical physical separation of members of the two parties within the institution:

> Hardly anybody lives here [in Washington, DC] anymore; we have always heard that when people lived here there were better relationships because either they went out to dinner or they saw each other, whether at church or at kids' soccer games or at kids' schools. Well, that doesn't really happen here anymore, and so it has to be very intentional . . . when we're not working here at the House, it has to be very intentional for us to find time or set aside time to be with people of the other party.

The dinners have "been helpful [for us] just to get to know each other better and to find some areas that we might be able to work on together," according to Representative Grace Meng (D-NY).

Sports offer women another arena for crossing party lines. The Congressional Women's Softball Game pits women in Congress against women reporters who work on Capitol Hill and raises money and awareness for young cancer survivors. Representative Debbie Wasserman Schultz

(D-FL), a breast cancer survivor, helped spearhead the effort, begun in 2009, in order to benefit an organization called the Young Survival Coalition. The team's first captains were Wasserman Schultz, Representative Jo Ann Emerson (R-MO), Senator Kirsten Gillibrand (D-NY), and Senator Susan Collins (R-ME). Congresswomen who are not part of the game can also join the cheerleading squad started by Representative Susan Brooks (R-IN).

The bipartisan nature of the women's team distinguishes it from the congressmen's baseball game, according to Representative Suzanne Bonamici (D-OR).[1] Congressmen from the two parties play against each other and sit in separate sections, whereas women legislators from the two parties join forces to play against women from the media. She noted, "To me it sort of exemplifies the difference in the more collaborative approach. Let's all form a team; we want to raise money for charities, let's figure out how to do that. Rather than saying, 'Let's play each other,' it's 'Let's play together.' "

Bonamici reached out to Representative Susan Brooks (R-IN) on a budget issue related to federal defenders and later, education, based on their mutual participation in the softball game and their shared committee work; Bonamici explained that she "found somebody who happened to be a woman, who I happened to get to know cheerleading together at the women's softball game, and we started going out to lunch together."

Softball teammates might even have success in transcending partisan differences on abortion rights. Representative Michelle Lujan Grisham (D-NM), who plays softball with Representative Martha Roby (R-AL), noted:

> And she's a real asset on our team. There are other things that I can work on with Martha Roby and for me—which I haven't spoken to her about in a long time, in fairness to her. You know, "If I can't get you on reproduction protection. . . and access to choice, let's work on family planning. [There has] got to be a way that you want to prevent unwed pregnancies. Come on, work with me here." And that opportunity largely comes because I spend four hours a week with

---

1. To date, two women have joined the men's baseball game.

her where she is trying to teach me to throw a softball because I'm terrible at softball and she's really good.

Travel builds relationships among women as well, as Representative Virginia Foxx (R-NC), explained:

> We're criticized for travel. It's this schizophrenic thing on the part of the public. The public says, "Well, we want y'all to get along." Well, how do you do that? You don't get along with somebody you don't know. And people don't understand the limits to our ability to get to know each other. Because again, people have no concept of our schedules. No concept.

One ongoing travel opportunity of consequence is a bipartisan women's trip to Afghanistan timed around Mother's Day, originated by Representative Susan Davis (D-CA), who served previously as chair of the House Armed Services Subcommittee on Military Personnel in 2009:

> I went into Afghanistan very early on. It was just a few months after we had gone there and I was with—I believe it was one other colleague, female colleague, and the men couldn't even talk with the women. And the women were so key in our understanding of what was going on in Afghanistan that I felt like, well, let's take a trip. Let's do it around Mother's Day and let's see where it goes. Let's see if we can make this something that we continue so that we send a clear message that we really care about what's happening.

According to Davis, the Mother's Day trip, which has become an annual event, facilitates American communication with Afghan women, can aid US intelligence, and helps support the American women currently serving in Afghanistan.

Republican women from the House concurred that the women's Afghanistan trip has fostered women's bipartisan ties and friendships. As a result of the trip, Representative Donna Edwards (D-MD) and Representative Cathy McMorris Rodgers (R-WA) formed the Afghan

Women's Task Force, a bipartisan group designed to assist Afghan women and provide mentorship. Representative Martha Roby (R-AL) noted the impact of the Mother's Day event as well, observing that its effects extended beyond policy toward Afghanistan: "Now does that mean we agree on policy? No. But we can talk about it. That happens to be a women's CODEL [co-delegation trip abroad], but that would be true of any opportunity to spend time with one another."

We saw in the preceding chapter that the Congressional Caucus for Women's Issues (CCWI) has had far less success recently in bridging party differences and championing a legislative agenda. But the caucus continues to bring women together to some degree, which can also help women bridge racial differences. Friendships across the aisle can result, as Representative Cynthia Lummis (R-WY) explained about her experience as CCWI co-chair:

> My co-chair was Gwendolyn Moore from Wisconsin, and if you were looking for two women who have almost nothing in common, you would probably match us up. You know, I'm a rural person, a rancher from a racially homogeneous state. Very few African Americans. And then Gwendolyn is African American, was a single parent, welfare mother who became . . . who educated herself and came to Congress from an urban area. Man, you know we were like [*laughing*] polar opposites, and in our case opposites attracted, because we had a great time together. I think we did good work together.

The friendships that arise from the women's caucus can result in policy cooperation. For example, Representative Lois Capps (D-CA) noted her policy collaborations on pediatric research with Representative Cathy McMorris Rodgers (R-WA), with whom she co-chaired the caucus. She observed that their ability to work together partly arises from their shared experiences as women:

> I don't know if men do this as well, but we have had to, by necessity I think, band together. We're more . . . I believe, we work as team members because there is a little bit of the stigma against

women . . . I go back to the day when I first ran, after my husband's death, and people said, "You're going to run for Congress? You're just a woman." Can you believe that?

Not all of the House women we interviewed said they participated in social activities such as dinners or softball games specific to women, often citing their busy schedules. Several, such as Representative Nita Lowey (D-NY), noted the time constraints of serving in Congress that precluded more informal interaction:

> It's a sad thing that we don't interact as much as we probably should. Some members do. . . I guess I'm so busy on Appropriations that other than with Kay Granger, I don't usually get very social in the evening. I go from six in the morning, and at nine, ten o'clock at night, that's it . . . that's it. But many people—I know them—they are bipartisan groups of women that go out to dinner, and they said to me just yesterday, "You will say yes one of these days." But I find I'm just so busy by the end of the day—I've had it.

Additional Reasons for Women's Greater Bipartisanship

Thus, all-women spaces can fuel women's bipartisan relationships. But our interviews revealed additional opinions about why women legislators are seen as more bipartisan than men. For instance, Representative Marsha Blackburn (R-TN) argued, "I think that women are more collaborative, and we seek the solution. Guys have a tendency to seek a win, and we seek a win-win to get to a solution."

Different motivations for running and serving in Congress may yield a distinctive work style. Representative Jackie Walorski (R-IN) noted that women "want to make a difference, not that men don't, but we are leaving our homes, we are leaving our families and we are coming here and saying, 'I want to fight for x. I'm leaving my whole world because

I'm that passionate about it.' Women are driven by passion, and they are very effective." In a similar vein, Representative Julia Brownley (D-CA) emphasized women's desire to "get things done":

Women, we're a much smaller group, and so I think we have a tendency to know each other better and obviously in most cases have like interests, and we work well together. So women just approach problem-solving . . . in a much different way than men do, and particularly at this level of government and public office, and we want to get things done.

Representative Marcia Fudge (D-OH) observed that women, "probably better than anyone else, know and understand our job, which is to take care of the people we serve." She noted that this desire to serve can help women find ways to work together:

When you come here and you understand why you are here, which most of us do, it is easier for us to work together. But when you come and you think that your job is to be the person that blows up the government, the person that shuts down the government, the person that is "No, no," no matter what it is, I think that that makes their lives so much more difficult.

Women senators also see a gender difference in legislative style. For example, Senator Kirsten Gillibrand (D-NY) told us:

I think it's part of our nature. We are often less concerned with credit, less concerned with partisan politics, less concerned with ideology and more focused on how you get something done and solving a problem. I think a lot of women in the Senate are practical and are quite talented at building consensus. So I think we get more done.

Representative Kathleen Rice (D-NY) said that women want agreement and lack interest in fighting for the sake of the fight, noting, "I just think that's how women are wired. We are multitaskers. I think our nature is to be solution-oriented, and if that means compromising and bending then that's what we do." Likewise, Senator Tammy Baldwin (D-WI) explained:

> More women go into politics to get something done, to solve a problem, to fix something than men do. Very few of my female colleagues got into politics because they just wanted to be a US senator. You know, they got in because there was something awry that they wanted to work on and . . . some of the stories are quite profound . . . We're not there for the power of politics.

Women usually escape the "ego trappings" of the office, according to Senator Debbie Stabenow (D-MI), and can be more successful as a result. She told us, "When you look at the things that have gotten done, the majority of them had at least one woman leading [them] . . . I think we are much more focused on solving problems and getting things done and less focused on the trappings of power, our name on a bill, all of the ego trappings with the job."

To a great extent, these views are consistent with research by the Center for American Women and Politics on gender differences among state legislators in their motivation for seeking office. Women state legislators are less likely than men to have had a long-standing interest in running; in contrast, they are more likely to have been recruited to run and more likely to be motivated by public policy concerns (Carroll and Sanbonmatsu 2013). Many of our interviews with women in Congress echo these findings. Among both sets of legislators, the evidence points to different pathways that lead women to become candidates. In the case of Congress, the perception of some women legislators is that such differences yield a difference in legislative purpose and leadership style, and a more pragmatic orientation overall.

Family considerations can also unite Democratic and Republican women. Representative Chellie Pingree (D-ME) observed that in her state legislative and congressional service "women are more likely to engage each other in conversations about their aging parents, their spouse, their children ... things that I think make a slightly stronger connection," leading to more bipartisanship among women. The theme of women's commonality around family status and motherhood animated many interviews, as we saw in a previous chapter.

Traditional Sources of Bipartisanship

Regardless of whether or not women legislators believed that women were more bipartisan than men, they commonly spoke with enthusiasm about their bipartisan initiatives, many of them undertaken with men. The reasons they offered for this work across the aisle were not necessarily gender-specific. Instead, more universal sources of congressional motivation appear to be at work.

Geographic considerations can certainly help women (and men) find common ground with members of the other party. Representative Cynthia Lummis (R-WY) told us, "Vermont is so liberal and Wyoming is so conservative, Libertarian-leaning conservative," but she conceded that rural issues aligned her perspective with that of Representative Peter Welch (D-VT). In the Senate, Debbie Stabenow (D-MI) has allied with Senator James Inhofe (R-OK): "He cares about infrastructure, water infrastructure, roads, bridges and so on. And we've been able to form a partnership around this issue of both helping Flint [Michigan] with the lead in the water crisis, but also activating a national loan program for water infrastructure projects." Even legislators who "probably vote in an opposite direction 99% of the time," in Stabenow's words, can overlap on vital issues facing their constituents.

Membership in a state congressional delegation and prior service in a state legislature can yield shared perspectives as well. Representative Lois Frankel (D-FL), who served with her colleague Representative Dan Webster (R-FL) in the state legislature before entering the House, explained that the two "absolutely have completely different political philosophies," but said those differences did not preclude their collaboration on port security and other important Florida issues. Similarly, Representative

Julia Brownley's (D-CA) bipartisan efforts stemmed from relationships with Republican congressional colleagues with whom she served in the California legislature.

Both formal and informal settings, from caucus and committee membership to travel on congressional delegation trips, can also bring members together (Baker 2015). For example, Representative Diane Black (R-TN) explained, "A lot of it is with Ways and Means, because I spend a lot of time with the members of that committee, so they are on the same committee. But others I have just gotten to know by maybe social events, going on CODELs." Representative Lois Frankel (D-FL) likewise noted that a trip facilitated her work with Representative Joe Wilson (R-SC) on sexual assault in the military.

Congressional scholars have long found differences in the extent to which partisanship characterizes the inner workings of committees (Fenno 1973). As Representative Yvette Clarke (D-NY) explained, today's opportunities for bipartisanship still depend on the committee as well as the issue at hand. She cited her collaboration with Representative Renee Ellmers (R-NC) on an amendment to the 21st Century Cures Act, legislation that passed during the 114th Congress, significantly expanding federal funds for medical research and reforming mental healthcare. According to Clarke, her time on the Homeland Security Committee was also a bipartisan experience.

Likewise, Representative Dina Titus (D-NV) observed that the committees on which she serves "just by definition aren't as ideological as some." With respect to the chair of one of her subcommittees, Representative Suzanne Bonamici (D-OR) noted, "We don't agree on every issue, but we have that history and sort of mutual respect in terms of understanding that there are possibilities to work together." Representative Diana DeGette (D-CO) argued that multiple interactions with Republicans through committee service have helped establish her reputation among those across the aisle as "a straight shooter." Although bipartisan opportunities vary from one committee to another, the women we interviewed usually found ways to work with other committee members and remarked that personal connections are possible despite polarization.

Not surprisingly, district characteristics can shape the intensity of members' dedication to bipartisan work. The women we interviewed who were elected from more competitive districts appeared especially likely to express a dedication to bipartisan activities. These members, who entered Congress fully aware of the polarized environment awaiting them, seemed well prepared and determined to find openings for interaction with members of the other party. Representative Elizabeth Esty (D-CT) has joined bipartisan breakfast and dinner groups; she also interacts with Republican members at the gym:

> And my own personal commitment means that I get up . . . not as a morning person, I got up at 5 a.m. and worked out every day for a year to get in good enough shape that I can get up at 5 a.m. on Thursday mornings to join Paul Ryan and a handful of other guys . . . who do a killer spin/exercise spin bike workout, half an hour, followed by 45 minutes of yoga, also with this group. I am the only woman who does it. There are only two Democrats who do it.

Like Esty, Representative Kathleen Rice (D-NY), who was serving her first term at the time of our interview, explained that she campaigned on a bipartisan theme. She noted, "When I was campaigning, I talked about the need to send more people like me to Washington. As effective as I was as DA [district attorney] because I didn't care what your political party was, I just wanted to get stuff done. So I reached across the aisle all the time." Bipartisan campaign commitments also characterized Republican women's candidacies in some cases. At the time of our interview, Representative Elise Stefanik (R-NY) was enjoying her first term in the House after winning an open seat previously held by a Democrat. She explained that her district is bipartisan and noted the significance of her age: "Millennials are less partisan than our parents' generation and have an expectation that government functions. We've come of age, unfortunately, when there's been so much gridlock—the 24/7 news cycle highlights that gridlock rather than celebrating some of the bipartisan compromises."

For institutional reasons, Democratic women members, as the minority in the House, arguably need bipartisan collaboration far more than their Republican colleagues. Democratic women have different strategic incentives for pursuing legislation. As Representative Cheri Bustos (D-IL) observed, "I know that I'm in the minority party, and we are in the minority by a lot of seats. So if we are going to have any legislative success, we had better figure out how we are going to work across the aisle." Likewise, Representative Elizabeth Esty (D-CT) explained the imperative of working with the majority party:

> I first go to a Republican because that's the only way things are going to get done here. I'm not interested in the headline or the press release, I'm interested in passing legislation that will help people. So if your goal is that, then you ought to be first going to a bipartisan sponsor, and that's what I do.

THE DYNAMICS OF BIPARTISANSHIP

The women we interviewed shared their strategies for working successfully across party lines in the face of powerful forces pushing the two parties apart in Congress. These strategies are familiar to students of Congress. But they merit attention because they illustrate the ways that members can adapt to a difficult environment and help explain how members are able to find job satisfaction today.

Being strategic about choice of issues is one way forward, as Representative Martha McSally (R-AZ) explained: "You know, just trying to figure out and assess and have your situation awareness. So figure out the environment that you are in." "I think our office is really savvy about trying to pick issues that we think we can win," explained Delegate Stacey Plaskett (D-VI) about her issue priorities. Similarly, Representative Marcy Kaptur (D-OH) noted, "I try to find ways to embed ideas, legislation, projects, to the extent I can, in legislation that is moving—amendments on bills that are moving."

Although she expressed her interest in electing more women—especially Democrats—as a way to overcome polarization, Representative Katherine Clark (D-MA) expressed a determination to be effective in the current environment:

[A]t the same time we are here right now, and so we've got to find issues, you know. So we were very strategic about looking at the opiate issue and focusing on neonatal abstinence syndrome, which affects these babies being born dependent on opiates, because we knew that that could cut across lines. We didn't know that we would get Mitch McConnell to be our lead co-sponsor in the Senate, which is kind of insane, but we are strategic in finding Republican co-sponsors and really working issues for them.

Being persistent helps, said Representative Niki Tsongas (D-MA), explaining that she had recently told a member of her staff, "We just have to remember we can't always get everything we want overnight. So we have made a change, we've gotten some good things in here, and we'll come back at it. We'll come back at it."

Some of the women spoke of a personal dedication to bipartisanship and outreach, as well as to civility—a characteristic in short supply nowadays. According to Senator Patty Murray (D-WA), her ability to work with Speaker Paul Ryan (R-WI) when he chaired the House Budget Committee depended on their personal relationship. She explained:

I think there are a couple of things that always are important when you're working with somebody across the aisle, because you walk into a room thinking they're on the other side. So I walk into the room thinking, "What do they need?" and earning their respect and having them earn mine. And part of that is what you say when you walk out of a room. So when Paul Ryan and I did the budget deal, we agreed that we wouldn't walk out of the room and trash the other person on whatever they said . . . or "Can you believe that he said this?" I mean having that basic trust of listening to each other is an important part of getting things done.

It is important to avoid personalizing conflicts with other members, according to Representative Elizabeth Esty (D-CT). She elaborated:

> I don't denounce people in person . . . I don't take to the floor, I don't name names, I don't embarrass or humiliate other members. And some people do that. They do that, that's part of what they see their role as or what plays well in their district. I don't think it's helpful and I think it gets in the way of us getting things done.

Representative Virginia Foxx (R-NC) expressed a similar sentiment about finding common ground, which was a theme throughout the interviews, noting "all of a sudden an issue comes up, and somebody again who's philosophically very different from you on most things agrees with you. And so you look for common ground. In fact, people spend a lot of time doing that." Connecting as people is critical. As Representative Ann Wagner (R-MO), said, "At the end of the day, we all want to be productive, we want to give back to society, we want to be safe and secure, we want our families to be able to have a shot at the American dream that we've all had." She concluded that "if you reach people at the human level, it's amazing how much you can accomplish."

In discussing how she was able to maintain her relationship with Representative Marsha Blackburn (R-TN) in light of their differences on reproductive rights, Representative Carolyn Maloney (D-NY) explained:

> Well, you know, we just do our own thing. You know she's on the floor for it and I'm on the floor against it. The Ryan budget was le-thal to a lot of programs in education and healthcare and for women. She's out there defending it. I'm out there attacking it. But it's not personal. I think the way to navigate it is to not make it a personal

attack. A lot of people make it a personal attack. But you attack the issue. And so . . . I'm not attacking her, I'm attacking the position you see.

In short, many of the women we interviewed spoke of their commitment to being civil and personable with their colleagues and reaching out to other members with whom they might typically differ on policy proposals. They contrasted their legislative and interpersonal style with that of other members.

For more junior members of the House, these types of efforts can be conscious and quite targeted. Representative Michelle Lujan Grisham (D-NM) explained her efforts to serve effectively in a bipartisan way, reaching out to her committee chairs to ask about the best way to serve:

And I did something that no one has ever done here, apparently . . . I met with every Republican chair of my committees. Day one, once I got assigned I made an appointment to see them all . . . And it was as if I had grown a tail. It took a long time to get those meetings scheduled . . . And that led to, actually, a relationship with a Republican named Reid Ribble, and we worked on bipartisan budget legislation.

Some of the women we interviewed talked about how they respond to the costs of, or the backlash from, being involved in bipartisan work. For example, Representative Kristi Noem (R-SD) explained that sometimes her policy disagreements are with other Republicans, and so she may want to work with Democratic members. She told us:

Sometimes I'm building coalitions with Democrats that think more like I do on a certain policy than maybe members of my own Conference. So that's something [where] I feel as though, when I take positions and I'm working on something, . . . I need to go back home and explain to people . . . why this is important and why we need to work together to get it done. And . . . those people who want to see you constantly battling the other political party, they are not going to be happy with you. But then I go meet with them and I tell them why it's important that we do it. So you can't really be in this job and be effective if you aren't bold enough to have those conversations.

CONCLUSION

This chapter has revealed much more evidence of bipartisan efforts, friendships, and commitments than one might have expected. Many women in Congress—of different ideological persuasions, from different geographic regions, and with varying racial/ethnic backgrounds—typically perceive themselves as more bipartisan than men, pointing to differences in approach and priorities. In documenting their perceptions, we add to other work on bipartisanship that has examined the recent, nearly overwhelming attention to polarization (Harbridge 2015).

Friendships among women across party lines are not always easy to establish, and they are no doubt easier to accomplish in the Senate than the House given the differences in size and rules between the two chambers. But through formal and informal means, including single-sex enclaves such as dinners and trips, many women in both chambers make vital connections. These bonds pave the way for the identification of shared interests and, often, bipartisan legislation. In part, women find each other across party lines because they're conscious of their minority status in a male-dominated institution.

Congresswomen's commitment to work across party lines helps them be effective actors within the House and the Senate. These findings complement research by Craig Volden, Alan E. Wiseman, and Dana E. Wittmer (2013, 2017), who show that women members of the minority party are more effective lawmakers than their male colleagues.

The interview data presented here reveal several mechanisms that can help explain those results. We turn in the next chapter to an examination of women's multifaceted contributions to the policy-related work of Congress—contributions that often result from their ability to work with members of both parties.

6

Altering Policy Agendas and Debates

Ask the women of the 114th Congress if the presence of women members has made a difference in Congress in recent years, and you will hear strong affirmations of "absolutely" and "without a doubt." Nearly all of the women members we interviewed identified ways they see women exerting a distinctive influence within our nation's legislature. Through their descriptions of where and how women's presence significantly affects legislative norms, processes, and outcomes, we come to understand more fully why women in Congress are so committed to having more women join them.

Representative Robin Kelly (D-IL) told us, "We are all part of, as I like to say, a stew. And yes there is the gravy of the United States and we all have a role, the carrots, the peas, the beef, and all that." She affirms that women, replete with their own diversity, are key ingredients in the congressional stew, adding flavors—and value—to the final dish. Altering the recipe for congressional decision-making changes not only outcomes but also the processes by which those outcomes are achieved—or how the final dish gets made. This chapter and the next outline the myriad ways women members see themselves contributing to institutional change, both symbolically and substantively. In these chapters we examine women's perceptions of why their presence matters in Congress.

Very few women members hesitated to assert that the presence of women members has made a difference in Congress in recent years. But for those who did, their reasons were largely about context and comparison with men. For example, Representative Vicki Hartzler (R-MO) told us, "You can find examples of women who have advanced bills that have been helpful. You can find examples of men [too], but I don't think it is based on gender." Other representatives noted the dominance of party affiliation in shaping all members' behavior and capacity to make legislative change, arguing, as Representative Zoe Lofgren (D-CA) did that "political ideology and party affiliation are *greater indicators* of activity than gender" (emphasis added). Representative Loretta Sanchez (D-CA) pointed to the underrepresentation of women in the Republican Party as indicative of the limitations on women's congressional influence. Asked if the presence of women members has made a difference in recent Congresses, she told us, "Not really, in some ways, not really. I mean I look at this leadership race that's going on the Republican side," going on to point out the exclusion of women from the race to select a new Speaker in the fall of 2015.

Partisan disparities and perceived polarization may temper some members' views that women can or do have a significant influence in Congress, but the overwhelming response among the congresswomen we spoke with was that they do make a difference, even in this polarized era. But how do we assess the type and magnitude of difference women make in legislative institutions? Existing research offers some possibilities.

First, some scholars have investigated gender differences in legislative effectiveness, whether evaluating bill passage, collecting more detailed indicators of legislators' ability to move agenda items through the legislative process, or identifying alternative measures of success such as securing federal funding for their districts (e.g., Bratton and Haynie 1999; Anderson, Box-Steffensmeier, and Sinclair-Chapman 2003; Jeydel and Taylor 2003; Anzia and Berry 2011; Volden, Wiseman, and Wittmer 2013, 2016; Volden and Wiseman 2018). While findings vary, few studies show that women legislators are any less effective than their male colleagues, and recent research indicates that women members of Congress are actually the most effective legislators when they are in the minority (Volden, Wiseman, and Wittmer 2013; Volden and Wiseman

2018). Beyond partisan differences, some studies have measured legislative success of minority women specifically, yielding mixed results. Orey et al. (2006) find that Black women state legislators are not any less likely than their colleagues to pass legislation, but Adams (2007) finds that Black women state legislators are collectively less likely than other groups to pass bills.

Confining measures of influence to legislative success, however, paints an incomplete picture of the significance of women's legislative representation. A robust literature has looked at the ways in which women's presence has affected legislative agendas, finding differences in the issues that women legislators bring to and prioritize in state legislatures and Congress (Dodson and Carroll 1991; Thomas and Welch 1991; Thomas 1994; Bratton and Haynie 1999; Reingold 2000, 2008; Carroll 2001; CAWP 2001; Bratton 2002, 2005; Swers 2002; Wolbrecht 2002; Bratton, Haynie, and Reingold 2006; Gerrity, Osborn, and Mendez 2007; MacDonald and O'Brien 2011; Minta and Brown 2014; Volden, Wiseman, and Wittmer 2016). For the most part, the literature demonstrates that women in legislatures are more likely than their male colleagues to give priority to issues, such as healthcare and children and families, associated with women's traditional caregiving roles in society, and to issues, such as reproductive health and women's rights, associated with the organized women's movement. As for Congress specifically, Michele Swers (2002) finds that women members of the 103rd and 104th Congresses were more likely than men to prioritize feminist issues on their legislative agendas, with gender differences most distinctive at the bill sponsorship stage. More recent analyses demonstrate that this finding has held over time (MacDonald and O'Brien 2011; Volden, Wiseman, and Wittmer 2016), within congressional districts (Gerrity, Osborn, and Mendez 2007), and in the US Senate (Swers 2013).

Some research has focused specifically on women of color. Michael Minta and Nadia Brown (2014) find that the presence of women, and specifically minority women, on House committees leads to increased attention to women's issues in committee hearings. However, they find that the presence of minority men is just as important in raising these issues, illuminating the significance of gender and racial diversity in promoting greater legislative responsiveness across communities.[1]

Work done at the state legislative level provides additional insights into the agenda-setting influence of minority women, finding that Black women's agendas are distinct from those of Black men and White women, encompass both Black and women's interests, and have coalesced around education, healthcare, and economic development (Barrett 2001; Bratton, Haynie, and Reingold 2006; Orey et al. 2006; Adams 2007; Brown and Banks 2014). Limited research on Latina state legislators finds that their policy preferences are also distinct from those of their peers (Bedolla et al. 2014; Rocha and Wrinkle 2011), though Luis Fraga et al. (2006) find similarities in substantive policy focus among Latinas and Latinos. Importantly, the literature on minority women's policy priorities challenges conceptions of "women's interests" or "women's issues" as existing along a singular axis. As Wendy Smooth argues in her work on Black women state legislators, "Fundamentally, women's interests must be envisioned as complex, varied, in flux, and divergent if we are to articulate a sense of their alignment with the ways women experience the world" (2011: 440).

Whether via explicit references to women or discussion of their own experiences as women, research shows that women in Congress also bring unique voices to legislative debates, and not just on issues deemed distinctly gendered (Levy, Tien, and Aves 2001; Swers 2002, 2013; Osborn and Mendez 2010; Pearson and Dancey 2011; Swers and Kim 2013; Dietrich, Hayes, and O'Brien 2017). In doing so, they expand the frames for and terms of debate in both the words they use and the legislation they offer (Dodson et al. 1995; Hawkesworth et al. 2001; Swers 2002, 2013; Walsh 2002). Women's voices and perspectives are rooted in personal and historical experience, each of which demonstrates *both* commonalities and diversity among women (Brown 2014; Brown and Gershon 2016).

1. Minta and Brown (2014) find that in the Senate, it is representation by White women that has led to more attention to women's issues (e.g., crimes against women, breast cancer prevention and treatment, federal responses to domestic violence against women), but the increase in minorities in Congress, mostly minority men, has yielded more attention to issues that indirectly affect minorities (e.g., social welfare) (Minta and Brown 2014, 267).

This recognition of diversity among women has been constrained by conceptual choices made in previous studies investigating the policy influence of women's descriptive representation in government. Much of this research has equated the substantive representation of women with legislative work on "women's issues," defined as activity related to women's traditional private sphere roles and responsibilities (e.g., caregiving: healthcare, education, childcare, social welfare); advocacy on issues that disproportionately impact women (e.g., domestic violence, sexual assault, pay inequity); and/or efforts to promote women's rights or, more explicitly, feminist policy initiatives (Dodson and Carroll 1991; Thomas 1991, 1994; Reingold 2000; Wolbrecht 2000; Carroll 2001; Bratton 2002, 2005; Swers 2002; Osborn 2012). Challenging this reliance on specific issues, other scholars have pushed for broader conceptions of "women's interests" rooted in similarities in women's experiences *as women* that either persist across time, space, and other politically relevant categories (Beckwith 2014) or exist in specific moments or contexts in which gender is especially salient (Young 1994; Weldon 2006).

Even these conceptions, however, can privilege the interests of particular subsets of women—such as White, heterosexual, and/or liberal women—as representative of and beneficial to all women. As Wendy Smooth contends, "The effects of framing interests as women's interests . . . obscures how issues affect women differently, particularly as it relates to the material consequences of race, class, and sexual identities" (2011: 437). She goes on to say, "Any progressive vision of women's interests must reject notions of those interests existing along a singular axis, or notions that limit women's interests to a set of issues that portray a sense of sameness among them" (440). While Smooth articulates a research framework that can "maintain possibilities for group mobilization," her critique of existing research on the substantive representation of women challenges researchers to understand and analyze women's interests as "complex, fluid, and varied" (437).

Research on ideological differences among women legislators further illuminates the importance of re-visioning, or at least expanding, our conceptions of women's interests in studying legislative representation. Across parties, women legislators express a sense of both responsibility and pride in representing women (see Chapter 2; see also Thomas 1994;

Carroll 2002). However, multiple studies point to partisan disparities in the degree to which women legislate on women's issues, often finding Democratic women most likely to support, act upon, or benefit from engagement on researcher-defined women's issues (Carroll 2001; Bratton 2002; Dodson 2006; Reingold 2008; Osborn 2012; Swers 2013). Tracy Osborn contends, "Perhaps this disparity reflects problems across studies in defining women's issues on partisan terms" (2014: 149).

Taking these critiques and concerns into account, we offer a different approach to analyzing the ways in which women's presence in Congress affects policy agendas and outcomes. In this chapter, we focus on the ways in which women members themselves describe their influence on policy agendas and debates. First we examine the role that women members say they play in agenda-setting by bringing forth new issues. We also explore the expanded agenda brought by women of color. Then we move beyond agenda-setting, turning to the distinctive perspectives women claim to bring to a broad range of issues and policy debates within Congress. Throughout, we highlight differences among women of different parties, races and ethnicities, and leadership roles.

In resisting the use of preconceived notions of what constitutes a "woman's issue" or "women's interests," we allow congresswomen to articulate the issues on which they view their presence, experience, perspective, and priorities as distinctly influential on policy agendas or debates. This approach, similar to those employed and championed in other recent research (Celis et al. 2008, 2014; Volden, Wiseman, and Wittmer 2016), both exposes and values the complexities inherent in women legislators' claims about their substantive representation of women. Moreover, it allows us to address the influence of intersecting and multilayered identities in the policy contributions of women in Congress.

AGENDA-SETTING: PRIORITIES AND PERSISTENCE

The women members we interviewed emphasized the ways in which women bring new issues to the congressional agenda, consistent with previous research on gender differences in bill sponsorship and policy prioritization. Senator Kirsten Gillibrand (D-NY) told us women have raised issues "that previously didn't get the light of day," and Representative Debbie Wasserman Schultz (D-FL) echoed, "There are just issues that would not have reached the top of the agenda without women there pushing to make sure." Moreover, congresswomen described the persistence with which women advocated for these issues, noting that they not only add issues to the agenda but work hard to keep them there.

Both Republican and Democratic women referenced changing the agenda as evidence of the difference women have made in Congress in recent years, but Democratic women did so with greater frequency and specificity, perhaps reflecting the differences in positional and within-party power between Republican and Democratic women. Representative Maxine Waters (D-CA) elaborated, "I'm saying that Democratic women have carried issues that men just didn't pay attention to or that were not [even] considered issues."

Empowering Women

There were several times when women in the 114th Congress used their political power to help empower other women. These efforts included introducing initiatives to aid the advancement of women in traditionally male-dominated occupations and institutions, to ensure that women's historical achievements are recognized, and to make sure women receive equitable pay in the workplace.

As one example, multiple women members we spoke with talked about the ways they had included the advancement of women in science, technology, engineering, and math (STEM) within larger policy debates and development. Representative Elizabeth Esty (D-CT) introduced legislation in the 114th Congress to promote women's entrepreneurship in the sciences, telling us, "Girls and women have been not completely shut out of, but often discouraged [from STEM fields]." On Equal Pay Day in 2016, Senator Mazie Hirono (D-HI) introduced the STEM Opportunities Act to combat barriers to women's inclusion in STEM fields. Hirono has a history of working on this issue; she told us about an amendment she offered on the 2013 immigration reform bill that would have provided additional opportunities for women to immigrate to the United States to counter the weight given to those with male-dominated STEM backgrounds. She explained that she started gathering support for her amendment from women "because I thought that they had experienced [these kinds of sex role stereotyping and expectations] themselves to some level and so they would understand that we need to give a fair shot to women to be able to come to our country without those kinds of weighted factors that they wouldn't be able to meet."

In the fall of 2016, Representatives Cynthia Lummis (R-WY) and Jackie Speier (D-CA) sent a letter to President Obama asking him to make a public call for the next secretary general of the United Nations to be a woman, writing, "It has been 70 years since this esteemed organization was formed on the promise of equal rights for all people and nations. It is time for that promise to be fulfilled and for a qualified woman to lead the United Nations." Lummis explained why she and Speier were easily able to work across party lines on this issue: "[It's] not supporting a specific woman, but acknowledging that it's important since women are a majority of all the people on the face of the earth, and that women's health, women's civil rights, women's voting rights are very much global human rights issues that we believe would get more attention if there were a woman secretary general." As women in a male-dominated legislative institution of their own, the women in Congress have seen firsthand the importance of women's leadership in policy debates.

The bipartisan work of Representatives Carolyn Maloney (D-NY) and Marsha Blackburn (R-TN) to support the creation of a National Women's History Museum was not quite as easy. Maloney described it as an incredibly "divisive" issue with staunch opposition from Republicans and conservative groups. Still, she credits Blackburn with defending the legislation to her caucus and for never folding in spite of the attacks she faced. Together, the women were able to move legislation forward to establish a congressional commission to study a national women's history museum through the House in May 2014. It took another year for the commission to become enshrined in law as a separate title to the National Defense Authorization Act of 2015. Maloney and Blackburn's work to move the museum's creation forward was rooted in their belief that women should be included and appreciated in American history. Representative Blackburn (R-TN) noted that one basis for their collaboration was the significance of their respective states in the fight for women's suffrage: "The push for winning the right to vote started in New York and the 19th Amendment was ratified by Tennessee, so we had the New York/Tennessee connection." And as Representative Maloney (D-NY) said to us, "Why should everybody have a museum except for women, for God's sake?"

On March 25, 2015, Senator Barbara Mikulski (D-MD) and Representative Rosa DeLauro (D-CT) reintroduced the Paycheck Fairness Act to address the gender gap in wages. Mikulski and DeLauro had introduced this legislation in every congressional session since 1997, and it was once passed in the House in 2009. Delegate Eleanor Holmes-Norton (D-DC) also reintroduced the Fair Pay Act in the 114th Congress, a complementary bill seeking to close the wage gap.[2] While legislation addressing gender inequities in pay had been introduced in Congresses prior to the 114th, this is an important policy area where congresswomen have demonstrated both leadership and persistence in promoting women's economic empowerment. Notably, Republican women—who have been unsupportive of the Democratic bills—have offered their own alternative legislation in recent Congresses. Senator Kelly Ayotte's (R-NH) Gender Advancement in Pay Act and the Workplace Advancement Act, sponsored by Senator Deb Fischer (R-NE) and Representative Lynn Jenkins (R-KS), were both introduced in the 114th Congress.[3]

2. In September 2016, Delegate Eleanor Holmes Norton (D-DC), Representative Rosa DeLauro (D-CT), and Representative Jerrold Nadler (D-NY) introduced a complementary bill—the Pay Equity for All Act —to limit employers' ability to ask questions about salary history during the hiring process.

3. Previous research (e.g., Dodson 2006; Swers 2013) suggests that Republican women have been urged by party leaders to provide a counternarrative to Democratic claims that their party does not support women's empowerment. Another example in the 114th Congress was the reintroduction of the FAMILY Act, providing paid family leave to workers, by Democratic Representative Rosa DeLauro (CT) and Democratic Senator Kirsten Gillibrand (NY), which was countered by Republican Representative Martha Roby's (AL) reintroduction of the Working Families Flexibility Act that would give private sector workers the option of using their earned overtime toward paid time off. The introduction of alternative bills such as these allows Republican women and men to offer support for the overall issue (women's economic

Just as GOP women have offered different plans for addressing pay inequity, women of color have contributed to these debates by emphasizing that disparities are most acute for minority women. Representative Alma Adams (D-NC) told us that legislators too often "just look overall at women" in crafting policy without recognizing how differently Black women are affected. Representative Linda Sánchez (D-CA) used the issue of pay inequity as an example, explaining:

> For White women it is 75 cents on the dollar. For Latina women it's like 54 cents on the dollar. So it is important to have women of color here, because while I'm sure that, and I'm not trying to overgeneralize here, White women see there is a pay gap, Latina women and Black women really feel the brunt of it because it is twice as bad for them as it is for White women. And so I think adding that perspective is very important; otherwise they might just stop if women got a pay raise that listed the 75 cents to the dollar, still leaving Black and Latina women way behind.

In resisting the homogenization of women, these women members of color promote an empowerment agenda that takes seriously the existing disparities in power *among* women.

Protecting Women and Children

When asked what women members of Congress have in common, Senator Kirsten Gillibrand (D-NY) said:

> We are all very different. We all have different priorities, different interests, different areas of expertise. But there does seem to be a commonality that we all do care about our families, we care about

empowerment and/or promoting work–family balance) without endorsing specific policies that they deem harmful to business interests.

our communities. There is an interest in protecting the most vulnerable and so there's common ground there. And so a lot of our legislation gets built from there.

Representative Doris Matsui (D-CA) similarly claimed, "I think women in
particular feel the need [to] . . . look around to see who might be left out,
and want to make sure that that person has a voice and can be heard." In
many cases, that means giving voice to women and children, according to
the women members we interviewed. In doing so, they claim, women add
new and critical items to the congressional agenda.

While Delegate Stacey Plaskett (D-VI) ceded that many men are likewise focused on fighting for the next generation, she argued of women, "I
just think that we go about it very differently." Perhaps that is due to the
caregiver role women so often embrace in describing their policy perspective and priorities. Representative Kristi Noem (R-SD) cited the national
security debates of the 114th Congress and argued that a "mom's perspective" always "made it a much more fruitful conversation." The "number
one priority" of every mom in the country, including congresswomen
who are moms, she claimed, "is that their kids are safe."

Representative Debbie Wasserman Schultz (D-FL), a mother of three,
combined a desire to empower veterans with her work to curb child exploi-
tation when she introduced and passed the Hero Act in the 114th Congress.
It creates an avenue for veterans to be trained as forensic specialists who
pursue child sexual predators online. Representative Marsha Blackburn
(R-TN) joined Democrat Lois Capps (D-CA) to secure a provision in the
21st Century Cures Act, passed in late 2016, that would ensure that children were included in clinical trials. These examples illustrate women
members of the 114th Congress giving voice to and seeking protection of
children, but women's efforts did not end at US borders.

Senator Jeanne Shaheen (D-NH) talked about the need to apply a gendered perspective to 114th Congress debates over US military withdrawal
from Afghanistan. She emphasized the importance of having members
who will ask, "What happens to women if we totally pull . . . our support
from our efforts there?" As we saw in the preceding chapter, women

members of the House and Senate have been particularly engaged in women's rights in Afghanistan, motivating questions like these in policy debates. Representative Debbie Wasserman Schultz (D-FL) provided another example of women members raising an international issue that might otherwise have gone unnoticed. On the day we interviewed her, she had just published an op-ed with her colleague Congresswoman Norma Torres (D-CA) about a law in El Salvador that mandates imprisoning women for killing their babies in the case of miscarriage (which is presumed to be a deliberate abortion). She asked, "What are the chances if she and I were not in Congress together that [this issue] would ever be elevated to the level that it was? . . . I mean, no offense, but some random man, some random White guy, is not going to be likely to write an op-ed like that or even have it be on their official radar."

Finally, throughout the 114th Congress, Representative Frederica Wilson (D-FL) was dogged in bringing attention to the more than 200 girls kidnapped in Nigeria by Boko Haram. Multiple women we interviewed cited Wilson's efforts. Representative Marcia Fudge (D-OH) used Wilson's persistence as an example of the difference women make in Congress, telling us, "We've got Frederica Wilson, who is constantly talking about bringing the girls home. That may not have been a mantra if she weren't here." Representative Maxine Waters (D-CA) added, "And she's working to keep this issue alive and to try and force more involvement from us, from the United States, in trying to get these girls back. So, no man would do that, you know what I'm saying?" While Black members of Congress have historically taken an interest in African affairs (Tillery 2011), this example highlights the gendered aspects of that work.

Addressing Sexual Assault and Harassment

Representative Elizabeth Esty (D-CT) cited women's life experiences as explaining the diversity that women add to the policy agenda. "Women's life experiences have made them more attuned to understanding the importance of some issues which maybe didn't get emphasized as much," she told us. An example of one of those issues is online sexual harassment. Asked about what motivated her introduction of the 2015 Prioritizing Online Enforcement Act, a bill that would compel the Department of Justice to enforce laws prohibiting online violence against women, Representative Katherine Clark began her answer by noting, "I don't think any woman who has ever run for any office isn't a little familiar with on-line harassment." It was the harassment faced by one of her constituents, though, and the apparent lack of prioritization by the FBI that fueled Clark's continued work on the issue. When she introduced her bill on the House floor in June 2015, she argued, "It is not ok to say to women that this is just the way things are, and it's not ok to tell women to change their behavior, withhold their opinions, or stay off the internet altogether just to avoid severe threats. When we don't take these cases seriously, we send the clear message that when women express an opinion online, they are asking for it."

Challenging dismissive claims about abuse victims has been central to many women members' work to combat myriad types of violence against women, as well as sexual assault of women and men. Asked specifically about whether men and women approach the issue of sexual assault in the military or on campuses differently, Senator Kirsten Gillibrand (D-NY), a champion of these issues, responded affirmatively:

I think it is easier for a female member to imagine what it's like to be victimized, to be disbelieved, disregarded, and retaliated against. It is something that they can imagine happening easier than many of our male colleagues who can't imagine ever being victimized or disbelieved or disregarded because they've never experienced that. I have experienced being disregarded many times in my ca-reer. Many times as a lawyer, being dismissed or disregarded or not believed or not trusted or not valued because of my gender, so I can imagine it. I can imagine what happens to a young woman when they say, "I don't believe you. It was consensual. You just regret what happened." I can imagine that happening. So I think there is a fun-damental difference between our world experiences that will allow us to empathize differently . . . I think it's easier to understand and easier to believe if you are a female member. That, of course, does not exclude some very empathetic male colleagues who have been amazing on this issue. And they do have empathy and they can imagine it and they can understand it. But I think, by and large, you will get more women who understand the issue or empathize more quickly than the male colleagues.

That empathy may also create a sense of responsibility among women members, as Representative Jackie Walorski (R-IN) explained: "When you get into [Congress] and have an opportunity to do your part to stop the violence against [women], . . . it is part of the responsibility I think that we bear as women." For Representative Ann Kirkpatrick (D-AZ), that empathy also breeds an anger that fuels action. "I'm a former prosecutor [who] prosecuted sexual assault cases, and I think that's an area where women in the House and the Senate really, really have shown leadership, whether it's on college campuses [or] in the military," she explained. "That's something that women are especially angry about."

Women members of the 114th Congress offered examples of legislative priorities that sought to address sexual assault both before and after it occurs. For example, Representative Suzanne Bonamici (D-OR) introduced the Teach Safe Relationships Act to improve the K–12 curriculum so that students learn the tenets of healthy relationships, with the goal of preventing campus sexual assault once they move on to college. Key elements of the bill, which was sponsored by Senators Claire McCaskill (D-MO) and Tim Kaine (D-VA) in the Senate, were integrated into the 2015 reauthorization of the Elementary and Secondary Education Act. Representative Debbie Wasserman Schultz (D-FL) worked across party lines with Representative Tom Marino (R-PA) to address the consequences of sexual assault. In the 114th Congress, they passed the Rape Survivor Child Custody Act to incentivize states to allow a woman who had a child after being raped to petition a court to terminate the rapist's parental rights by using a clear and convincing evidence standard. Wasserman Schultz explained that the process of meeting the "outrageous standards" set in most states prior to the law's passage to terminate rapists' parental rights "would revictimize the woman again and again."

At least 10 women members we spoke with credited women in Congress with bringing the issue of sexual assault in the military and on college campuses to the legislative table in the 113th and 114th Congresses. For Representative Dina Titus (D-NV), these issues represent items on the agenda "that would never be there if we were still waiting for a man to put them on there." But it also took positional power for women to ensure that their attention to sexual assault issues had a direct effect on legislative agendas. Senator Jeanne Shaheen (D-NH) echoed many public reports on the role of Senate women in investigating sexual assault in the US military:

> I think it's no small thing that, now that we have seven women on the Armed Services Committee, that sexual assault in the military has come to the forefront and it has stayed there . . . and there was unanimous support for about 30 provisions to look at how to address sexual assault in the military, and I think that was because the women on the Armed Services Committee made that an issue.

It was in the 113th Congress that a record seven women first served on the traditionally male-dominated Senate Armed Services Committee. Seven women also served on the 26-member committee in the 114th Congress, continuing to raise this issue as a committee priority. As committee member Senator Kirsten Gillibrand (D-NY) explained, "[H]aving seven women on the Armed Services Committee I think really pushed the issue to the forefront and didn't let it diminish." Senator Mazie Hirono (D-HI), another committee member, said of the record number of women on the Armed Services Committee:

> I think we really pushed that issue to the point where now when the military leadership comes, they should be prepared to respond to questions from us as to what is happening in the military . . . with sexual assault . . . "What are you doing regarding retaliation, because we know that still occurs?" So they have to be ready to answer those

questions, which I have a feeling they really didn't have to do very much before.

She added, "That is to me a shining example of how women with our different perspectives . . . you could say that we may bring to the table different priorities."

It is important to note, though, that women's perspectives on how to best curb sexual assault in the military are not uniform. Senators McCaskill and Gillibrand, both Democratic women on Armed Services, publicly disagreed on legislation to best address adjudication of sexual assault claims by military members. But it was the shared passion to address the problem that united them. Women also came together across party lines to address this issue; in the 113th Congress, McCaskill was joined by Republican Senators Kelly Ayotte (NH) and Deb Fischer (NE), as well as other members of the Armed Services Committee, to push forward her legislation requiring a civilian review of military sexual assault cases if a prosecutor and commander disagree over whether to litigate. Earlier in that Congress, Representative Ann McLane Kuster (D-NH) joined forces with Democrat Loretta Sanchez (CA) and Republican Representative Jackie Walorski (IN) to include H.R. 1864, which strengthened protections for whistleblowers who report sexual violence in the military, in the National Defense Authorization Act. Kuster and Walorski, both members of the House Committee on Veterans' Affairs, also teamed up on legislation to make victims of military sexual trauma eligible for Department of Veterans Affairs beneficiary travel benefits, reintroducing this legislation most recently in 2017. As Kuster noted in her conversation with us about sexual assault in the military, "We continue to talk about it. We continue to bring it up."

Kuster's persistence on this issue included her work to address sexual assault on college campuses. She joined her House colleagues to cosponsor the Campus Accountability and Safety Act in the 114th Congress and lent her own story to debates over campus sexual assault in June 2016. On an evening when House members were expressing their solidarity with a woman ("Emily Doe") who had been sexually assaulted by a Stanford University swimmer, who received a mere six-month sentence for his rape, Kuster began her remarks by setting a scene:

> I'm going to start my remarks tonight 40 years ago, on a cold winter night, at a prestigious college campus, this time on the East Coast. I was an 18-year-old student. I was going to a dance. The dance was at a fraternity, and I intended to enjoy the evening with my friends. We danced. We listened to music. We enjoyed the evening, and we enjoyed the party—until one young man assaulted me in a crude and insulting way, and I ran, alone, into the cold, dark night.

She continued, "I have never forgotten that night. I was filled with shame, regret, humiliation, while he was egged on by everyone at that party standing by." Kuster went on to detail two other instances of sexual assault she has experienced in her lifetime, noting that she shared her stories for the first time "because they are all too common" (Henneberger 2016). In her remarks on the House floor, Kuster recognized the work of her Republican male colleague Ted Poe (TX) in addressing this issue. When we spoke with her, Kuster emphasized the role that women can play in bringing more men to the cause. She explained, "We need to help our colleagues have that opportunity to be a part of the solution, whether it's in the military, on college campuses, in this society generally. And by the way, most of our colleagues are husbands of women, they are fathers of daughters, they have nieces and close friends that they care about." She talked about women's capacity to start conversations without "accusing men generally" and believes, "When you start to have these conversations on that personal level, you will immediately connect and find converts to the cause."

Women's Health

Women members have also drawn from their own experiences to keep women's health on the legislative agenda. Representative Rosa DeLauro

(D-CT), a survivor of ovarian cancer, described her illness as an impetus for her to seek a committee assignment addressing health-related issues. When she got to Congress more than two decades ago, she joined women members of both parties to fight for women to be included in clinical trials at the National Institutes of Health (NIH). "[W]e thought we had settled that when I got here a while ago," she told us in 2016, "and then to our chagrin, [we] find out that that's not the case [and] we're still, you know, dealing with this issue." She explained that the women in Congress are still waging the battle to protect women's health, calling the issue "a stepchild" in research and policy.

Representative Debbie Wasserman Schultz (D-FL), a breast cancer survivor, has frequently spoken out about her experience and used it to motivate legislative action to address young women's capacity to protect their breast health; the EARLY Act, which created a Centers for Disease Control and Prevention–administered education and outreach campaign highlighting cancer risks for young women and women with high-risk racial or ethnic backgrounds, was signed into law in 2010 and reauthorized in 2014.

Talking about the particular health challenges facing the Black community, Representative Gwen Moore (D-WI) used breast cancer as an example where "[y]ou'd have to be more concerned about African American women." She explained, "Because of the lack of healthcare and access, they are diagnosed later, so there is greater morbidity, greater mortality." Similarly, Representative Lucille Roybal-Allard (D-CA) pointed out the "specific needs of Latinas" across issues, including healthcare: "Whether you are talking about explaining policies in healthcare or education, there's a different way of approaching a Latino family than maybe a White family from the South or the Midwest." Representative Robin Kelly (D-IL) prioritized this type of cultural competence as chair of the Congressional Black Caucus's Health Braintrust in the 114th Congress, in which, she told us, "all the health policy runs through me." Among the group's priorities was "raising awareness on African American women's healthcare," including "advancing research with respect to life-threatening diseases such as breast and cervical cancers, sexually transmitted infections, and HIV."[4]

It is with these layered perspectives and priorities that women approached the most significant healthcare debate of the past half century. While it happened prior to the 114th Congress, many of the Democratic women members we interviewed spoke about the role of women in their party in debates over the Affordable Care Act (ACA) in 2010. Specifically, women across chambers touted the critical role of chamber leaders in the fight—Senator Patty Murray (D-WA), then-chair of the Senate Health, Labor, Education, and Pensions (HELP) Subcommittee on Employment and Workplace Safety (and Democratic Conference Secretary), and then-Speaker Nancy Pelosi (D-CA). It was these women who held the line on preserving reproductive health benefits included in the bill. As Senator Jeanne Shaheen (D-NH) told us:

> I remember when we were working on the Affordable Care Act, and Patty Murray came in and talked to the women, and she said she had gotten a call from then–majority leader Harry Reid at night about trying to reach an agreement on what was going to be in the bill and she said, "I went in and what they were talking about doing was taking out all of the section that applied to women's health." [That section included] parity in terms of how much the insurance companies can charge, access to reproductive health, provisions that provide for prevention for women. [Murray] said, "And I told him, 'No, you're not going to do that. You do that and we are not going to vote for it.'"

Representative Rosa DeLauro (D-CT) credited Pelosi and a small group of women Democratic colleagues with taking the same stand in the House:

> The Affordable Care Act would not have happened without Nancy Pelosi ... There were maybe five or six of us in the meeting where our

4. See "114th Congress Priorities" for the Congressional Black Caucus's Health Braintrust: https://cbcbraintrust-kelly.house.gov/114th-congress-priorities.

male Democratic colleagues said, . . . "Well, let's not [include reproductive health] . . . because of the Catholic bishops." And, you know, "Well, let's let it go and let's adjust it at another time," and so forth. It wasn't "no," it was "hell no." And it was Nancy [Pelosi] with myself, Louise [Slaughter] . . . Nita [Lowey]. Tammy Baldwin was here at the time, Diana DeGette . . . [We said,] "No, we're not going down that road again." But you've got a leader who isn't gonna sell it down the river, you know . . . who's gonna stand up to what it was.

Representative Barbara Lee (D-CA) was also in that group of women holding the line on reproductive health access in the House, in addition to being a key player in negotiating health equity provisions in the ACA. As she told us:

I was chairing the Black Caucus then and was part of the team that helped negotiate on that, and I remember meeting with the president. It was the chair of the Black Caucus, myself, the co-chair of the Progressive Caucus, Congresswoman Lynn Woolsey. Then we had Congresswoman Lucille Roybal-Allard, who was chairing the Hispanic Caucus, and in the room was Congressman Mike Honda from the Asian Pacific American Caucus, and the president. And I looked around and . . . it was mostly women over here with President Obama, so that was really kind of cool. We made a real impact on the Affordable Care Act.

The members of the Tri-Caucus, which unites the CBC, Congressional Hispanic Caucus (CHC), and Congressional Asian Pacific American Caucus (CAPAC), continued to seek greater health equity across race and gender after the ACA was passed. In 2011, for example, Lee and other caucus chairs introduced the Health Equity and Accountability Act to enhance federal data collection and reporting, strengthen accountability and evaluation, provide better mental health services, address social determinants of health, provide culturally and linguistically appropriate healthcare, promote health workforce diversity, and improve health outcomes for women, children and families. The bill also prioritized addressing high-impact minority diseases like HIV/AIDS, hepatitis B, diabetes, and cancer, and would have created a new Office of Minority Health at the Department of Veterans Affairs.[5] The bill did not pass in 2011, but another woman member—Representative Robin Kelly (D-IL)—was the lead sponsor in its reintroduction in 2016. She was joined by six original co-sponsors, of whom four were Democratic women of color.

In her work on gender adaptability of prosthetic limbs, Representative Niki Tsongas (D-MA) provided another example of a woman raising an issue specific to women's health that men may not have considered. After speaking with a male survivor of the Boston Marathon bombing who voiced suspicion about how well prosthetic limbs fit women, Tsongas raised a number of policy questions about this issue for women amputees in the general population and in the military. Among other things, she offered a provision in the 2015 National Defense Authorization Act (NDAA) that would require the Department of Defense (DoD) to brief Congress on DoD's ability to provide the best prosthetics for women amputees. Tsongas cited this as an example of the difference women make in Congress, arguing, "Those questions would never get asked without us here . . . We bring a different view. My guess is we bring our unique views to everything else we talk about."

Abortion Access and Funding

But women's views are far from uniform across policy debates. Republican and Democratic women members' policy advocacy and efforts on abortion access and funding demonstrate the ways that partisanship and ideology can sharply divide women, which we noted previously with respect to the challenges of the current polarized era. Nonetheless, our interviews

5. "Barbara Lee, Tri-Caucus Members Introduce the Health Equity and Accountability Act," Press release, Office of Representative Barbara Lee, September 16, 2011. http://lee.house.gov/news/press-releases/barbara-lee-tri-caucus-members-introduce-the-health-equity-and-accountability-act.

revealed that women's passion for this issue persists across party lines, along with their perception that they are the most credible members to speak about it. Unlike many of the issues already discussed in this chapter, this issue would not likely be absent from the agenda if women were absent from Congress. But congresswomen indicate that they bring an urgency and authenticity that would be missing in abortion-related debates if only men were included.

Republican women referenced the distinct voice that women bring to anti-abortion efforts. They described the issue as personal to women in a way that it cannot be for men. Representative Vicki Hartzler (R-MO) told us, "[Women] certainly have knowledge about some issues from their personal experience . . . Women by nature . . . have dealt with pregnancy, so that's why . . . it's a natural fit for women to share their perspective on [pro-life issues]." Representative Martha Roby (R-AL) described Republican women's desire to be out front on this issue as "a natural thing," adding, "It's because the women who do speak out on this feel very passionate about that." She noted that there are men "who feel as passionately about defending the unborn as the women do," but other Republican women cited the value of empowering women within the Republican Conference to lead on this issue. Representative Diane Black (R-TN) emphasized just how intimate a decision about abortion is for women, suggesting, "This is a very personal decision, a very personal situation for a woman, and I think that women feel that it is hard for men to put themselves in a position that frankly they can never be in."

Representative Susan Brooks (R-IN) said that this credibility contributed to abortion debates being a "particular area of influence for Republican women." In two prominent examples of this influence in the 114th Congress, Republican women were credited with pushing back against their party's plan to introduce a 20-week abortion ban without exceptions for unreported rapes (they later supported a revised ban in May 2015), and Representative Marsha Blackburn (R-TN)—a longtime pro-life advocate—led the Select Investigative Panel on Infant Lives to investigate fetal tissue procurement and donation facilitated by medical providers, including Planned Parenthood.

Democrats selected an equally passionate pro-choice champion as their ranking member on this Select Investigative Panel in Representative Jan Schakowsky (D-IL). In fact, all but one of the Democrats selected for the panel were women.

While most took positions in these debates that were essentially the opposite of those of Republican women members, Democratic women in the 114th Congress agreed that their personal stake in abortion policy and politics made them the most effective advocates in legislative debates. Echoing Hartzler, Representative Suzanne Bonamici (D-OR) stated simply, "Women obviously look at [abortion] differently from men . . . I think for women it's much more personal. Because women get pregnant and men don't." Senator Barbara Boxer (D-CA) elaborated:

> It's not that women are better than men. We're not; we're equal to men, equally good and equally bad. But we bring with us a life story experience, and you know when the men get out there on the floor and talk about the joys of childbirth, fine, but they never gave birth, and we know how joyful it is, but also how difficult it is and what you face when there is a problem with your pregnancy. So just there alone . . . we [congresswomen] can authenticate the experience that women are having outside [of Congress].

Representative Carolyn Maloney (D-NY) explained how women's personal experiences with reproduction spur their passion in policy debates on abortion, telling us, "They can feel it, you know." Representative Lois Capps (D-CA) explained why women play a prominent role in abortion debates, saying, "Because it's our bodies and we also know the burden of an unplanned pregnancy—either from one's own experience or from seeing it within our families and our wider community." As examples, in 2011, Representative Gwen Moore (D-WI) shared her experience with an unintended pregnancy at age 18, and Jackie Speier (D-CA) talked on the House floor about her own abortion to make a strong case against defunding Planned Parenthood. Through storytelling, these women lent an authenticity to their position that could not be matched by their male colleagues.

In the 114th Congress, Democratic pro-choice congresswomen channeled that passion into putting up a strong defense against efforts to curb abortion access. But they also put forth proactive, instead of reactive, legislation that sought to make the positive case for publicly funding abortions. In July 2015, Representative Barbara Lee (D-CA) introduced the EACH Woman Act to ensure coverage for abortion care in public and employer-provided health insurance programs. Pro-choice caucus chair Representative Diana DeGette (D-CO) credited Democratic women of color with leading the effort on the bill and reframing the abortion access debate to ask, "Why shouldn't every woman, rich or poor, in this country be able to get the access to a full range of healthcare services that she needs?" The legislation addresses the very real intersections of class, race, and gender in women's access to abortion, as well as women's ability to take on the economic, health, or other demands of an unintended pregnancy. It also demonstrates the value of women's presence and perspectives, as diverse as they are, in congressional debates over issues like this that most directly affect women's lives.

RACE AND GENDER: AN EXPANDED AGENDA BROUGHT BY WOMEN OF COLOR

Trying to identify an exclusive set of issues that most directly affect women's lives is not merely difficult, but fruitless. Just as women's lived experiences vary greatly, so do the issues that they deem most important. Wendy Smooth illustrates this in her research on Black women state legislators. She finds, "Legislators articulated a political agenda reflecting crosscutting issues that were not easily codified along a single issue axis," adding, "Instead, the legislators articulated their legislative priorities as complex and multifaceted" (2011: 436). We found similar articulations of policy priorities among the minority women we interviewed in Congress. Delegate Stacy Plaskett (D-VI) argued that the issues important to congresswomen of color are "very different than White women's issues . . . because our experiences in America have been enormously

different than [theirs]." But other congresswomen characterized minority women's agendas as both inclusive of and expanding beyond the
issues deemed most important by White women or men. For example,
Representative Lucille Roybal-Allard (D-CA) explained:

> I want economic opportunity; I want to have good schools, educa-
> tion. All the same things that every American would want regard-
> less of where you're from. And I think that . . . if you were to talk to
> any of my Latina colleagues, they would say that. But in addition to
> that, part of that agenda is recognizing that there are doors that still
> have to be opened to Latinas and minorities in general that are either
> closed or just cracked open a little bit, and so I think that's where we
> [Latinas] focus and try and make sure that whatever we are dealing
> with, that those doors can be opened wide. And not just in token
> ways, but in really meaningful ways.

Representative Bonnie Watson-Coleman (D-NJ) was more explicit in
explaining that women of color "have an expanded agenda." She added,
"I think that we recognize that we are dealing with two issues: race
and gender. And that . . . we obviously see it from those perspectives."
Representative Barbara Lee (D-CA) characterized this as "an added layer"
or, more specifically, "added value" that Black women bring to legislating.
She said, "Okay, so we have our agenda which is very similar to women,
all women, but then on top of that we have the unique perspective that we
bring coming from the African American experience."

Criminal Justice Reform

Lee pointed to one example of an added layer that Black women bring
to congressional agendas: "Mass incarceration—Black women see [this]
as a priority, whereas White women may or may not see it as a priority."
Representative Gwen Moore (D-WI) put this issue in economic terms for
Black families:

Right now everybody is feeling so relieved, for example, that the economy is recovering. [But] we got African American male unemployment over 50%. That has an impact on families. We live in a community where we have the largest incarceration rates among African American men in the country. So that means that we have lots more children, but without the family formation, without the income.

Racial bias in the criminal justice system does not only affect women's and families' economic security. As Delegate Plaskett (D-VI) reminded us, criminal justice issues "are issues that Black women . . . in particular really are sensitive to, because it's our children that are being killed; it's our sons and daughters that are being incarcerated." Representative Robin Kelly (D-IL) spoke about this issue as a Black woman with police officers in her family, as well as a member of Congress from Chicago, when she described the "lack of trust" between community members and police. She has advocated for community policing and diversity on police forces as key reforms to foster trust and public safety.

In advocating for this reform agenda, Black women have often aligned with their Black male peers in Congress. But Representative Karen Bass (D-CA) provided an example of Black women's distinctive contributions to debates over criminal justice reform, consistent with Orey et al.'s (2006) finding that Black women legislators' propensity to advance certain interests-specifically those of Blacks and women-differs not only from White women and men, but also from Black men. Bass told us, "My concern about [criminal justice reform legislation] is that it's moving and it forgot gender, so it forgot girls and women. And so one specific thing I would like to accomplish would be to insert legislation that is specific for girls and women in the criminal justice reform [bill]." While advocating for attention to the impetus of abuse in girls' route to incarceration in the 114th Congress, Bass noted that her advocacy was being received well. "I think it was one of those things that the guys went, 'Oops,'" she explained, adding, "And I think that that's one of the reasons why women have to be in the legislature."

168

A SEAT AT THE TABLE

Guns

Representative Brenda Lawrence (D-MI) talked about Black congresswomen's advocacy on the issue of gun control. She described her motivation as personal and political: "I have lost a second cousin to gun violence, but I see it every day and it's African Americans. And so it's not an agenda, but . . . I think the passion to directly legislate and bring these issues up so they are in the forefront, I think that is what you will see from African American women." Lawrence represents an urban, majority-minority district that includes parts of Detroit, a city ranked fourth in the number of nonfatal shootings per capita in 2015. Representative Robin Kelly's (D-IL) district includes parts of Chicago, the US city with the highest number of nonfatal shootings overall in 2015 and the twelfth-highest number of nonfatal shootings per capita among 68 major cities (Mirabile 2016). Kelly described the strategies she employed to bring attention to the gun violence confronted by her constituents on a daily basis. She explained, "[I]t's not just about the mass shootings. It's about the individuals." Kelly introduced H.R. 224 in 2015 to require the surgeon general to submit to Congress an annual report on the effects of gun violence on public health. She also sought to bring the Democratic Caucus's attention to gun violence that has been ignored, such as when she refused to stand during congressional moments of silence in honor of mass shootings since 2014. She told us, "I'm not going to do it anymore, because we stand up, sit down, and do nothing," adding, "I'm not going to be a part of this charade."

About seven months after we interviewed Kelly, her Democratic colleagues joined her in sitting down to speak out against gun violence in another way. As noted in Chapter 4, members of the Democratic Caucus staged a sit-in on the House floor in June 2016 to protest Republican inaction on legislation to curb gun violence. Public reports highlighted the role that another White woman member, Representative Katherine Clark (D-MA), played by providing the initial impetus for the action. Just as the House was set to hold another moment of silence for victims of the mass shooting at the Pulse nightclub in Orlando, Clark approached her colleague, Representative John Lewis (D-GA), with frustration—similar to Kelly's—that members weren't doing enough to push the issue of gun control. It was Lewis, an icon of the civil rights movement, who suggested the more dramatic strategy of taking over the House floor, which the Democrats did for 25 hours. Dozens of members joined Clark and Lewis at the sit-in, but Lewis praised Clark for her leadership, calling her "the initiator and pillar of the whole effort" (Helman 2016).

While women of color have not advocated for gun control legislation alone, as Clark's example illustrates, they have challenged the narratives around and responses to gun-related violence. Congresswomen like Representatives Brenda Lawrence (D-MI) and Robin Kelly (D-IL), who represent areas with high rates of gun violence among and affecting primarily communities of color, seek to expand congressional attention to daily gun violence tragedies across all communities, not just mass shootings at sites where gun violence is less common. The degree of gun violence in districts represented by minority women is important in explaining their orientation to the issue, but so are personal, and distinctive, experiences with gun violence and the criminal justice system.

Immigration

Like criminal justice reform and gun control efforts, immigration reform was a major issue looming in the 114th Congress, even though major legislation on the issue was not passed. And while there was great gender and racial and ethnic diversity among the members engaged on these issues, the congresswomen we interviewed pointed to a special urgency and empathy among specific groups of women. For example, Representative Robin Kelly (D-IL) told us, "I think that when you look at violent crime, who's in jail, I'm sure it's [disproportionately] close to Black and Brown [people]," explaining her prioritization of those issues. She continued, "But I think that, let's say, even though immigration's very important to me, I'm sure it's more important to Latinas." Representative Linda Sánchez (D-CA) agreed, arguing:

It's a little bit different, because . . . there are issues that disproportionately impact Latina women. So like our immigration policy and
separating families, most White women don't have to worry about
that, but Latina women do. Most African American women don't
have to worry about that, but Latina women do if they have a family
of mixed status. So there are certain issues that . . . are unique to
Latina women that—it is not to say that every White or Black woman
doesn't experience that; I'm sure a Caribbean immigrant family
experiences that, but it just disproportionately impacts Latinas.

Stemming from the recognition of that disproportionate impact, Latina
congresswomen described distinctive contributions they made to what
was included on the immigration reform agenda and what was discussed
in reform debates.

According to Representative Lucille Roybal-Allard (D-CA), "I
think with Latina women, we focus on those things from our own personal experience. Plus the whole issue of immigrant women and children is something . . . that we focus on and help our colleagues to gain
a better understanding of where they are coming from and why they are
coming here." In line with their intersectional identities as Latinas and
caregivers, Representative Ileana Ros-Lehtinen (R-FL) explained, "We're
more family-oriented when we look at immigration." For Ros-Lehtinen,
that orientation stems from her own experience fleeing Cuba as a refugee
with her family at age eight. Senator Mazie Hirono (D-HI), herself an immigrant from Japan, shared a similar orientation based on personal experience. Recalling her time on the Senate Judiciary Committee during
debates over comprehensive immigration reform, she explained, "I would
say mine was the only voice in [the Judiciary] Committee that spoke for
the importance of family unity [in debates over immigration reform].
And so I brought [that voice] . . . not only as a woman but also as an immigrant. And this is why it is important to have minority representation
on all of these committees. Because you have different life experiences,
different perspectives, and women certainly bring that to any committee
they are on."

In the 114th Congress, Representative Zoe Lofgren (D-CA), herself a champion of immigration reform and family unity, credited Roybal-Allard with leading the Congressional Women's Working Group on Immigration Reform, which has infused special concerns or challenges facing women and children into immigration policy debates. Beyond family unity, the group worked to address conditions faced by immigrant families at detention centers. Lofgren, the ranking member on the House Judiciary Subcommittee on Immigration and Border Security, also championed this issue directly with the Obama administration. She told us that progress was made in the 114th Congress on the issue thanks, in part, to another woman positioned to make policy change. Talking about then–Secretary of Health and Human Services Sylvia Burwell, Lofgren said, "She took it personally. She's a mother herself. I think to some extent she was imagining her own child by themselves in some cement holding cell."

Of course, party divisions are hard to ignore on immigration policies. Even with respect to questions of family unity, Republican women members were not generally any more likely than Republican men to support reforms that would provide paths to citizenship or legalization of young people brought to the United States illegally by their parents ("Dreamers"). Representative Ros-Lehtinen (R-FL), the only Republican woman immigrant to serve in the 114th Congress, told us, "We're still a ways off from that. I'm in favor of it, but I know that I don't represent the bulk of the party and . . . women GOP members either."

After describing the diversity of issues that Black women prioritize on the congressional agenda, Representative Maxine Waters (D-CA) stated, "But in addition to that, we take on everything." Existing research backs up her claim, finding that Black and Latina women legislators feel a responsibility to represent women and multiple minority groups—which often translates into legislative agendas that span issues advancing women's and minority interests (Carroll 2002; Tate 2003; Bratton, Haynie, and Reingold 2006; Fraga et al. 2006; Orey et al. 2006; Brown 2014; Brown and Banks 2014). Nadia Brown and Kira Hudson Banks, in work on Black women, define this as a "race/gender advantage" that minority women bring to legislative work; they argue, "Black women are uniquely positioned to use their intersecting raced and gendered identities to advocate for the needs of racial/ethnic minorities, women, and specifically minority women—what we refer to as intersectionally marginalized populations" (2014: 166). Our evidence of minority congresswomen's contributions to policy agendas and debates bolsters this claim, demonstrating the ways in which they contribute to an agenda identified as most attentive to "women's interests," while also expanding both that agenda and agendas commonly associated with communities of color.

BEYOND AGENDA SETTING: VOICES AND PERSPECTIVES ON A WIDE RANGE OF ISSUES

Women not only bring new issues and help to expand the legislative agenda, but change policy conversations on the full range of issues being debated in Congress. Often drawing on their own life experiences, women offer diverse perspectives in congressional debates on a variety of issues far beyond those specifically related to women. Representative Diane Black (R-TN) agreed: "I believe that women look at issues differently than men do and that's just the way we are. We come at things in a different way, and since 52% of the population is female it behooves us to make sure that we have a voice, a woman's voice in the discussions." Senator Susan Collins (R-ME) explained that this is why it is important to have women represented on every Senate committee. She said, "I think that's helping. Again, not because we think alike, but women bring different perspectives, different life experiences, and that's very healthy for an informed debate on issues."

Senator Jeanne Shaheen (D-NH) added, "Women's life experiences are different from men's. They're not better. They're not worse. But they are different. It is important for us to have people who have those experiences at the table so we can talk about those and we can respond to the challenges that half of the population in this country face." Representative Donna Edwards (D-MD) responds to claims by "the guys" that they care equally about women's issues by conceding, "Okay, but we can speak for ourselves." Representative Debbie Dingell (D-MI), knowingly referencing

Carol Gilligan's work, said of women in Congress, "I think we do have a different voice."

House Democratic Leader Nancy Pelosi (CA) described women legislators as using their voices to expand opportunities for everyone, not just women, emphasizing, "To recognize the dignity and worth of every person . . . [is] an important role for women to play." Diversity of perspective is not limited to gender, however. As Representative Katherine Clark (D-MA) reminded us, "[O]ur democracy is dependent on us being reflective of the American people, and a majority of Americans are women and we should reflect that . . . whether it's people of color, different religions, you know, we are stronger as a Congress and a democracy when we really represent people." Her colleague, Representative Virginia Foxx (R-NC), emphasized the value of ideological diversity among women, noting, "Diversity generally excludes conservatives. And I'm kinda sensitive to that. But, I think, you know, and I say this a lot, you need lots of different perspectives. We need people who have been carpenters. We need people who have been electricians. We need farmers. You know, we need different perspectives. And women bring a perspective." Racial and ethnic diversity is also essential, as we have demonstrated in this chapter, and that means also recognizing differences *among* women of color.

In this section, we draw from our interviews with women veterans, Black, Latina, and Asian American women to illustrate the multifaceted aspects of congresswomen's identities, experiences, and perspectives, and how they translate into shaping policy conversations. We also describe how congresswomen almost universally credited their caregiving experiences with shaping the voices and priorities they bring to congressional agendas. While these are just a sampling of the multilayered identities women bring to legislative work, they exemplify the importance of complicating narratives about the difference women make in political institutions generally and in Congress specifically. As Nadia Brown notes, "identity is not static" and its influence must be considered in specific contexts (2014: 7). For the congresswomen we interviewed, sometimes that influence includes injecting gender and intersectional perspectives into debates over policies rarely deemed women's issues.

Women Veterans

Representative Tulsi Gabbard (D-HI) provided an example of how diversity of perspective can come from the intersection of multiple identities, including gender. Gabbard, one of four women combat veterans to serve in the 114th Congress and a member of the House Armed Services Committee, explained how important her voice and the voices of her female colleagues were for debates in the 114th Congress over women serving in military combat roles:

> The opportunity to bring voice to the many women who have served and sacrificed so much for our country comes with great responsibility. Many of my colleagues on the House Armed Services Committee have not served in the military, and some have misguided views about women in the military that don't reflect the realities of the contributions women have been making for generations. I appreciate the opportunity to not only share my own perspective, but to share the experiences and voices of the many women who have and continue to serve our nation in uniform.

Gabbard added, "Serving with Tammy Duckworth on the [Armed Services] Committee enabled us to bring our own stories and experiences into the conversation." She concluded, "Having someone with a seat at the table to share this perspective helps to advance the progress and fairness we are advocating for."

Representative Ileana Ros-Lehtinen (R-FL) credited her colleague Martha McSally (R-AZ) with being a "trailblazer" on issues related to women's participation in all sectors of the armed forces. McSally drew upon her own experience as the first woman fighter pilot to fly in combat and the first to command a fighter squadron in combat in acting on behalf of her women compatriots in 2016. After the army cited space limitations in 2015 and revoked the rights of members of the World War II Women Airforce Service Pilots (WASP) to be buried in Arlington National Cemetery, McSally introduced a bill (along with Democratic

Representative Susan Davis of California) that became law, reversing the army's decision. A companion bill in the Senate was co-sponsored by Senator Joni Ernst (R-IA), who served in the Army Reserve and the Iowa National Guard, and Senator Barbara Mikulski (D-MD). McSally explained how the issue was personal for her:

> I remember when I showed up to become a fighter pilot and there was really nobody to look up to, and these three women showed up at a meeting . . . it was a fraternity of military pilots called the Daedalians. At the time we [women] weren't even allowed to be Daedalians, but they showed up and sat down and started talking to me . . . and they were these amazing, feisty, funny, strong women who just encouraged me in my journey, which was so meaningful for me.

When she heard that the WASP members' rights to have their remains buried at Arlington were being revoked, she described being "infuriated" and getting to work immediately on seeking an administrative or legislative solution. Joking about the importance of having a woman veteran lead this bill, she quipped to a supportive male colleague, "I get to lead on this because I have ovaries and wings."

Latinas

In their volume on the "distinct identities" that women of color bring to American politics, Brown and Gershon argue, "The unique intersectional location that women of color inhabit impacts how they operate within and view American politics" (2014: 8). In addition to the evidence of congresswomen's influence on agenda-setting, our interviews suggest that their intersectional perspectives contribute much-needed insights to a range of issues and debates. As Representative Linda Sánchez (D-CA) described earlier, Latina congresswomen have engaged on issues like immigration with knowledge and credibility that is rooted in their

Latina identity. But their "added value" to congressional debates is not limited to that issue. Representative Roybal-Allard (D-CA) noted how minority women bring different experiences of discrimination to legislative discussions:

> Because even though we share experiences as women, and as I mentioned earlier as wives, mothers, and sisters, the experiences are still different in many ways, and those of us who are minority or from minority communities have experienced discrimination in a different way, not just because we were women, but also because we were, in my case, a Mexican American or others . . . Puerto Rican, or Asian—whatever it happens to be. So again, it's those experiences that we bring to the policymaking table.

In practice, those diverse experiences contribute to better policy, she argued. For example, "When things are being developed—whether it's material that should be in Spanish, there are certain ways that things should be worded so that they actually are meaningful and reach the target audience."

Roybal-Allard described this type of work as educating congressional colleagues, something she has done since she entered Congress in the early 1990s, especially in distinguishing among Latino communities. She told us:

> When I first got here in '93, there were only three Latinas: me, Mexican American; Nydia Velázquez, the first Puerto Rican; Ileana Ros-Lehtinen; and a handful of Latino men. I literally had to explain to my colleagues on both sides of the aisle what the difference was between me and Nydia. [They'd say,] "You're Latino . . . you speak Spanish. What is the difference between you [two]?" So we literally had to explain that I come from a different country, or background from a different country, and Nydia comes from a territory, Ileana comes from Cuba, and [we] had to explain that difference.

While she observed that her colleagues are "much more exposed to minorities" today, Latinas continue to educate their colleagues on issues, constituencies, and cultures to which they may not have otherwise been exposed or attentive.

Asian American Women

Senator Mazie Hirono (D-HI) described a similar role she plays as an Asian American woman in Congress, and as the only Asian American woman—or minority woman—in the Senate in the 114th Congress. Talking about the difference it makes to have more women of color in Congress, she said, "[T]he fact that a lot of my colleagues had never actually encountered someone like me" made for some interesting encounters. For example, she explained:

> I am an Asian person, [and] there are still people who have certain notions about how Asians are—that I am quieter. I don't beat my chest and I'm not out there . . . all of that, and they are sort of surprised when I swear, for example. I do a lot of swearing actually, and they say, "Wow. We didn't know." "No, no, no" [I say]. "How do you think we got here?"

But Hirono has not just challenged her colleagues' and constituents' stereotypical notions about Asian American women's behavior. A Japanese American herself, Hirono noted, "There are still a lot of people in our country who don't understand that during World War II we interned 120,000 Japanese Americans, disrupted their lives and in many ways destroyed their lives and took away lands, and they were sold at a mere pittance, and the impact that that has had on our community." She went on to say that this historical context is important in dealing with issues of race and immigration in a "humane, enlightened way." Hirono's legislative work in the 114th Congress with another Asian American congresswoman, Representative Grace Meng (D-NY), including an effort to strike the word "oriental" from federal laws, reflects how that enlightened perspective translated into policy results.[6]

Black Women

When we asked Black women in the 114th Congress whether they had a policy agenda different from other women members of their party, they frequently suggested that they have a different perspective rather than a different agenda. Representative Joyce Beatty (D-OH) responded, for example, "I don't know if it is a different agenda; we bring a different cultural view and diversity to the agenda." Part of that view is rooted in historical discrimination. Beatty explained, "We have a long history of differences that this government and the world placed on us strictly because of our color."

Representative Marcia Fudge (D-OH) alluded to this shared history, telling us, "We grew up at a time where things were difficult, and we worked very hard," adding, "There are those who believe that people like me shouldn't be here." Of those people, Fudge contends, "They don't realize our stories," which influences how they perceive public policies drafted today to address economic and education inequality. Representative Beatty (D-OH) elaborated on that viewpoint, explaining that while "feeding a child is feeding a child," the stigma around government assistance too often varies by the race of those being helped: "Your Black person who needs help from the government—they are told that they are on welfare. A White farmer that gets help, it's called a subsidy. So for me, we don't go in with an even playing field." Noting these disparities, Beatty emphasized, "It is very personal to me." That experience is especially personal to Representative Barbara Lee (D-CA), who told us that her own time on public assistance motivated her to break down barriers that create untenable conditions for women, and especially women of color, like her.

6. See https://www.hirono.senate.gov/press-releases/hirono-meng-bill-to-strike-term-oriental-from-federal-law-headed-to-president.

Representative Gwen Moore (D-WI) agreed that "African American women find themselves dealing with the same issues," but added, "perhaps with greater urgency." She explained, "No matter what the issue is, Black women find themselves at the bottom of that spectrum ... So I don't know [that] we have different issues, it's just deeper; [as somebody said,] when America gets a cold, Black people get pneumonia." Representative Robin Kelly (D-IL) was more specific, saying of African Americans, "We are at the bottom of so many things," from housing and wages to incarceration. Representative Brenda Lawrence (D-MI) cited key gender differences *within* the Black community, explaining, "The things that we encounter as an African American woman are different from what an African American male will encounter, and so ... when I talk about education of girls I know what it feels like, the barriers that girls have, and also African Americans." According to Lawrence, it is on issues like these, and those mentioned earlier—like women's health, pay equity, criminal justice reform, and immigration—that the "double-minority" status experienced by Black women in Congress provides a valuable perspective that is distinct from that of other women and Black men. Lawrence noted that Minority Whip Steny Hoyer (D-MD) explained his decision to appoint her as a senior whip because she would be able to bring that perspective to Democratic leadership, a responsibility she has enjoyed. Talking specifically about the need to unite around challenges faced by Black girls, Representative Donna Edwards (D-MD) called on Black women to play a more activist role in policymaking that will affect them. She urged, "[T]here is nobody else to carry that voice here in the Congress unless it is going to be Black women to bring other people along."

Edwards's comments reflect the passion that Representative Brenda Lawrence (D-MI) told us Black women members bring to congressional work. Responding to our question about a distinctive Black women's agenda, she pointed out, "[I]t's not an agenda, but you will see African American [women] rise up" to combat racism and sexism while addressing the diversity of issues that affect their communities and families. Representative Gwen Moore (D-WI) rose up in September 2015 to reintroduce the RISE Out of Poverty Act to overhaul the welfare system in ways that better accommodate the needs of those receiving assistance. Moore was one of those recipients before coming to Congress, adding authenticity to her goal "to peel back the rhetoric from the reality of the program" (Covert 2015).

That authenticity was a thread in our conversations with Black women members, who made explicit connections between their personal experiences with government and their government service. Representative Maxine Waters (D-CA) stated emphatically, "It does not make a difference what leadership role you're in; all that you are is what has happened to you and what you have experienced throughout your world and throughout your life." For her, being raised in a community where she saw neighbors evicted from their homes guided her policy work on predatory lending in 2008. In the 114th Congress, as the ranking member of the House Committee on Financial Services, Waters continued to bring that experience to debates over housing, lending, and financial opportunity.

In the Republican-dominated 114th Congress, Waters also discussed counting on her Financial Services Committee colleague Representative Joyce Beatty (D-OH) to ensure that the Office of Minority and Women Inclusion, an office she included in the Dodd-Frank financial reform legislation of 2010, would continue its work to promote the inclusion of women and minorities at all levels of the Security and Exchange Commission's workforce. Beatty did that work, leveraging her position on the committee with a shared passion for combatting the "historical disadvantages" that she feels the government has placed on her community. Importantly, though, Beatty cautioned against telling a single or short-sighted story of the Black women in Congress. With great pride, she stated:

> We're not only the conscience of the Congress, we're also the brilliance and the intelligence of the Congress, because we want people to know that we are more than Black people standing there fighting for a cause. We are scholars . . . Probably out of our caucus, 75% of them are attorneys and nurses and [have] advanced degrees and have held some of the most prestigious jobs in the country. So

we just don't come with hard luck stories; we come with a lot of skills and a lot of credentials to do our job.

Beatty's comments reaffirm the ways in which Black women serving in the 114th Congress not only changed the conversations and expanded the policy agenda, but also disrupted stereotypes associated with gender and race, as well as the image of congressional leadership.

Caregivers

Across party lines, one of the most common perspectives that women members referenced in their interviews was that of caregiver. As noted in Chapter 2, the congresswomen in our study described the distinct experiences and perspectives they bring as mothers, grandmothers, and/ or caregivers to elderly parents. Multiple women members talked about the "tug and pull," "juggle," or need for women to "balance multiple balls" at home and work in ways that shape both their experience and input in legislative conversations. Senator Heidi Heitkamp (D-ND) joked, "I doubt somehow that [Senator] Pat Leahy is folding laundry [while on his conference call], but we have different life experiences and that enriches the organization."

Representative Kristi Noem (R-SD) was more specific about why women's experiences juggling multiple responsibilities are essential to policymaking. Speaking about the women voters she represents and with whom she empathizes, she explained:

They are not just working jobs, they are caring for their parents, they are raising children, they are making their household budgetary decisions, they are making the healthcare decisions for their family, they are feeling stressed and stretched in many different directions. And that perspective needs to be at the table when we are talking about bills and legislation. We don't get the luxury of having tunnel vision and focusing on one thing. We have to multitask.

Noem's colleague Representative Renee Ellmers (R-NC) talked about the significance of this distinct perspective in the Republican Party's policy discussions. Asked about the difference the presence of women has made in her party's caucus, she said:

> We know that women in the household—moms and wives—across this country are the ones who are paying bills and taking care of healthcare for their families, and making sure that it all works. So we knew that we had to have a more personal conversation and really speak to women with the understanding that this affects people on a personal level. And it's not just about dollars and it's not just big billions and trillions of dollars. It's about how it affects every family. So because we became more [aware] of that conversation, I've seen a real change in the way that we are all articulating this—women in the Congress and men in the Congress.

Representative Marcia Fudge (D-OH) reiterated the value of integrating this perspective into policy discussions across party spaces: "I think it is really important that people who are basically caregivers, that people who basically run our households, are the people who make decisions about what goes on in those households."

Women's caregiving roles and household responsibilities do not disappear once they are elected to Congress, but women do arrive with increased power to alter policy in ways that seek to ease those burdens for women and men nationwide. In describing her own experiences caring for school-aged children, a mother with Alzheimer's, and a father who suffered from a stroke, Representative Katherine Clark (D-MA) explained that she relates differently than other members might to issues around medical research, funding, and policies to provide home healthcare. Representative Elizabeth Esty (D-CT), who also shared that her mother was suffering from early-onset Alzheimer's disease, agreed, "That can't help but change your experience and thinking that this is really important." She elaborated on the direct applicability to a bill passed in the 114th Congress:

So if you look at something like the 21st Century Cures Act, which we passed in the House, women were at the forefront of that because again . . . whether it is caring for a severely disabled child or a child who has childhood leukemia or dealing with parents who are aging and [have] Alzheimer's . . . women still bear the lion's share of that [burden], and that includes women in Congress who probably still bear the lion's share of those efforts.

For congresswomen, she concluded, those experiences translate into greater understanding of the problems facing caregivers and additional motivation to do something about it. For Representative Doris Matsui (D-CA), who sits on the House Energy and Commerce Committee dealing with Social Security, a key problem is accounting for caregiving work in providing women long-term financial security. She listed multiple questions she continues to ask in legislative debates:

How do we change [Social Security] to really make sure that we're accounting for that? Because women live longer, [and] they made less money because they had to step out of the workforce. Their pay was lower, right? And they live longer. So what do you do, because they're not gonna make as much money as a contemporary male, right?

Matsui joined 25 other Democratic women members and 17 Democratic men as an original co-sponsor of Representative Nita Lowey's (D-NY) Social Security Caregiver Credit Act of 2015, a bill reintroduced in the 114th Congress to include caregiving work in Social Security calculations for compensation.

Many women's orientation to policymaking, then, appears to be particularly influenced by their familial roles and responsibilities. As Senator Heidi Heitkamp (D-ND) told us, "I think there is more kind of a sense of a greater responsibility for the family that women have." Representative Terri Sewell (D-AL) pointed to family issues among the "common interests" between Republican and Democratic women, even if they take different approaches to addressing them. Representative Lois Capps (D-CA) was even more direct: "I see everything framed with health and family issues, and if it is anti-family, then I'm going to oppose it. Again, I think I do that as a woman."

But women's roles within and perceptions of family are far from universal, despite public policy that too often adheres to a singular norm or ideal of family structure. Representative Linda Sánchez (D-CA) provided a clear example of how her own complex experience caused her to change the conversation in a debate over childcare in the House Ways and Means Committee:

> We were having the discussion once in a hearing in Ways and Means about how difficult it is to find affordable childcare. I am a working mom. I mean, I had a son while I was a member of Congress and I've had to raise him and obviously work in a job that is very demanding [and] that requires more than just nine to five hours. And I heard a Republican colleague, [a] white male Republican colleague, mutter under his breath [while] I was passionately advocating for tax credits, "Well Jesus, can't the grandparents watch the kids?" I heard the utterance and I said let me answer [that] often misunderstood idea that somehow grandparents can watch children for working mothers. I said, ". . . I'm a working mother. Both of my parents have Alzheimer's and I am a part-time caregiver for both, so it isn't always the case that grandparents can watch kids . . . If that was your experience, you were fortunate, but many people in America don't have that luxury."

Drawing on this exchange from an earlier Congress to illuminate the importance of having women in Congress today, Sánchez concluded:

> You know, you just assume that everybody else has the same arrangement, and until somebody stands up and says, "No, that is not the reality for many in this country. That's not my reality," they don't ever consider that perspective. It just never even crosses their mind. So I feel like my role as a woman on the committee is very important because I don't just speak for myself, I speak for many

similarly situated women . . . [Were I] not there, that perspective [would be] totally absent from the debate.

Sánchez shared how this perspective shaped her legislative priorities and participation in the 114th Congress, merging her positional power on the committee with her passion to help working families. She talked about the importance of "looking at the tax code in terms of ways in which we can help alleviate some of the economic uncertainty and provide some help to working women in particular with respect to childcare, the need for quality affordable childcare," adding, "That is something that I continue to work on." In the 114th Congress alone, Sánchez sponsored the Support Working Parents Act of 2015, the Alzheimer's Beneficiary and Caregiver Support Act, and legislation to amend the Social Security Act to improve Social Security benefits for widows and widowers in two-income households, each seeking to accommodate changing family structures in federal policymaking.

These perspectives are illustrative of the ways in which "women's experience of care work might give rise to political competencies or political values," as Fiona MacKay investigates in her volume on women politicians and the ethic of care (2001: 4). Consistent with Joan Tronto (1993), she emphasizes care as a practice by women, not an innate disposition of women. That practice is socially and historically contingent on gendered and raced expectations of who is responsible for care. In the United States, responsibility for care has rested on women, with distinctive care experiences and expectations for women across race and ethnicity, class, and generation (see Hill Collins 2000). Those experiences underlie many of the comments made by the congresswomen we interviewed, which, in line with MacKay's (2001) work, illuminate an ethic of care as one form of difference women's presence makes in congressional policymaking.

CONCLUSION

Women members of Congress view their contributions to legislative work as multifaceted. They highlight the issues that they bring to, and work

to keep on, the legislative agenda, particularly those that have a disproportionate effect on women. But the significant influence of women on
agenda-setting is not limited to policies traditionally deemed "women's
issues." Instead, congresswomen emphasize the ways in they expand
conceptions of women's interests to encompass the unique needs and
concerns of women situated at various intersections of experience and
identity. Moreover, their comments demonstrate the ways in which
women's voices change policy conversations that are not typically or
solely identified as women's issues. That is a point that many women we
interviewed felt it was important to make. Poignantly, Representative
Roybal-Allard (D-CA) explained, "I think everything is a woman's issue
because whether you talk about foreign policy, it's our sons and daughters who would end up going to war." Her Republican and Democratic
colleagues, like Representative Ann Wagner (R-MO), echoed that sentiment. "I think all issues are women's issues," Wagner told us. "We just may
come at them from a different perspective, and . . . from living our lives
and the complexity of it all, we may have a different approach to so many
different issues."

As our interviews demonstrate, women add value to legislative
conversations by bringing their diverse gender experiences, as well as a
multitude of other experiences and identities, to Congress. Of course,
while there are multiple areas where women spoke with a louder or more
distinctive voice in the 114th Congress, their voices were also key to the
breadth of policy debates not covered in this chapter. Here, we chose to
focus on congresswomen's characterizations of their *distinctive* influence
on congressional agendas and debates. In the next chapter, we continue
this examination of women's contributions by highlighting the difference
congresswomen believe they make on congressional structures, processes,
and policy outcomes.

7

Changing the Institution, Image, and Exercise of Power

In our interview with Representative Terri Sewell (D-AL), she told us:

> [T]o measure our success in getting bills passed is not, I think, the best way to view our success. I think that [to measure] the impact of women—women of color and women generally—you have to expand your matrix, if you will, in order to really be able to fully appreciate the difference that women have made in this House.

Expanding the matrix of measures used to determine the significance of women's congressional representation—and underrepresentation—includes recognizing the ways in which women alter policy agendas and change policy conversations well before legislative votes, as we did in the preceding chapter. But Sewell's call for fully appreciating the difference women have made in Congress also requires attention to extra-legislative effects of women's representation and power.

In this chapter, we investigate how women in Congress view their collective contributions to the institution, finding that they perceive that the significance of their presence goes beyond their policy agendas and perspectives. Our interviews reveal that women pose challenges to institutional structures, norms, and expectations in conducting their congressional work. These challenges reflect the diversity among women in

Congress, who offer distinct approaches and effects based on ideology, party, and racial and ethnic identities. Differences in women's influence also persist within institutional power constructs, whether exhibited across chambers, based upon seniority, or exercised within caucuses or committees.

CHANGING THE FACE OF CONGRESSIONAL LEADERSHIP

In making the case for greater descriptive representation of women and minorities in politics, Jane Mansbridge argues that the "presence or absence in the ruling assembly of a proportional number of individuals carrying the group's ascriptive characteristics shapes the social meaning of those characteristics in a way that affects most bearers of those characteristics in the polity" (1999: 649). In other words, women and minority representatives disrupt expectations of what it means to be a member of Congress, while also expanding perceptions of what is possible among those populations with shared identities. Nirmal Puwar (2004) adds that the presence of "newcomers" to a legislative institution highlights the dominance of White men in the foundations, function, and face of the institution.

More than a decade ago, Representative Linda Sánchez was a newcomer whose identity as a 33-year-old Latina provided a stark contrast to the 409 White male members of the 108th Congress (Amer 2004). As she walked the halls of Congress in those early days, she was acutely aware that her presence was rare; she was one of just seven Latinas in the 108th Congress, and the only Latina under 40 years old. At that time, the average age of all members of Congress was 54.9 (Amer 2004). Sánchez recounted being stopped repeatedly at security checkpoints in the Capitol to show her member identification, despite wearing her member pin and even after multiple instances of proving herself to be an elected representative. Describing how this felt, she told us:

When you are walking with male colleagues and the male colleagues are waved through and they're stopping you, the subtle message that they are sending is that these people belong here and you don't, which angered me because I had won an election just like they had to be here and represent my district. They would say, "Isn't that cute? They think you're an intern." They were very good-natured about it, but it was humiliating.

Sánchez soon took action. First, she called out one of the security guards for reinforcing norms of who should or does hold congressional office. She explained, "One day I [got] really annoyed . . . I looked at [the policeman] and said, 'You know, White men are not the only members of Congress. There are women who are members. You know there are Hispanic and Black members too.'" Soon enough, she took her complaints to the top. She recounted:

One day I got tired of it and I marched into the Sergeant at Arms Office who is in charge of security for the complex and I said, "Hey look—I'm not asking to be treated better than my colleagues. I'm asking to be treated the same, because this is humiliating when you are walking with constituents and . . . the Capitol police don't treat you like a member. How are your constituents supposed to have faith and confidence that you are taken seriously?"

The Sergeant at Arms took action, circulating a photo of Representative Sánchez among the Capitol police and warning them not to ask her for her identification again. Things got better for her from then on, but even in 2016 she was not convinced that new women members were not subject to the same skepticism. Her story provides a concrete example not only of how stubborn the image of congressional leadership is, but also how important it is to have women disrupting it. "I feel like you have to kind of push [the idea that members of Congress are diverse] so people's thinking and attitudes change," Sánchez told us.

Sánchez's efforts to normalize leadership by women, including leadership by women of color, took place inside the institution of Congress, but women's legislative representation also has an effect outside congressional chambers, according to the women we interviewed. House Democratic Leader Nancy Pelosi (CA) explained, "It is really important for women in the country to see that someone who may have shared their experience—whether it is to be a working mom or whatever it happens to be—[has] a voice at the table." Pelosi raises an important point about the democratic legitimacy that may be ceded to a governing body that better represents the people it serves. Representative Ileana Ros-Lehtinen (R-FL) shared this perspective, telling us, "[Y]ou want the people of the United States to look at this legislative body and say, 'Oh they represent me.'" In addition to legitimacy, both women also point to the empathy fostered between members and constituents as an added value of greater diversity among members.

That diversity is not limited to race and gender. For Representative Renee Ellmers (R-NC), electing more Republican women provides a necessary challenge to "the stereotypical picture of a Republican in Congress [as] an older, graying, nondescript White man in a gray suit." In addition to altering the image of Republican members, Ellmers added, "I want the face of the Republican Party to show more women as well, because I really do believe that we are . . . very representative of the American people in our thinking on issues, especially issues that deal with families." Her Republican colleague, Representative Marsha Blackburn (R-TN), said that electing more conservative women to Congress sends another important message to voters. She told us, "Every day someone realizes that there is a Republican woman who is elected, it sends a message that . . . it has happened here, it can happen in your district also."

Blackburn alludes to the potential for greater diversity in Congress—particularly among women—to alter perceptions of efficacy, especially among women who look to women members as role models. Research has investigated whether having more women in office or on the ballot sparks greater interest, engagement, or efficacy among women voters or constituents, yielding mixed findings. While Lawless (2004) finds few independent symbolic effects of women's presence in Congress on female constituents, particularly on political efficacy and engagement, Campbell and Wolbrecht (2006) find evidence of a role model effect on adolescent girls when women political leaders are made visible to them. Their findings complement Burns, Schlozman, and Verba's conclusion that "[t]he more it looks as if politics is not simply a man's game, the more psychologically involved with politics women are" (2001: 347). Atkeson and Carrillo's (2007) findings at the state legislative level also suggest that higher proportions of women officeholders increase women citizens' external efficacy.

When we asked about opportunities distinct to women in Congress, the most common response was related to women members' capacity to inspire more women to run for elected office. Representative Kathleen Rice (D-NY) answered, "I would be surprised if every other one of my colleagues didn't say that they felt an enormous responsibility as a role model for young women." She was right. Representatives Elise Stefanik (R-NY) and Terri Sewell (D-AL) provided more concrete examples of how they have sought to inspire and encourage women to be politically engaged. Stefanik told us:

[Y]ou have to be aware that you're a role model for women, and that's something that I've taken to heart. And I'm constantly meeting with young women who reach out to our office, whether they're from the district or they get in contact from across the country, to encourage them to step up to the plate and add their voices to the conversation.

Likewise, Sewell explained:

It is about making this job accessible to people who you represent. And I firmly believe that part of that is a mentoring of young women . . . because if I spark the imagination of one woman who wouldn't have otherwise thought of [herself] as a policymaker, I am hopefully creating a pipeline of other women who will join the ranks of the elected.

Representative Susan Brooks (R-IN) noted that girls and women are not the only beneficiaries of seeing women in power. She said, "I think that we have to change the mindset not only of girls in encouraging them to run or consider leadership; we have to change the minds of boys and boys who support girls."

Senator Barbara Boxer (D-CA) agreed that seeing women in positions of authority was good for little girls *and* boys, and her colleague from California, Representative Anna Eshoo (D-CA), provided an illustration of this effect, sharing a story:

> My dentist in Palo Alto has an assistant and she has sons and they planned a trip to Washington and they did come . . . And so I took the boys . . . onto the floor of the House. We were in session when I was voting and all of that. And so their mother was telling me last week when I went in to have a checkup that . . . the younger son said to her, as he was attempting to write a thank you note to me, he said . . . "Well, I have a question," and she said, "What's your question?" He said, "Can boys become Congresswomen?" [*Laughing*] So you know what? That just more than made my day. Because for that little boy, . . . that's the way he saw Congress. That's the way he saw Congress. And it is more than an aha moment to me. It was very powerful to me, you know, really; my eyes filled up with tears when I heard his mother share that with me.

Representative Ann Wagner (R-MO) was clearly touched by a similar reminder of the power of role modeling, so much so that she has framed in her office a note written by her daughter, Mary Ruth, when Wagner worked in presidential politics. In the note, a very young Mary Ruth writes that when she grows up she wants to work for the president like her mom.

In talking about what difference it makes to have more women of color in Congress, Representative Joyce Beatty (D-OH) discussed a similar influence women members like her have on how young people see Congress. She explained, "[Having more women of color in Congress] makes a difference when little African American girls can dream that they, too, can serve in Congress." The limited research on the symbolic effect of seeing minority women as political elites yields similarly positive results; Stokes-Brown and Dolan (2010) find that the presence of Black women candidates for Congress increases Black women's likelihood of engaging in political proselytizing and voting. But Beatty described how she conveys a message to young people today that she could not fathom in her own childhood. "I never thought as a little girl that I would be sitting in the United States Congress. You know I was just hoping I would graduate from high school and get a job and be a good citizen, because I'm [a] first-generation college [graduate]," she told us. She then noted the privilege she feels in being able "to sit there and vote on the most important issues that are before us and that run this country, and to go back home and sit in the classroom or to sit in the neighborhood center and be able to honestly say, 'Somebody in this room—lots of you—can do this, and yet do greater things.'" Beatty added that having more women of color in Congress has an influence not only on communities or children of color. Just as Boxer and Eshoo emphasized the importance of boys seeing women in positions of power, Beatty discussed the benefit of seeing minority women in leadership roles for girls and women of all races and ethnicities.

Representative Michelle Lujan Grisham (D-NM) noted that, in addition to inspiring young people, congresswomen have an opportunity to "create normalcy" regarding women's political leadership, assuring the public that "the earth didn't stop revolving around its axis" with women at the helm. Relatedly, Representative Suzan DelBene (D-WA) described the importance of increasing the number of women in legislative leadership roles to alter expectations of women's political opportunities and appropriateness in positions of power:

Women who are chairs of committees, who are leaders in caucuses are critically, critically important . . . [N]ot only does it break existing barriers that are there, but it provides role models that hopefully allow the next woman to pursue a certain job, or a particular office, or be . . . a CEO of a company or the president of the United States.

In these comments, the women in the 114th Congress recognize the importance of simply changing the image of congressional representation to include women, in all their ideological, racial, and ethnic diversity. While more symbolic than substantive, the effect of this change matters in the perceptions of who is deemed powerful within and outside of congressional walls.

CHANGING INSTITUTIONAL RULES AND STRUCTURES

Accommodating women in Congress has occurred in even more overt ways in recent decades, altering both actual structures and institutional rules. Some of the women members we spoke with described the dominance of masculinity they found upon entering congressional settings. Representative Niki Tsongas (D-MA) explained, "When I first got here, I said I felt like I was going from the playing field to the locker room. There's a physicality to it . . . [H]ad women been part of this all along, it would not have evolved like that. It would have been different." One way it would have been different, according to Representative Terri Sewell (D-AL), is that there would have been a women's restroom near the House floor. "Until Speaker Pelosi became the speaker of the house, women members of the House of Representatives had to walk pretty far to go to the bathroom," she explained, adding, "This is just a practical difference that we have made in the House of Representatives. Now we have a bathroom literally right off the House floor that we did not have up until her ascension as speaker of the house."

Women members might also have been allowed in the Senate swimming pool if it had not been a male-only space over decades of men's dominance in the chamber. Instead, only in the past decade have the rules been changed to allow women senators to swim alongside their male colleagues (Mundy 2015). And while men could not bar women from the chamber floor, Senator Barbara Mikulski (D-MD) recalls leading the move to eliminate an informal rule enforced by male leaders requiring women to wear skirts on the Senate floor. It was not until 1993 that Mikulski and her female colleagues donned pantsuits and trousers while conducting Senate business. While these changes may appear trivial, they challenge practices that marked women as "other" and thus helped uphold inequities in gender power.

Globally, organizations like the Inter-Parliamentary Union, independent researchers, and governments have begun to define and evaluate "gender-sensitive" parliaments, identifying rules and structures that better facilitate gender equality in access to the institution and in the experiences of men and women members (see, e.g., Palmieri 2011; Childs 2016). Their recommendations go beyond building bathrooms to, for example, changing legislative schedules, providing childcare, and creating lactation rooms, all with the intent of fostering greater interest among women aspirants for office and more positive experiences for and retention of women who are serving (Krook and Norris 2014). The Congress and state legislatures in the United States have been slow to adopt similar institutional accommodations, but our conversations with congresswomen provided some indications that they recognize the value of structural change.

For example, in October 2015, Delegate Eleanor Holmes Norton (D-DC) wrote a letter to the secretary of the Smithsonian Institution, David Skorton, calling for designated lactation spaces for employees at all Smithsonian facilities. Skorton quickly confirmed that those spaces would be provided, in accordance with federal law. Noting that she went further to draft a bill that would require accommodations for nursing mothers who are tourists in federal buildings, Norton asked, "Is that because I'm a woman? A man could easily have done this with an understanding of that." But she added, "I don't [know], but it's an example . . . it might be more meaningful to somebody like me." Another example of the same style of accommodation was presented to us while we interviewed Representative Lois Capps (D-CA). During the interview, one of Capps's staff members walked into a room attached to the congresswoman's office to pump. Capps stopped the interview to explain, "We have a special need for a very young mom whose baby is waiting for her breast milk when she gets home . . . So this is part of the daily schedule. It's accommodating women."

The challenges of balancing work and family go beyond providing a site for breastfeeding mothers, as discussed in Chapter 3. But the presence of women in Congress, many of whom come to the institution with experiences as mothers and primary caregivers, can spark dialogue about strategies for better accommodating individuals' private and public needs—whether for staffers, members, visitors, or the public—via the legislative policy that members make.

CHANGING THE EXERCISE OF POWER

When Representative Karen Bass (D-CA) told us, "[I]n general, [I] think that women work differently," she raised another dimension on which the influence of women's presence can be evaluated in Congress. Previous research has identified differences in men and women state legislators' leadership styles, finding women to be more integrative and less aggressive (Kathlene 1994; Rosenthal 1998). Similarly, comparative literature has found distinct, and less adversarial, work styles among women parliamentarians (Norris 1996; Bochel and Briggs 2000; MacKay 2001; Childs 2004). As Sarah Childs (2004) notes, however, this difference is likely not determined by legislators' sex, but instead reflects differences in gender performance that are rooted in gender role socialization and expectations.

Our interviews indicate that these differences in how women "do politics" within legislatures might also be explained by what motivates their legislative service. Over and over we heard women in Congress say that they are there to get things done. They credit what they perceive as their results-oriented approach with facilitating policy achievements, and they also believe their strong commitment to finding policy solutions distinguishes them from many of their male counterparts.

Senator Barbara Boxer (D-CA) characterized women senators as "problem-solvers, rather than problem-makers," adding, "And we have problem-makers among senators who are men. We have none among women." Senator Debbie Stabenow (D-MI) echoed her claim, as discussed in Chapter 5, arguing that women's focus on solving problems comes before their concern about amassing power. Of course, the institutional structure and culture of the Senate, which is by design less adversarial and more collaborative than the House, helps to foster this approach to policy-making among all members. But women in the House shared similar claims, despite the contentiousness that often constrains representatives' behavior. Republican leader Representative Cathy McMorris Rodgers (R-WA) observed that a woman's instinct, unlike a man's, "is to be a problem solver." Representative Ann Wagner (R-MO) called women "doers" who "look for others to work with us to make [things] happen." Alma Adams (D-NC) also called women "doers," invoking the oft-quoted words of Margaret Thatcher, "In politics if you want something said you ask a man, but if you want something done you ask a woman." Representative Marsha Blackburn (R-TN) even called conservative women "the leaders of the Get 'er Done Caucus."

Perhaps more important than the perception that women *do* get things done is an understanding of how and why they approach congressional work in this way. Multiple women in Congress claimed that members' prioritization of achievement over ego differs by gender. Representative Cathy McMorris Rodgers (R-WA) said, "[I] believe that women are maybe less motivated by what might be next on the career ladder versus actually wanting to make a difference, wanting to make an impact for the long term." Even more succinctly, Representative Anna Eshoo (D-CA) said, in line with research on women's motivation to run for office, "I don't think women come here to be somebody. I think we come here to get things done." Multiple women explained that they feel women members, themselves included, are less concerned about seeing their names on a bill than getting legislation of importance to them passed.

Women's prioritization of policy outcomes over political advancement and credit-taking is likely related to the strong commitment they have to the issues that motivate their public service in the first place. Representative Yvette Clarke (D-NY) described the difference women have made in Congress this way: "I think women bring a laser-like focus to issues, and we're pretty determined to get things done and we see . . . all the issues as bread and butter issues, as issues that really will impact on families and communities." Her House colleague Marcia Fudge (D-OH) was even more specific, suggesting, "We want to be able to go home and say, 'Look—this is what we did for Head Start or this is what we did for K–12 today or this is what we did for child nutrition.' . . . I mean, we want to get things done."

With less concern about claiming short-term and individual political credit, women—according to some members we interviewed—are able to take a more comprehensive approach to policymaking. Representative Cynthia Lummis (R-WY) explained, "I think men are more inclined to legislate towards the next election, and women are more inclined to legislate well beyond the next election." She cited the costs of this approach to policy outcomes: "When you don't have . . . as many people who are looking beyond the election, I think we get some more short-sighted policies," adding, "If we had more women, I think we'd have an opportunity to look farther out and do better planning." Representative Marsha Blackburn (R-TN) raised a similar point, arguing, "I think that men have a tendency to push forward; women have a tendency to completely define the problem and then find a way forward. So the approach is different." Defining the problem requires looking at things "broadly, deeply, and [with] forward vision," according to Representative Doris Matsui (D-CA), who credited women with listening well in preparation for policymaking.

House Democratic Leader Nancy Pelosi (CA) described women's prioritization of listening as "part of the beauty of women's leadership." She explained, "Women don't waste time . . . So if you are having a meeting, . . . you want to hear what people have to say, you want to build some consensus to take you to the next step." This approach requires humility, according to Pelosi: "We have a certain level of humility that we can learn from what people are saying, so you listen." It also promotes a less adversarial style of engaging with constituents and colleagues, something that some congresswomen, such as Representative Ileana Ros-Lehtinen (R-FL), described as more common among women: "I think women are not as conflict-oriented, and they try to reach a consensus and they don't relish the fight and the drama of opposing, clashing ideas." Other women members noted that relating to their colleagues with civility and humanity makes conflict less likely, something noted in Chapter 5 as also facilitating bipartisanship.

These strategies for seeing results are likely often employed for partisan goals, but they are also consistent with women's willingness to work across party lines. As Representative Tulsi Gabbard (D-HI) argued, women members "bring people together around a common solution and do our best to deliver results." Those common solutions require compromise, something the women we interviewed fully understood and accepted as necessary to the outcome—policy change—that they most wanted. Senator Claire McCaskill (D-MO) perceived women's approach in this way:

I think that we are just more wired to try to figure out a way to accomplish something, to be pragmatic, to get it done. And if that means we have to swallow something we really want to do or leave something on the sidelines that we really wanted to get passed, I think women are more willing to do that for the greater good.

Representative Linda Sánchez (D-CA) agreed:

I would say that, generally speaking, women legislators look to ways in which people may not get 100% of what they want, but people don't lose 100%. So they are more willing to work on things where . . . a Democrat might get 30% of what they want and the Republicans get 70% of what they want but . . . they don't tend to be as extreme as the men—which is all or nothing, you know, winning at any cost.

McCaskill and Sánchez were not alone in talking about women's pragmatism, which likely stems from the experiences they bring with them to Congress, some specifically gender-related. For Representative Terri Sewell (D-AL), that pragmatism comes from being the only Democrat in Alabama's congressional delegation. She explained, "If I don't work with my colleagues from [Alabama] to promote [legislation], I'm not going to get anything done. So I believe in compromise. I believe in the spirit of negotiating." For Representative Renee Ellmers (R-NC), being a nurse shaped the way she approached policymaking. She told us, "[F]or me it's about fixing the problem to the best optimal position we can get to, and that's really from my nursing background in healthcare, that you are not always working in a perfect situation, but you got to get the best outcome you can. And that's why it's easy for me to understand that you are never going to 100%."

Other women tied their pragmatism back to their experiences with juggling demands of work and family. Representative Elizabeth Esty (D-CT) noted that adaptability is something to which women are accustomed in their personal and professional lives before coming to Congress. She explained, "It's not always been an easy path, and so you've had to be more adaptable and creative in figuring out how to get things done, and so I find that, as a whole, the women tend to be a little more pragmatic about what that might involve." Representative Louise Slaughter (D-NY) agreed that women are used to tackling multiple demands to achieve results: "[We] run a household of family members, knowing that we have to keep the peace and the environment has to be clean and everyone has to be fed and educated. So that's just a given with all of us. We don't have to learn that."

Passage of the Every Student Succeeds Act in the 114th Congress provides an excellent example of women's pragmatic approach. As a member of the conference committee on the bill, Representative Susan Davis (D-CA) said that women's presence there made a difference because they were among those "willing to give up their egos in many ways for the greater cause." Davis also credited the leadership of Senator Patty Murray (D-WA), the ranking member on the Senate's Health, Education, Labor, and Pensions (HELP) Committee, with playing a key role in making the necessary compromises to ensure the bill's passage. Murray worked closely with the Republican chair of the committee, Senator Lamar Alexander (R-TN), to negotiate a far overdue reauthorization of the nation's K–12 education law after years of failed attempts. It was Murray, according to public reports, who told Alexander that approaching reauthorization in the 114th Congress in the same way as before would not work. She made the case that the two of them had to draft the bill together, not start from a Republican draft and negotiate from there. Murray warned Alexander that the process would be difficult, requiring "really listening to each other, working it, member by member, line by line, idea by idea" (Layton 2015).

Alexander conceded, and the two drafted a bipartisan bill that was signed into law in December 2015. In an interview with the *Washington Post*, Alexander credited Murray with offering "good advice," and added, "I gave up something, but I gained more—not only a working relationship with her but a lot of support from the Democratic members of the committee" (Layton 2015). Murray also concluded that the rewards of compromise outweighed the costs of concession in the policy process. Upon the bill's final passage, she reflected, "As the chairman knows, I've had to give up lots of things I didn't want to, but so has every member here. And that is how we make our country a better place and show the young people of this country who are coming up behind us that democracy works" (Chacko 2015).

Murray's positional power as the ranking member on the Senate committee tasked with education policy was an equally important factor in her drive to compromise and thus secure a positive policy outcome. Other women in the Senate referenced how women members' motivation to see results has a greater effect when they are in seats of power and leadership. For example, both Senator Susan Collins (R-ME) and Senator Kirsten Gillibrand (D-NY) talked about the success of recent major pieces of legislation that were ushered into law through committees with women at the helm. Gillibrand cited Senator Debbie Stabenow's (D-MI) leadership in the Agriculture Committee as instrumental in the passage of the Farm Bill in the 113th Congress, and Collins talked about her own work leading the Housing and Transportation Appropriations Subcommittee with Senator Murray in 2014. She proudly noted, "We always produced the bill, always. Even though we didn't agree on every issue, we would work together to achieve consensus on a bill." In the 114th Congress, Gillibrand pointed to Senator Barbara Boxer's leadership in bringing about a much overdue reauthorization of the transportation bill in December 2015. As the ranking member of the Senate Committee on Environment and Public Works, Boxer worked with Republican Chair

James Inhofe (R-OK) to pass the Fixing America's Surface Transportation (FAST) Act, representing one of the most significant and complex pieces of legislation to make it through the 114th Congress. Reflecting on these women Senate leaders' accomplishments, Gillibrand explained, "[E]ach of these women senators are really good at their jobs and they really care about getting things done. Not the partisan politics as much, [but] much more about actually helping the people they represent, and it makes me really proud."

In the House, Democratic women repeatedly praised Minority Leader Nancy Pelosi (D-CA) for her leadership style and success. Representative Jan Schakowsky (D-IL) called Pelosi "focused on a mission," "tireless," and "relentless," crediting these traits and her leadership skills with delivering results. Likewise, Representative Rosa DeLauro (D-CT) distinguished Pelosi as a leader who is "willing to fight to make sure there is a win." This is consistent with Peters and Rosenthal's evaluation of Pelosi as displaying "task ambition," a type of ambition they perceive as gendered and they define as "[using] political opportunities to accomplish specific objectives" rather than "focusing on the attainment of office as a fulfillment of one's personal ambition" (2010: 197). But does being a woman shape Pelosi's approach or effectiveness? Some members we spoke with said yes. Representative Judy Chu (D-CA) noted how Pelosi's style is reflective of that of other women members:

> [Pelosi] has an uncanny ability to really read where the members are coming from. She is the best vote counter of all time, and it's just not because she does the mechanical vote counting; it's because she can read where the members are coming from. So I do believe that women members have a greater ability to develop the relationships and also to read the body language and intent of other members.

Similarly, Representative Jackie Speier (D-CA) argued, "I think her success as a great vote counter, as [a person with] an ability to bring divergent groups to the table, has a lot to do with her XX chromosome.

I think those are qualities that women tend to have in greater abundance than men."

Another benefit of Pelosi's leadership, according to Democratic women in the House, is her focus on empowering other women. Representative Grace Meng (D-NY) told us:

> Leader Pelosi makes a very intentional effort to make sure that women are always included whatever the discussion is, so that's something that she prides herself on and she shows through her actions and . . . making sure that at any given major conversation or discussion, that it's not just men around the table. So she's really very good about that.

Pelosi affirmed that those efforts are intentional. "I do want to give the women the opportunity to show their stuff," she explained, "[to show] that they have the four things we say about leadership: they have a vision, they have knowledge and therefore their judgment is respected, they have a plan [so] they think strategically, and they are able to convey that passion." Peters and Rosenthal quantify Pelosi's influence on expanding opportunities for women on committees, finding that the number of committee leadership positions held by women increased under her party leadership despite a decline in women's overall seniority from previous congresses (2010: 217–18).

Not all Democratic women were as confident that the Democratic Party fully valued women's, and particularly minority women's, leadership, but almost no one was directly critical of Pelosi. Republican women in the House touted the advancements of women in their party's leadership, but offered fewer direct examples of how the actions of Republican women in leadership positions in the 114th Congress reflected distinctive leadership styles or priorities. Across both parties and chambers, however, there was little doubt among congresswomen that seniority and leadership posts—whether in their party or on committees—provide women with greater power and more opportunity to realize their commitment to get policy-related results.

CONCLUSION

How might Congress be affected if there were more women in office? Representative Lois Frankel (D-FL) told us, "I really, truly believe the more women that are in Congress, the better this country will be. I really do believe that." Other women members we interviewed were more specific about what the positive effects of greater women's representation would be, whether these would be more balanced debate, more long-term planning, or a more comprehensive approach to legislating. Arguing that women members are more likely to reject the "my-way-or-the-highway attitude" so dominant in Congress, Representative Debbie Wasserman-Schultz (D-FL) told us, "If we had more women, not just in Congress, but who have the authority to make big decisions and who are in power positions to make things happen, we can get bigger things done."

Our reliance on interview data means we cannot directly test Wasserman-Schultz's claim or the claims of the other congresswomen cited in this chapter. However, we have been able to document their widely shared perceptions that as women they value policy over power, achievement over ego, and pragmatism over politics and that these characteristics have contributed to their policy successes.

As we showed in the case of women senators, women's influence varies by the positions and power they hold. That may explain why Representative Louise Slaughter's (D-NY) response to our question about the difference women have made in Congress included, "We still don't have an awful lot of women in strong leadership positions, and we should." Like Wasserman-Schultz, Slaughter raises the possibility that having more women not only in Congress, but also in congressional leadership roles, would make even more of a difference than we have seen thus far.

The difference women make is not limited to getting things done through legislation. This chapter also highlights members' beliefs in the symbolic effects of and structural changes that result from women's presence in Congress. Congresswomen argue that there is value in citizens seeing women—and particularly women of diverse ideologies, races and ethnicities, and ages—in positions of political power. Women members of

Congress not only act as role models for young women, but also challenge and alter institutional images and expectations of political leadership in ways that affect both women and men. Women have also been responsible for changing rules and structures to better accommodate women within government, creating better conditions—in the most literal sense—for women to succeed.

In this and the preceding chapter, the women members of the 114th Congress discussed multiple ways in which women are making a difference in congressional work, from changing the policy agenda and adding diverse voices to legislative debate, to bringing styles and motivation to Congress that help get things done. Women add value to congressional debates, processes, and outcomes in myriad ways, but this does not mean that they work in a uniform manner or from a singular perspective. Rather, listening to women members describe in their own words why, how, and in what ways they influence Congress reveals that their influence is just as complex, context-dependent, and multifaceted as the influence of the men with whom they serve.

Together, the insights from congresswomen make a positive case for women's inclusion and empowerment not only in the US Congress, but in political offices at all levels nationwide. We elaborate upon this conclusion in our next and final chapter.

8

Conclusion

Representation Matters

Late into the night on July 27, 2017, Senators Lisa Murkowski (R-AK) and Susan Collins (R-ME) sat together on the Senate floor while debate concluded on the Republican majority's attempt to repeal and replace the Affordable Care Act. The two women sat apart from members of their own party, who were otherwise unified in supporting a "skinny repeal," and from Democrats, who were universally opposed to the bill. As the night wore on into the following morning, Murkowski and Collins were joined by Senator John McCain (R-AZ), who—with dramatic flair—cast the deciding vote against the repeal effort. McCain, who had returned to Washington, DC, only days earlier after emergency brain surgery and a subsequent cancer diagnosis, garnered much of the immediate attention, and even credit, for the legislative upset. But it was Murkowski and Collins's steadfast commitment to sustainable policy reform instead of a short-term political win that positioned them as the key players in efforts to achieve healthcare reform in 2017.

Republican Party leaders appeared to have underestimated the strength of these women. No women senators were included in a 13-member Republican working group that drafted repeal options, and the White House spent little to no time lobbying Murkowski or Collins for their votes. In fact, in recalling the minutes leading to the final vote, Senator Collins told the *New York Times* that Vice President Mike Pence addressed her for the first time that week. "All of the sudden someone tapped on my back and it was the vice president," Collins said. "He obviously had heard that John [McCain] has decided to vote no. He was well aware of my vote and Lisa's position, and he was there to talk to John." She added, "He said, 'Boy, are you tough,' but he softened it by putting his arm around me as he said it" (Flegenheimer, Martin, and Steinhauer 2017). After the bill failed, Democratic Senate Leader Chuck Schumer (NY) praised Collins and Murkowski for that toughness. He told reporters, "They were amazing. Women are in so many instances stronger than men. They brag less about it, but they are. And last night sort of proved that."

Thirty months, and one Congress, after Senator Murkowski talked about the "hardiness of women" on the Senate floor, these women senators displayed their hardiness in another way. But more than proving their resilience, this moment in the 115th Congress is illustrative of many of the findings from our interviews with congresswomen across chambers and parties in the Congress that preceded it. Collins and Murkowski's behavior was motivated by how they perceived their representational role and whom they felt responsible to represent in the Senate. They took on the challenges of navigating an institution—and legislative process—dominated by men and partisanship. And they seemed to prioritize achievement over ego and policy over politics in exercising their legislative leadership, a style that the congresswomen in our study told us sets them apart from men.

THE VALUE OF TALKING TO WOMEN

Our interviews with more than three-fourths of all women members of the 114th Congress provide details and nuance that help explain the context within which Collins and Murkowski were operating in 2017. In over 40 hours of interviews, congresswomen shared perspectives on their representational roles; discussed their experiences in a gendered, raced, and partisan institution; and described what motivates their legislative priorities and behavior. Existing scholarship has often focused on more formal measures—such as roll call votes or floor speeches—to evaluate gender differences in legislative behavior or impact. First-person accounts like those presented in this book are rarer, particularly at the congressional level. Our findings contribute significantly to existing work; they speak to the motivation behind women's observable behaviors and the informal ways in which women's experiences, identities, and approaches to leadership matter to the daily work of the US Congress.

The qualitative approach we take also allows us to better distinguish the ways in which women's representation varies based on the multilayered identities, experiences, and motivations that women bring to their roles. Too little research has been done on the distinct influence of women of color in legislatures, especially in Congress, and too often the work done to investigate differences by legislators' gender says little about intersections with race and complexities arising from party, geography, chamber, or seniority. Throughout this book, we have sought to illustrate how and where categories of identity and experience operate simultaneously for women members, complicating prevailing narratives and highlighting the value of challenging single-axis analyses of gender and representation. These categories of identity operate within a congressional institution that is at the same time gendered, raced, and partisan. Those dynamics shape both formal and informal rules, norms, structures, and processes, creating diverse conditions for those tasked with navigating them.

Taken together, the insights congresswomen share in our chapters support the claim that women's representation matters in congressional debates, processes, and outcomes. In spite of challenges they face as "space invaders" in a male-dominated institution prone to partisan gridlock, women members find myriad ways to have a meaningful structural, symbolic, and substantive impact in Congress. The value-added of women's representation is neither uniform across all women nor interchangeable among them. As our interviews illustrate, the perspectives, experiences, and influence of women in Congress are just as complex, context-dependent, and multifaceted as those of the men with whom they serve.

THE SCHOLARLY DEBATE ABOUT WOMEN
IN CONGRESS

Recognizing and illustrating this complexity of identity among women in Congress are among our most important contributions to existing scholarship on women's legislative representation. Previous studies of women in Congress have focused on the difference women make *as women* and on the sites in which their behavior or rhetoric differs most from men. Some of our findings bolster that research, even though we do not engage in a comparison between women and men; the congresswomen we interviewed told us that they offer distinctive—and more collaborative— work styles, that they advocate for policy issues that most directly affect women, and that they contribute more authentic perspectives and voices to distinctly gendered legislative debates.

But our findings take this research further by distinguishing among women in the various ways in which their representation matters. In elaborating upon the plurality of congresswomen's perspectives, voices, and positions, we seek to push scholarship on women in Congress further beyond gender dichotomies and a nearly exclusive focus on "women's issues." By allowing congresswomen to articulate the issues on which they believe their impact is distinct, instead of limiting our analyses to a predetermined set of "women's issues," we are better able to assess the influence of intersecting and multilayered identities in congresswomen's policy contributions. Our interviews revealed that two of the factors that most complicated a singular narrative of women's congressional representation are party and race/ethnicity. These are also the sites upon which we make more specific contributions to existing research; our interviews provide insights into the distinctive experiences, perspectives, and influence of women of color and Republican women.

Women of Color

More women of color served in the 114th Congress than in any previous Congress. Scholarship in women and politics today increasingly takes the racial and ethnic diversity of the group "women" into account, and intersectional analyses as well as studies of women of color are growing in number an influence.

Our interviews contribute to these debates and to the relatively small number of studies looking specifically at congressional experience and influence through lenses of *both* race and gender (e.g., Tate 2003; Hawkesworth 2003). The women of color we interviewed typically strive to represent multiple communities. The desire to represent women and people of color is often part of what motivates their legislative behavior. Consistent with past research, they also bring an intersectional perspective as women of color—or typically as Black, Latina, or Asian American women. This perspective permeates their jobs as legislators and is not limited to a specific issue agenda.

We also find evidence of heterogeneity within the category "women of color," which speaks to the need for further research on this group of women in American politics. Some women of color in Congress noted the import of ethnic, geographic, and occupational differences operating within racial groups, as well as their personal experiences with immigration and their representation of immigrant communities. And while women of color in Congress are almost all Democrats, we also found some evidence of racial differences cutting through the "Democratic women" umbrella. While recent research on party differences among women in studies of legislators is a step forward, scholars need to be more attentive to racial differences within each party.

Some of the women we interviewed mentioned challenges that they viewed as unique to congresswomen of color, whether in getting to or serving in Congress, and some said that racial barriers are harder to surmount than any barriers created by gender. While women in Congress must contend with racial, gender, and intersectional barriers, they are not without influence. Nor are they without determination. Our interviews showed that women of color in Congress are proud of their roles and take great satisfaction in serving their communities.

Republican Women

In recent years, scholars have become increasingly interested in the election and behavior of Republican women. As the Republican Party has moved from the minority to the majority in Congress and most state legislatures, understanding the influence of women legislators means understanding the behavior of Republican women. Limited research looks specifically at the distinctive ways in which Republican women experience and influence Congress (e.g., Dodson 2006; Swers 2002, 2013). We contribute to this body of knowledge in several ways.

While Republican women differ from one another in many ways, our research suggests that Republican women enjoy a sense of camaraderie within their party. But they also face challenges in exercising informal and formal influence given their dramatic underrepresentation among Republicans in Congress. We find that Republican women are cognizant of their minority status as women within their party, but they take great pride in their collective role as women within their conference. Relatedly, we find that Republican women typically note challenges and opportunities that women in Congress face. While gender consciousness is often associated with Democratic women legislators, who are more often allied with feminist organizations than Republican women are, we see that Republican women in Congress are cognizant of their distinctive status as women. Some voiced experiences with gender bias among voters; others noted their opportunity and responsibility to act as role models for girls and women. They would like to help elect more women from their party to Congress.

Interestingly, the Democratic women we interviewed also expressed interest in seeing more Republican women elected. They remarked on how few Republican women serve in Congress and especially in the House. Some wondered whether their Republican female colleagues are sufficiently valued by the Republican Party and expressed hope that Republican women will achieve the leadership positions they deserve.

MAKING THE CASE FOR WOMEN'S REPRESENTATION

In assessing women's political power today, many women in Congress told us that there remains significant room for progress. With women holding just one-fifth of the seats in Congress, one of the most significant limitations on their congressional influence is that there are simply too few of them. Moreover, there are too few women in positions of power, a reality made especially stark by the dearth of women in the majority party.

Representative Yvette Clarke (D-NY) told us, "Let me say this, I think that women are doing very well, that we've made a lot of gains, but I don't think that we should put a flag in it and say we've arrived because I think there is far more that we can and should do." Part of that work, she noted, is engaging and educating women in the electorate to amplify their voices and use their power to make change. That work is facilitated, in part, by proving that women's political representation matters. Representative Clarke (D-NY) said, "We will run into women who will say, 'Well, so what you're a woman in Congress? That's no big thing.' But actually, it is."

In addition to contributing greater nuance and evidence to scholarship on gender, race, partisanship, and representation, the 83 congresswomen we interviewed in the 114th Congress make a strong case for why their representation is a "big thing," and—even more important—why electing more women to Congress and to legislatures nationwide is a necessary step to creating a more representative democracy.

Women Are Resilient in the Face of Obstacles to Entering and Exercising Power in Congress

The obstacles confronting congresswomen, according to our interviews, are greatest at the campaign stage. Consistent with research on women's paths to elected office, women in Congress told us that overcoming challenges to winning office as women is often more difficult than navigating gender-based challenges inside the House or Senate. Many also celebrated progress over time in the acceptance and treatment of women in Congress.

Still, our interviews provide evidence that congresswomen operate within an institution where they remain apart from the norm. Like women in other male-dominated professions, women in Congress sometimes struggle to be heard and taken seriously, are more often asked to prove themselves as capable and credentialed for the job, and are tasked with negotiating work and family demands that are less likely to burden their male peers. These hurdles to full acceptance, inclusion, and power can be higher for Republican women and women of color, who are both fewer in number and confront race and party stereotypes that interact with gender expectations in ways that further set them apart from institutional norms of leadership.

There are times when the gendered culture of Congress is particularly hard to ignore. Examples are not limited to those in the 114th Congress. Within the first seven months of the 115th Congress, Senator Elizabeth Warren (D-MA) was silenced by Majority Leader Mitch McConnell (R-KY) on the Senate floor while reading a letter from Coretta Scott King opposing attorney general–nominee Jeff Sessions's earlier nomination to the federal judiciary; Senator Kamala Harris (D-CA) was reprimanded by male committee members for too aggressively questioning Attorney General Sessions (who claimed she was making him nervous); and Senator Susan Collins (R-ME) was threatened by Representative Blake Farenthold (R-TX) for her opposition to the July 2017 healthcare repeal bills. "If it was a guy from South Texas I might ask him to step outside and settle this Aaron Burr-style," Farenthold told a local radio host. Farenthold's comments not only marked women as "other" in an institution dominated by men, but perpetuated masculine norms of engagement that have historically excluded, or even targeted, women. The attempts to silence women like Warren and Harris, while their male Democratic colleagues were permitted to—in the case of Warren—read the same letter on the Senate floor, and—in the case of Harris—aggressively question a cabinet official, also reveal persistent disparities in the balance of gender power in today's Congress. While these examples of gender bias were more overt than most shared by the congresswomen in our study, they act as reminders that women in Congress operate in an environment that was established by and for men.

But the women we interviewed assured us that they are both accustomed to navigating gendered and raced terrain and more than capable of clearing hurdles to their congressional leadership and success. They discussed "beating back" attempts to undermine their power, talked about powering through the bias, and described strategies to maximize their political influence in spite of barriers that remain. Instead of seeing their underrepresentation only as a challenge, some women in Congress noted that women have worked to create both institutional and policy change by harnessing the power in the numbers they *do* have.

Representative Anna Eshoo (D-CA) told us, "When you get up in the morning, the first thing you have to do is put your feet on the ground and put [your] suit of armor on and come here [to take on] the battles that are worthy of being taken on." Sometimes the suits of armor worn by congresswomen deflect the gender biases in institutional norms and expectations that might distract them from more important policy battles awaiting them.

Women Get Things Done, Even in a Polarized Political Environment

At other times, congresswomen's armor is utilized in battles to break through partisan gridlock. This was particularly true in the 114th Congress, where high levels of party unity, divided government, and an impending presidential election contributed to its status as the third least productive congress in the nearly seven decades in which records on bill enactment have been kept ("Vital Statistics" 2017). The congresswomen we interviewed largely confirmed that partisan polarization creates a difficult work climate. But minority legislators—Democrats in the 114th Congress—were particularly, and understandably, more troubled and frustrated by the problems that partisanship presents.

While acknowledging the hurdles that partisanship erects, women outlined strategies they adopt for clearing them. Women in the minority play a strong defense and look to alternative sites for policy influence, such as legislative oversight. Congressmen utilize similar strategies to pursue their legislative agendas in the face of partisan stalemate.

Men and women also seek to break the gridlock by reaching across party lines. While these efforts are deemed newsworthy less frequently than instances of legislative brinksmanship and impasse, the congresswomen we interviewed shared many examples of working with members of the opposing party to promote shared policy interests. Their insights complicate narratives of unbridled polarization in today's Congress and also point to opportune sites for fostering cross-party efforts—from formal settings like congressional committees and CODELs to informal, and largely social, gatherings among members. In speaking to congresswomen, we found that single-sex spaces—including dinners, trips, and sporting events—provided distinct opportunities for them to build relationships with each other that were later useful in policymaking settings. These personal relationships seem easier to forge in the Senate than in the House given institutional differences and the smaller number of women senators. But friendships are forged in both chambers.

Whether presented to men or women members, these opportunities for cross-party collaboration must be based upon some shared policy goals. Thus, an important obstacle to collaboration is the undeniable fact that there are some policies on which women in the Republican and Democratic Parties will rarely, if ever, agree; the stark divide among women in the 114th Congress on abortion provides a clear example. Opportunities for cross-party collaboration also rely upon members' willingness to compromise. The majority of congresswomen we interviewed, regardless of party, told us that they believe they are more likely than their male counterparts to both create and capitalize on opportunities for bipartisan collaboration. They explained that women's proclivity for bipartisanship might arise from the ties that bind them *as women,* whether life experiences like motherhood or shared minority status in a male-dominated institution.

Women See Themselves as Having a Distinctive Work Style
That Prioritizes Results and Values Collaboration
and Consensus

At least a quarter of the women we interviewed emphasized that their
results-oriented approach to congressional leadership distinguishes them
from their male colleagues and motivates them to reach across party lines
to get things done. They said they prioritized policy results over political
wins, making them more likely to take on the political risks of bipartisanship to achieve the policy outcomes that motivated them to run for office
in the first place.

Of course, women in Congress do not ignore political realities or
overlook significant ideological divides in seeking policy results. Our
interviews reveal congresswomen's electoral motivations to work—or not
work—across party lines, particularly among members in swing districts.
They also point to limits on women's willingness to collaborate with
members of the other party when ideological differences are too vast and
when chances for success—partly reliant upon the positional power of a
cross-party partner—are low.

Still, in a polarized environment where progress in enacting policies
appears to be hampered by political disincentives to compromise, the
results-oriented approach that women leaders tout as distinct from the
approach of their male colleagues has the potential to grease the wheels
of legislative bodies and foster greater confidence among the public in our
democratic institutions.

Women Bring Distinctive and Diverse Perspectives
to Legislative Debates and Agendas, Often Rooted
in Their Own Experiences

Women in Congress are also motivated by representational goals rooted
in their beliefs about who they "stand for" in the House or Senate. In many
ways, congresswomen perceive their representational roles in similar

ways to men; they stand for the constituents who live in the district or state from which they were elected and are influenced by occupational and personal experiences that they bring to their legislative work. But the women we interviewed also expressed a commitment to represent diverse groups of women in their legislative work and cited the value of having their lived experiences *as women* represented in legislative deliberation and decision-making.

Sometimes that commitment translates into bringing issues of particular importance to women to the legislative agenda and prioritizing them, consistent with much of the existing scholarship on the impact of women in state and federal legislatures. When we asked women in the 114th Congress whether and how the presence of women has made a difference in Congress, many mentioned their promotion of policies that empower women or address women's health. They described congresswomen's leadership, credibility, and passion on policies to curb sexual assault on college campuses and in the military, as well as on abortion access and funding. Even where the women in our study disagreed on policy positions and solutions, as was most evident in their discussions of abortion policy, they identified a distinct value of being women that affected how and to what degree they engaged with and influenced these policy debates. These findings lend support to research connecting women's descriptive representation to the substantive representation of women in policymaking bodies like the US Congress.

But the women we interviewed also made clear that influences on their legislative behavior cannot be attributed to gender alone; the experiences and perspectives that congresswomen bring to their representational work vary across and within race and ethnic groups and/or generational, class, regional, or ideological divides. We highlight the distinctive voices that women of color contribute to policy debates, rooted in their unique perspectives and experiences as minority women. These women members have also expanded legislative agendas to complicate conceptions of "women's issues" and raise policy issues that are of particular importance to—and affect women uniquely within—communities of color. The specific policy debates within the 114th Congress on which we focus—criminal justice reform, immigration, gun control, and abortion—are just a few examples of where the multilayered identities and interests that motivate congresswomen's work. They also reveal the ways in which women legislators may bring a gender lens to bear on policy issues not traditionally perceived as gendered.

Making the case for women's presence in Congress means recognizing the value-added of their representation and also noting what is lost when they are not there. The congresswomen we interviewed believe that there are issues that would be left unaddressed and perspectives overlooked were it not for their presence, passion, and persistence.

Women Act as a Voice for the Voiceless, Using Their Power as Elected Officials to Advocate for Those Who Are Too Often Ignored in the Halls of Power

Existing research provides some evidence that women legislators are more likely than their male colleagues to rely on and respond to constituents as they conduct their work (Carey, Niemi, and Powell 1998; Beck 2001; CAWP 2001; Epstein, Niemi, and Powell 2005) and that women in power boost citizens' perceptions of government responsiveness and their own capacity to influence government policy (Atkeson and Carrillo 2007). Our interviews with women in Congress lend support and context to these findings; in explaining their representational responsibilities, a number of congresswomen cited their commitment to being a voice for the voiceless. The voiceless, according to them, include groups who have been marginalized from power and whose interests are too frequently overlooked due to a dearth of money, access, or seats at policymaking tables. They include, among others, the economically disadvantaged, individuals not represented by lobbyists, children, and the unborn.

Those individuals who bear the brunt of caregiving responsibilities—women, regardless of class, race, generation, and region—have also historically been among the voiceless in Congress. But the congresswomen we interviewed frequently pointed to their roles as mothers, grandmothers, and caregivers as motivating them to focus on the impact of policy on children and family and/or bring issues to policy agendas that highlight struggles associated with care work, which have been historically relegated to the private sphere. These roles not only guide their representational behavior in ways distinct from their male counterparts, but also create commonalities among women in Congress that they credit with helping to facilitate relationships across party lines.

The commitment of congresswomen to give voice to the voiceless contributes to the case for more women in government. Increasing women's legislative representation will expand the representativeness of American democracy—not just for women, but for other populations that have been excluded from the halls of political power.

Elected Women Alter Institutional Structures and Images of Leadership to Accommodate Women

The congresswomen we spoke with shared examples of the ways in which their presence in Congress has contributed to institutional change. As more women have been elected to Congress, they have succeeded in altering both physical structures and institutional rules that were not initially created to accommodate women. Thanks to congresswomen, there are now women's restrooms located near the House and Senate floors, women are no longer excluded from the congressional swimming pool, outdated dress codes have been changed, and in government buildings the needs of nursing mothers are better addressed.

The women we interviewed also discussed the value of citizens seeing women—particularly women diverse in ideology, race and ethnicity, and age—in positions of political power. Women in Congress act as role models for young women in the course of their daily work, and many congresswomen we interviewed also pointed to their efforts to inspire and encourage more women to participate in politics and perhaps run for office themselves. These efforts contribute to institutional change by promoting shifts in power away from White men, both in actual numbers and in institutional expectations of who can and should have a seat at the congressional table when policy is made.

WOMEN'S CONGRESSIONAL REPRESENTATION MATTERS

In the days leading up to the Senate's contentious vote on a "skinny repeal" of the Affordable Care Act in the 115th Congress, Senator Lisa Murkowski (R-AK) was reportedly threatened by Secretary of the Interior Ryan Zinke with the loss of federal support for economic development projects in her state if she failed to fall in line with her party. Not long before that, President Trump himself tweeted that Murkowski had "let the country down" with her vote against an earlier repeal bill. Asked by a reporter to comment on these attacks and what they may mean for her reelection, Murkowski responded, "Every day shouldn't be about winning elections. How about just doing a little bit of governing around here?! That's what I'm here for."

Our interviews with women in the 114th Congress indicate that Murkowski is not alone. The women we spoke with share a commitment to governing, a limited tolerance for institutional dynamics that distract them from it, and an ability to overcome obstacles that may stand in the way of meeting their representational and legislative goals. Congresswomen are in no way above politics; like their male colleagues, they are astute strategists in navigating political terrain. They are partisans who bring strong ideological perspectives to legislative debates. But those perspectives are intertwined with the distinct and diverse perspectives they bring as women to congressional work.

Future research will continue to measure women's legislative impact in more objective terms and in direct comparison with men. But what we have offered here are insights from women legislators themselves about their experiences in, disruption of, and influence on an institution in which they were not originally intended to serve. In telling their stories, we have identified the ties that bind women in Congress together, as well as the factors that set them apart from each other. We have revealed the ways in which both getting to and serving in Congress can be hard for women, but they have both assured and showed us that it is worth it. The congresswomen we interviewed reiterated and illustrated time and again that it matters that they are there and that being a woman in Congress is a "big thing." Whether looking at women's congressional service across history or in a single Congress, we find it hard to disagree with them.

The CAWP Study of Women in the 114th Congress includes interviews with 83, or 77%, of the women members of the 114th Congress. Our response rate was 81% among women members of the US House and 65% among women senators, with more success among Democratic than Republican women (12 of 14 Democratic women senators participated in interviews, compared with 1 of 6 Republican women senators). We had a strong response rate across the two parties (84% for Democrats and 59% for Republicans, including delegates). We also had a strong response rate for women of color (80% of Black women participated, compared with 67% of Latinas and 57% of Asian American women, including delegates).

The average interview was 32 minutes in length. Eighty percent of interviews were between 22 and 42 minutes in length, with one interview lasting more than one hour and two interviews lasting less than 15 minutes. All interviews were conducted by one of a team of five interviewers, including the four principal investigators on this project (three Rutgers professors and CAWP's director) and one senior graduate research assistant. The interview protocol included priority questions that were almost always asked of each woman legislator; supplementary questions that were asked when time allowed; and member-specific questions about policy in the 114th Congress. We sought to ask this set of priority questions during every interview:

In addition to representing your district as a whole, are there particular people or interests inside or outside your district that you feel a commitment to work on behalf of here in Congress?

We know there are many items on your agenda, but what is the one
   thing you would most like to accomplish during this Congress?
How has the current environment of party polarization affected
   your ability to pursue your goals?
Do you think the women in this Congress are more or less likely
   than the men to work together across party lines? Why?
Do you think the presence of women members has made a
   difference here in Congress in recent years? If so, how? If not,
   why not?

List of Congresswomen Interviewed

Rep. Alma Adams (D-NC)
Sen. Tammy Baldwin (D-WI)
Rep. Karen Bass (D-CA)
Rep. Joyce Beatty (D-OH)
Rep. Diane Black (R-TN)
Rep. Marsha Blackburn (R-TN)
Rep. Suzanne Bonamici (D-OR)
Sen. Barbara Boxer (D-CA)
Rep. Susan Brooks (R-IN)
Rep. Julia Brownley (D-CA)
Rep. Cheri Bustos (D-IL)
Rep. Lois Capps (D-CA)
Rep. Judy Chu (D-CA)
Rep. Katherine Clark (D-MA)
Rep. Yvette Clarke (D-NY)
Sen. Susan Collins (R-ME)
Rep. Susan Davis (D-CA)
Rep. Diana DeGette (D-CO)
Rep. Rosa DeLauro (D-CT)
Rep. Suzan DelBene (D-WA)
Rep. Debbie Dingell (D-MI)
Rep. Donna Edwards (D-MD)
Rep. Renee Ellmers (R-NC)

Rep. Anna Eshoo (D-CA)

Rep. Elizabeth Esty (D-CT)

Sen. Dianne Feinstein (D-CA)

Rep. Virginia Foxx (R-NC)

Rep. Lois Frankel (D-FL)

Rep. Marcia Fudge (D-OH)

Rep. Tulsi Gabbard (D-HI)

Sen. Kirsten Gillibrand (D-NY)

Rep. Gwen Graham (D-FL)

Rep. Kay Granger (R-TX)

Rep. Vicky Hartzler (R-MO)

Sen. Heidi Heitkamp (R-ND)

Sen. Mazie Hirono (D-HI)

Rep. Eddie Bernice Johnson (D-TX)

Rep. Marcy Kaptur (D-OH)

Rep. Robin Kelly (D-IL)

Rep. Ann Kirkpatrick (D-AZ)

Sen. Amy Klobuchar (D-MN)

Rep. Ann McLane Kuster (D-NH)

Rep. Brenda Lawrence (D-MI)

Rep. Barbara Lee (D-CA)

Rep. Zoe Lofgren (D-CA)

Rep. Nita Lowey (D-NY)

Rep. Michelle Lujan Grisham (D-NM)

Rep. Cynthia Lummis (R-WY)

Rep. Carolyn Maloney (D-NY)

Rep. Doris Matsui (D-CA)

Sen. Claire McCaskill (D-MO)

Rep. Cathy McMorris Rodgers (R-WA)

Rep. Martha McSally (R-AZ)

Rep. Grace Meng (D-NY)

Sen. Barbara Mikulski (D-MD)

Rep. Gwen Moore (D-WI)

Sen. Patty Murray (D-WA)

Rep. Grace Napolitano (D-CA)

Rep. Kristi Noem (R-SD)

Del. Eleanor Holmes Norton (D-DC)

Rep. Nancy Pelosi (D-CA)

Rep. Chellie Pingree (D-ME)

Del. Stacey Plaskett (D-VI)

Rep. Kathleen Rice (D-NY)

Rep. Martha Roby (R-AL)

Rep. Ileana Ros-Lehtinen (R-FL)

Rep. Lucille Roybal-Allard (D-CA)

Rep. Linda Sánchez (D-CA)

Rep. Loretta Sanchez (D-CA)

Rep. Jan Schakowsky (D-IL)

Rep. Terri Sewell (D-AL)

Sen. Jeanne Shaheen (D-NH)

Rep. Louise Slaughter (D-NY)

Rep. Jackie Speier (D-CA)

Sen. Debbie Stabenow (D-MI)

Rep. Elise Stefanik (R-NY)

Rep. Dina Titus (D-NV)

Rep. Niki Tsongas (D-MA)

Rep. Ann Wagner (R-MO)

Rep. Jackie Walorski (R-IN)

Rep. Debbie Wasserman Schultz (D-FL)

Rep. Maxine Waters (D-CA)

Rep. Bonnie Watson Coleman (D-NJ)

Acker, Joan. "From Sex Roles to Gendered Institutions." *Contemporary Sociology* 21, no. 5 (1992): 565–69. doi:10.2307/2075528.

Adams, Greg D. "Abortion: Evidence of an Issue Evolution." *American Journal of Political Science* 41, no. 3 (July 1997): 718–37. doi:10.2307/2111673.

Adams, Kimberly S. "Different Faces, Different Priorities: Agenda-Setting Behavior in the Mississippi, Maryland, and Georgia State Legislatures." *Nebula* 4, no. 2 (June 2007): 1–38.

Aday, Sean, and James Devitt. "Style over Substance: Newspaper Coverage of Elizabeth Dole's Presidential Bid." *Harvard International Journal of Press/Politics* 6, no. 2 (2001): 52–73. doi:10.1177/108118001129172134.

Ainsworth, Scott H., and Thad E. Hall. *Abortion Politics in Congress*. New York: Cambridge University Press, 2011.

Alduncin, Alexander, Sean Q. Kelly, David C. W. Parker, and Sean Theriault. "Foreign Junkets or Learning to Legislate? Generational Changes in the International Travel Patterns of House Members, 1977–2012." *Forum* 12, no. 3 (2014): 563–77.

Allen, Peter, David Cutts, and Madelaine Winn. "Understanding Legislator Experiences of Family-Friendly Working Practices in Political Institutions." *Politics & Gender* 12, no. 3 (2016): 549–72. doi:10.1017/S1743923X16000040.

Amer, Mildred. "Black Members of the United States Congress: 1870–2004." Congressional Research Service, 2004.

Anderson, William D., Janet M. Box-Steffensmeier, and Valeria Sinclair-Chapman. "The Keys to Legislative Success in the U.S. House of Representatives." *Legislative Studies Quarterly* 28, no. 3 (2003): 357–86.

Angevine, Sara. "Representing All Women: An Analysis of Congress, Foreign Policy, and the Boundaries of Women's Surrogate Representation." *Political Research Quarterly* 70, no. 1 (2017): 98–110. doi:10.1177/1065912916675737.

Anzia, Sarah F., and Christopher R. Berry. "The Jackie (and Jill) Robinson Effect: Why Do Congresswomen Outperform Congressmen?" *American Journal of Political Science* 55, no. 3 (2011): 478–93.

Atkeson, Lonna Rae. "Not All Cues Are Created Equal: The Conditional Impact of Female Candidates on Political Engagement." *Journal of Politics* 65, no. 4 (2003): 1040–61. doi:10.1111/1468-2508.t01-1-00124.

Atkeson, Lonna Rae, and Nancy Carrillo. "More Is Better: The Influence of Collective Female Descriptive Representation on External Efficacy." *Politics & Gender* 3, no. 1 (2007): 79–101. doi:10.1017/S1743923X0707002X.

Baker, Ashley. "Reexamining the Gender Implications of Campaign Finance Reform: How Higher Ceilings on Individual Donors Disproportionately Impact Female Candidates." *Modern American* 2, Fall (2006): 18–23.

Baker, Ross K. *Friend and Foe in the U.S. Senate.* New York: Free Press, 1980.

———. *Is Bipartisanship Dead? A Report from the Senate.* Boulder, CO: Paradigm Publishers, 2015.

Banwart, Mary Christine. "Gender and Candidate Communication: Effects of Stereotypes in the 2008 Election." *American Behavioral Scientist* 54, no. 3 (2010): 265–83. doi:10.1177/0002764210381702.

Banwart, Mary Christine, and Mitchell S. McKinney. "A Gendered Influence in Campaign Debates? Analysis of Mixed-gender United States Senate and Gubernatorial Debates." *Communication Studies* 56, no. 4 (2005): 353–73. doi:10.1080/10510970500319443.

Barrett, Edith J. "Black Women in State Legislatures: The Relationship of Race and Gender to the Legislative Experience." In *The Impact of Women in Public Office*, edited by Susan J. Carroll, 185–204. Bloomington: Indiana University Press, 2001.

———. "The Policy Priorities of African American Women in State Legislatures." *Legislative Studies Quarterly* 20, no. 2 (1995): 223–47. doi:10.2307/440449.

Beck, Susan A. "Acting as Women. The Effects and Limitations of Gender in Local Governance." In *The Impact of Women in Public Office*, edited by Susan J. Carroll, 49–67. Bloomington: Indiana University Press, 2001.

Beckwith, Karen. "Plotting the Path from One to the Other: Women's Interests and Political Representation." In *Representation: The Case of Women*, edited by Maria C. Taylor-Robinson Michelle M. Escobar-Lemmon, 19–40. New York: Oxford University Press, 2014.

Bedolla, Lisa Garcia, Katherine Tate, and Janelle Wong. "Indelible Effects: The Impact of Women of Color in the U.S. Congress." In *Women and Elective Office: Past, Present, and Future*, 3rd ed., edited by Sue Thomas and Clyde Wilcox, 235–52. New York: Oxford University Press, 2014.

Bejarano, Christina E. *The Latina Advantage: Gender, Race, and Political Success.* Austin: University of Texas Press, 2013.

Binder, Sarah A. *Minority Rights, Majority Rule: Partisanship and the Development of Congress.* New York: Cambridge University Press, 1997.

———. "Polarized We Govern?" Washington, DC: Brookings Institution, 2014. https://www.brookings.edu/research/polarized-we-govern/

———. *Stalemate: Causes and Consequences of Legislative Gridlock.* Washington, DC: Brookings Institution Press, 2003.

Bobo, Lawrence, and Franklin D. Gilliam. "Race, Sociopolitical Participation, and Black Empowerment." *American Political Science Review* 84, no. 2 (1990): 377–93. doi:10.2307/1963525.

Bochel, Catherine, and Jacqui Briggs. "Do Women Make a Difference?" *Politics* 20, no. 2 (2000): 63–68. doi:10.1111/1467-9256.00113.

Boehner, John, and Mitch McConnell. "Now We Can Get Congress Going." *Wall Street Journal*, November 6, 2014. http://www.wsj.com/articles/ john-boehner-and-mitch-mcconnell-now-we-can-get-congress-going-1415232759.

Bowen, Daniel C., and Christopher J. Clark. "Revisiting Descriptive Representation in Congress: Assessing the Effect of Race on the Constituent–Legislator Relationship." *Political Research Quarterly* 67, no. 3 (2014): 695–707. doi:10.1177/1065912914531658.

Brady, David W., John Ferejohn, and Laurel Harbridge. "Polarization and Public Policy: A General Assessment." In *Red and Blue Nation?*, edited by Pietro S. Nivola and David W. Brady, 107–33. Washington, DC: Brookings Institution Press, 2008.

Bratton, Kathleen A. "Critical Mass Theory Revisited: The Behavior and Success of Token Women in State Legislatures." *Politics & Gender* 1, no. 1 (2005): 97–125.

———. "The Effect of Legislative Diversity on Agenda Setting: Evidence from Six State Legislatures." *American Politics Research* 30, no. 2 (2002): 115–42.

Bratton, Kathleen A., and Kerry L. Haynie. "Agenda Setting and Legislative Success in State Legislatures: The Effects of Gender and Race." *Journal of Politics* 61, no. 3 (1999): 658–79. doi:10.2307/2647822.

Bratton, Kathleen A., Kerry L. Haynie, and Beth Reingold. "Agenda Setting and African American Women in State Legislatures." *Journal of Women Politics & Policy* 28, no. 3–4 (2006): 71–96.

Brewer, Mark D., Mack D. Mariani, and Jeffrey M. Stonecash. "Northern Democrats and Party Polarization in the U.S. House." *Legislative Studies Quarterly* 27, no. 3 (2002): 423–44. doi:10.2307/3598571.

Brooks, Deborah Jordan. *He Runs, She Runs: Why Gender Stereotypes Do Not Harm Women Candidates*. Princeton, NJ; Princeton University Press, 2013.

Brown, Nadia. *Sisters in the Statehouse: Black Women and Legislative Decision Making*. New York: Oxford University Press, 2014.

Brown, Nadia, and Kira Hudson Banks. "Black Women's Agenda Setting in the Maryland State Legislature." *Journal of African American Studies* 18, no. 2 (2014): 164–80. doi:10.1007/s12111-013-9260-7.

Brown, Nadia E., and Sarah Allen Gershon. *Distinct Identities : Minority Women in U.S. Politics*. New York: Routledge, 2016.

Burke, Edmund. *Reflections on the Revolution in France: And on the Proceedings in Certain Societies in London Relative to That Event*. William Porter, 1790.

Burns, Nancy, Kay Lehman Schlozman, and Sidney Verba. *The Private Roots of Public Action: Gender, Equality, and Political Participation*. Cambridge, MA: Harvard University Press, 2001.

Burrell, Barbara. *A Woman's Place Is in the House: Campaigning for Congress in the Feminist Era*. Ann Arbor: University of Michigan Press, 1994.

———. *Gender in Campaigns for the U.S. House of Representatives*. Ann Arbor: University of Michigan Press, 2014.

———. "Political Parties, Fund-Raising, and Sex." In *Legislative Women: Getting Elected, Getting Ahead*, edited by Beth Reingold, 41–58. Boulder, CO: Lynne Rienner, 2008.

Bystrom, Dianne G., Terry A. Robertson, and Mary Christine Banwart. "Framing the Fight: An Analysis of Media Coverage of Female and Male Candidates in Primary

Races for Governor and U.S. Senate in 2000." *American Behavioral Scientist* 44, no. 12 (2001): 1999–2013. doi:10.1177/00027640121958456.

Bystrom, Dianne G., Terry Robertson, Mary Christine Banwart, and Lynda Lee Kaid, eds. *Gender and Candidate Communication: VideoStyle, WebStyle, NewStyle.* New York: Routledge, 2004.

Campbell, David E., and Christina Wolbrecht. "See Jane Run: Women Politicians as Role Models for Adolescents." *Journal of Politics* 68, no. 2 (2006): 233–47. doi:10.1111/j.1468-2508.2006.00402.x.

Carew, Jessica Denyse Johnson. "'Lifting as We Climb'? The Role of Stereotypes in the Evaluation of Political Candidates at the Intersection of Race and Gender." Ph.D. dissertation, Duke University, 2012. https://dukespace.lib.duke.edu/dspace/handle/10161/5527.

Cargile, Ivy A. M. "Latina Issues: An Analysis of the Policy Issue Competencies of Latina Candidates." In *Distinct Identities: Minority Women in U.S. Politics*, edited by Nadia E. Brown and Sarah Allen Gershon, 134–50. New York: Routledge, 2016.

Canon, David T. *Race, Redistricting, and Representation.* Chicago: University of Chicago Press, 1999.

Carey, John M., Richard G. Niemi, and Lynda W. Powell. "Are Women State Legislators Different?" In *Women and Elective Office: Past, Present, and Future*, edited by Sue Thomas and Clyde Wilcox, 87–102. New York: Oxford University Press, 1998.

Carmines, Edward G., and James A. Stimson. *Issue Evolution: Race and the Transformation of American Politics.* Princeton, NJ: Princeton University Press, 1989.

Carroll, Susan J. "Representing Women: Congresswomen's Perceptions of Their Representational Roles." In *Women Transforming Congress*, edited by Cindy Simon Rosenthal, 50–68. Norman: University of Oklahoma Press, 2002.

———, ed. *The Impact of Women in Public Office.* Bloomington: Indiana University Press, 2001.

———. *Women as Candidates in American Politics*, 2nd ed. Bloomington: Indiana University Press, 1994.

Carroll, Susan J., and Kira Sanbonmatsu. *More Women Can Run: Gender and Pathways to the State Legislatures.* New York: Oxford University Press, 2013.

Casellas, Jason Paul. *Latino Representation in State Houses and Congress.* New York: Cambridge University Press, 2011.

CAWP. "Women State Legislators: Past, Present, and Future." New Brunswick, NJ: Rutgers University, Center for American Women and Politics, Eagleton Institute of Politics, 2001. http://cawp.rutgers.edu/sites/default/files/resources/stlegpastpresentfuture.pdf.

Celis, Karen, Sarah Childs, Johanna Kantola, and Mona Lena Krook. "Constituting Women's Interests through Representative Claims." *Politics & Gender* 10 (2014): 149–74.

———. "Rethinking Women's Substantive Representation." *Journal of Representative Democracy* 44, no. 2 (2008): 99–110.

Chacko, Sarah. "Conferees Finish Work on No Child Bill; House Vote Next." *CQ Roll Call*, November 19, 2015. http://www.cq.com/doc/news-4793964?0.

Charles, Nickie. "Doing Gender, Practising Politics: Workplace Cultures in Local and Devolved Government." *Gender, Work & Organization* 21, no. 4 (2014): 368–80. doi:10.1111/gwao.12042.

Childs, Sarah. "A Feminised Style of Politics? Women MPs in the House of Commons." *British Journal of Politics & International Relations* 6, no. 1 (2004): 3–19. doi:10.1111/j.1467-856X.2004.00124.x.

———. *The Good Parliament*. University of Bristol, July 2016. http://www.bristol.ac.uk/media-library/sites/news/2016/july/20%20Jul%20Prof%20Sarah%20Childs%20The%20Good%20Parliament%20report.pdf.

Cohen, Cathy J. "Portrait of Continuing Marginality: The Study of Women of Color in American Politics." In *Women and American Politics: New Questions, New Directions*, edited by Susan J. Carroll, 190–213. New York: Oxford University Press, 2003.

Collins, Patricia Hill. *Black Feminist Thought: Knowledge, Consciousness, and the Politics of Empowerment*. New York: Routledge, 2008.

Connelly, William F., Jr., and John J. Pitney. *Congress' Permanent Minority?* Lanham, MD: Rowman & Littlefield, 1994.

Cook, Philip J., and Kristin A. Goss. *The Gun Debate : What Everyone Needs to Know*. Oxford: Oxford University Press, 2014.

Covert, Bryce. "Congresswoman Pushes Back against Paul Ryan's Welfare Reform with Her Own Plan." *Think Progress*, September 14, 2015. https://thinkprogress.org/congresswoman-pushes-back-against-paul-ryans-welfare-reform-with-her-own-plan-b94b62d9c877/.

Crawford, Mary, and Barbara Pini. "The Australian Parliament: A Gendered Organisation." *Parliamentary Affairs* 64, no. 1 (2011): 82–105. doi:10.1093/pa/gsq047.

Crenshaw, Kimberlé. "Demarginalizing the Intersection of Race and Sex: A Black Feminist Critique of Antidiscrimination Doctrine, Feminist Theory and Antiracist Politics." *University of Chicago Legal Forum* 140 (1989): 139–167.

———. "Mapping the Margins: Intersectionality, Identity Politics, and Violence against Women of Color." *Stanford Law Review* 43, no. 6 (1991): 1241–99.

Crespin, Michael H., and Janna L. Deitz. "If You Can't Join 'Em, Beat 'Em: The Gender Gap in Individual Donations to Congressional Candidates." *Political Research Quarterly* 63, no. 3 (2010): 581–93. doi:10.1177/1065912909333131.

Dabelko, Kirsten la Cour, and Paul S. Herrnson. "Women's and Men's Campaigns for the U. S. House of Representatives." *Political Research Quarterly* 50, no. 1 (1997): 121–35. doi:10.2307/449031.

Darcy, R., Janet Clark, and Susan Welch. *Women, Elections, and Representation*, 2nd ed. Lincoln: University of Nebraska Press, 1994.

Dietrich, Bryce J., Matthew Hayes, and Diana Z. O'Brien. "Pitch Perfect: Vocal Pitch and the Emotional Intensity of Congressional Speech on Women." Working Paper, 2017. http://www.brycejdietrich.com/files/working_papers/DietrichHayesOBrien.pdf.

Ditonto, Tessa. "A High Bar or a Double Standard? Gender, Competence, and Information in Political Campaigns." *Political Behavior* 39, no. 2 (2017): 301–25. doi:10.1007/s11109-016-9357-5.

Ditonto, Tessa M., Allison J. Hamilton, and David P. Redlawsk. "Gender Stereotypes, Information Search, and Voting Behavior in Political Campaigns." *Political Behavior* 36, no. 2 (2014): 335–58. doi:10.1007/s11109-013-9232-6.

Dittmar, Kelly. *Navigating Gendered Terrain: Stereotypes and Strategy in Political Campaigns*. Philadelphia: Temple University Press, 2015.

Dodson, Debra L. *The Impact of Women in Congress*. New York: Oxford University Press, 2006.

Dodson, Debra L., and Susan J. Carroll. "Reshaping the Agenda: Women in State Legislatures." New Brunswick, NJ: Rutgers University, Center for American Women and Politics, 1991. http://cawp.rutgers.edu/sites/default/files/resources/reshapingtheagenda.pdf.

Dodson, Debra L., Susan J. Carroll, Ruth B. Mandel, Ronnee Schreiber, and Katherine E. Kleeman. "Voices, Views, Votes: The Impact of Women in the 103rd Congress." New Brunswick, NJ: Rutgers University, Center for American Women and Politics, Eagleton Institute of Politics, 1995. http://cawp.rutgers.edu/sites/default/files/resources/voices_views_votes.pdf.

Dolan, Julie. "Support for Women's Interests in the 103rd Congress." *Women & Politics* 18, no. 4 (1997): 81–94. doi:10.1300/J014v18n04_05.

Dolan, Kathleen. "Do Women Candidates Play to Gender Stereotypes? Do Men Candidates Play to Women? Candidate Sex and Issues Priorities on Campaign Websites." *Political Research Quarterly* 58, no. 1 (2005): 31–44. doi:10.2307/3595593.

———. "Symbolic Mobilization? The Impact of Candidate Sex in American Elections." *American Politics Research* 34, no. 6 (2006): 687–704. doi:10.1177/1532673X06289155.

———. "The Impact of Gender Stereotyped Evaluations on Support for Women Candidates." *Political Behavior* 32, no. 1 (2010): 69–88. doi:10.1007/s11109-009-9090-4.

———. *When Does Gender Matter? Women Candidates and Gender Stereotypes in American Elections*. New York: Oxford University Press, 2014.

Dolan, Kathleen, and Michael Hansen. "Blaming Women or Blaming the System? Public Perceptions of Women's Underrepresentation in Elected Office." *Political Research Quarterly* Forthcoming.

Dolan, Kathleen, and Timothy Lynch. "The Impact of Gender Stereotypes on Voting for Women Candidates by Level and Type of Office." *Politics & Gender* 12 (2016): 573–95.

Dolan, Kathleen, and Kira Sanbonmatsu. "Gender Stereotypes and Attitudes Toward Gender Balance in Government." *American Politics Research* 37, no. 3 (2009): 409–28.

Dovi, Suzanne. "Preferable Descriptive Representatives: Will Just Any Woman, Black, or Latino Do?" *American Political Science Review* 96, no. 4 (2002): 729–43.

———. *The Good Representative*. Malden, MA: Blackwell, 2007.

"Do Women Represent Women? Rethinking the 'Critical Mass' Debate." *Politics & Gender* 2, no. 4 (2006): 491–92. doi:10.1017/S1743923X06211140.

Dunaway, Johanna, Regina G. Lawrence, Melody Rose, and Christopher R. Weber. "Traits versus Issues: How Female Candidates Shape Coverage of Senate and Gubernatorial Races." *Political Research Quarterly* 66, no. 3 (2013): 715–26. doi:10.1177/1065912913491464.

Eagly, Alice H., and Linda L. Carli. *Through the Labyrinth: The Truth about How Women Become Leaders*. Boston: Harvard Business Review Press, 2007.

Epstein, Michael J., Richard G. Niemi, and Lynda W. Powell. "Are Women State Legislators Different?" In *Women and Elective Office: Past, Present, and Future*, 2nd ed., edited by Sue Thomas and Clyde Wilcox, 94–109. New York: Oxford University Press, 2005.

Escobar-Lemmon, Maria C., and Michelle M. Taylor-Robinson. *Representation: The Case of Women*. New York: Oxford University Press, 2014.

Eulau, Heinz, John C. Wahlke, William Buchanan, and Leroy C. Ferguson. "The Role of the Representative: Some Empirical Observations on the Theory of Edmund Burke." *American Political Science Review* 53, no. 3 (1959): 742–56. doi:10.2307/1951941.

Fenno, Richard F. *Congressmen in Committees*. Boston: Little, Brown, 1973.

———. *Going Home: Black Representatives and Their Constituents*. Chicago: University of Chicago Press, 2003.

———. *Home Style: House Members in Their Districts*. Boston: Little, Brown, 1978.

Filipovic, Jill. "Why Aren't the Extra-Effective Women of the U.S. Senate Getting the Credit They Deserve?" *Cosmopolitan*, April 14, 2015. http://www.cosmopolitan.com/politics/a39014/women-who-get-stuff-done/.

Fiorina, Morris, and Matthew S. Levendusky. "Disconnected: The Political Class versus the People." In *Red and Blue Nation? Characteristics and Causes of America's Polarized Politics*, edited by Pietro S. Nivola And David W. Brady, 49–71. Washington, DC: Brookings Institution Press, 2006.

Flegenheimer, Matt, Jonathan Martin, and Jennifer Steinhauer. "Behind Legislative Collapse: An Angry Vow Fizzles for Lack of a Viable Plan." *New York Times*, July 28, 2017. https://www.nytimes.com/2017/07/28/us/politics/john-mccain-health-care-senate-collapse-skinny.html.

Foerstel, Karen, and Herbert N. Foerstel. *Climbing the Hill: Gender Conflict in Congress*. Westport, CT: Praeger, 1996.

Fox, Richard L. "Congressional Elections: Women's Candidacies and the Road to Gender Parity." In *Gender and Elections: Shaping the Future of American Politics*, 2nd ed., edited by Susan J. Carroll and Richard L. Fox, 187–209. New York: Cambridge University Press, 2010.

———. *Gender Dynamics in Congressional Elections*. Thousand Oaks, CA: Sage, 1997.

Fraga, Luis Ricardo, Lind Lopez, Valeri Martinez-Ebers, and Ricardo Ramirez. "Gender and Ethnicity: Patterns of Electoral Success and Legislative Advocacy among Latina and Latino State Officials in Four States." *Journal of Women Politics & Policy* 28, no. 3–4 (2006): 121–45.

Frederick, Brian. "A Longitudinal Test of the Gender Turnover Model among U.S. House and Senate Members." *Social Science Journal* 52, no. 2 (2015): 102–11.

———. "Are Female House Members Still More Liberal in a Polarized Era? The Conditional Nature of the Relationship between the Descriptive and Substantive Representation." *Congress & the Presidency* 36 (2009): 181–202.

———. "Gender and Patterns of Roll Call Voting in the U.S. Senate." *Congress & the Presidency* 37, no. 2 (May 25, 2010): 103–24. doi:10.1080/07343460903390711.

———. "Gender and Roll Call Voting Behavior in Congress: A Cross-Chamber Analysis." *American Review of Politics* 34 (2013): 1–20. doi:10.15763/issn.2374-7781.2013.34.0.1-20.

———. "Gender Turnover and Roll Call Voting in the US Senate." *Journal of Women, Politics & Policy* 32, no. 3 (2011): 193–210. doi:10.1080/1554477X.2011.589281.

Freeman, Jo. "Whom You Know versus Whom You Represent: Feminist Influence in the Democratic and Republican Parties." In *The Women's Movements of the United States and Western Europe: Consciousness, Political Opportunity, and Public Policy*, 215–44. Philadelphia: Temple University Press, 1987.

Fridkin, Kim, and Patrick Kenney. *The Changing Face of Representation: The Gender of U.S. Senators and Constituent Communications*. Ann Arbor: University of Michigan Press, 2014.

Fridkin, Kim L., Patrick J. Kenney, and Gina Serignese Woodall. "Bad for Men, Better for Women: The Impact of Stereotypes during Negative Campaigns." *Political Behavior* 31, no. 1 (2009): 53. doi:10.1007/s11109-008-9065-x.

Fulton, Sarah A. "Running Backwards and in High Heels: The Gendered Quality Gap and Incumbent Electoral Success." *Political Research Quarterly* 65, no. 2 (2012): 303–14.

Gallup. "Congress and the Public." n.d. http://www.gallup.com/poll/1600/Congress-Public.aspx.

Gay, Claudine. "The Effect of Black Congressional Representation on Political Participation." *American Political Science Review* 95, no. 3 (2001): 589–602.

———. "Spirals of Trust? The Effect of Descriptive Representation on the Relationship Between Citizens and Their Government." *American Journal of Political Science* 46, no. 4 (2002): 717–33.

Gerrity, Jessica C., Tracy Osborn, and Jeanette Morehouse Mendez. "Women and Representation: A Different View of the District?" *Politics & Gender* 3, no. 2 (2007): 179–200. doi:10.1017/S1743923X07000025.

Gershon, Sarah. "When Race, Gender, and the Media Intersect: Campaign News Coverage of Minority Congresswomen." *Journal of Women, Politics & Policy* 33, no. 2 (2012): 105–25. doi:10.1080/1554477X.2012.667743.

Gertzog, Irwin N. *Women and Power on Capitol Hill: Reconstructing the Congressional Women's Caucus*. Boulder, CO: Lynne Rienner, 2004.

Gill, LaVerne M. *African American Women in Congress: Forming and Transforming History*. New Brunswick, NJ: Rutgers University Press, 1997.

Green, Matthew N. *Underdog Politics: The Minority Party in the U.S. House of Representatives*. New Haven, CT: Yale University Press, 2015.

Han, Hahrie, and David W. Brady. "A Delayed Return to Historical Norms: Congressional Party Polarization after the Second World War." *British Journal of Political Science* 37, no. 3 (2007): 505–31. doi:10.1017/S0007123407000269.

Harbridge, Laurel. *Is Bipartisanship Dead? Policy Agreement and Agenda-Setting in the House of Representatives*. New York: Cambridge University Press, 2015.

Hardy-Fanta, Carol, Pei-te Lien, Dianne Pinderhughes, and Christine Marie Sierra. *Contested Transformation: Race, Gender, and Political Leadership in 21st Century America*. New York: Cambridge University Press, 2016.

Hawkesworth, Mary. "Congressional Enactments of Race–Gender: Toward a Theory of Raced–Gendered Institutions." *American Political Science Review* 97, no. 4 (2003): 529–50.

Hawkesworth, Mary, Kathleen J. Casey, Krista Jenkins, and Katherine E. Kleeman. "Legislating by and for Women: A Comparison of the 103rd and 104th Congresses."

New Brunswick, NJ: Rutgers University, Center for American Women and Politics, 2001.

Hayes, Danny, and Jennifer L. Lawless. "A Non-Gendered Lens? Media, Voters, and Female Candidates in Contemporary Congressional Elections." *Perspectives on Politics* 13, no. 1 (2015): 95–118. doi:10.1017/S1537592714003156.

Heldman, Caroline, Susan J. Carroll, and Stephanie Olson. "'She Brought Only a Skirt': Print Media Coverage of Elizabeth Dole's Bid for the Republican Presidential Nomination." *Political Communication* 22, no. 3 (2005): 315–35. doi:10.1080/10584600591006564.

Helman, Scott. "Katherine Clark: The Woman Who Brought Congress to a Standstill." *Boston Globe*, December 14, 2016. https://www.bostonglobe.com/mag-azine/2016/12/14/katherine-clark-the-woman-who-brought-congress-standstill/VWoi3lG28DE7FtWJudlJMM/story.html.

Henneberger, Melinda. "Sexual Assault a Personal Issue for Rep. Ann Kuster." *Roll Call*, June 22, 2016. http://www.rollcall.com/news/opinion/sexual-assault-a-personal-ordeal-for-rep-ann-kuster.

Hero, Rodney E., and Robert R. Preuhs. *Black–Latino Relations in U.S. National Politics: Beyond Conflict or Cooperation.* New York: Cambridge University Press, 2012.

Hetherington, Marc J. "Putting Polarization in Perspective." *British Journal of Political Science* 39, no. 2 (2009): 413–48.

Hill Collins, Patricia. *Black Feminist Thought: Knowledge, Consciousness, and the Politics of Empowerment,* 2nd ed. New York: Routledge, 2000.

Howard, Jim. "New Congress Opens with Display of Bipartisanship." *St. Louis Public Radio*, January 7, 2015. http://news.stlpublicradio.org/post/new-congress-opens-display-bipartisanship.

Hulse, Carl. "Newly Empowered, Mitch McConnell Promises an End to 'Gridlock.'" *New York Times*, November 5, 2014. https://www.nytimes.com/2014/11/06/us/poli-tics/victory-assured-gop-to-act-fast-in-promoting-agenda-in-congress.html.

Inter-Parliamentary Union. "Women in Parliaments: World and Regional Averages." 2018. http://www.ipu.org/wmn-e/world.htm.

Jacobs, Lawrence R., and Theda Skocpol. *Health Care Reform and American Politics: What Everyone Needs to Know.* Oxford: Oxford University Press, 2010.

Jamieson, Kathleen Hall. *Beyond the Double Bind: Women and Leadership.* New York: Oxford University Press, 1995.

Jenkins, Shannon. "A Woman's Work Is Never Done? Fund-Raising Perception and Effort among Female State Legislative Candidates." *Political Research Quarterly* 60, no. 2 (2007): 230–39. doi:10.1177/1065912907301682.

Jeydel, A., and A. J. Taylor. "Are Women Legislators Less Effective? Evidence from the US House in the 103rd–105th Congress." *Political Research Quarterly* 56, no. 1 (2003): 19–27.

Jones, Charles O. *The Minority Party in Congress.* Boston: Little, Brown, 1970.

Junn, Jane, and Nadia E. Brown. "What Revolution? Incorporating Intersectionality in Women and Politics." In *Political Women and American Democracy,* edited by Christina Wolbrecht, Karen Beckwith, and Lisa Baldez, 64–78. New York: Cambridge University Press, 2008.

Kanthak, Kristin, and George A. Krause. *The Diversity Paradox: Political Parties, Legislatures, and the Organizational Foundations of Representation in America.* New York: Oxford University Press, 2012.

Karpowitz, Christopher F., and Tali Mendelberg. *The Silent Sex: Gender, Deliberation, and Institutions.* Princeton, NJ: Princeton University Press, 2014.

Kathlene, Lyn. "Power and Influence in State Legislative Policymaking: The Interaction of Gender and Position in Committee Hearing Debates." *American Political Science Review* 88, no. 3 (1994): 560–76. doi:10.2307/2944795.

King, David, and Richard Matland. "Sex and the Grand Old Party: An Experimental Investigation of the Effect of Candidate Sex on Support for a Republican Candidate." *American Politics Research* 31 (2003): 595–612.

King, Deborah K. "Multiple Jeopardy, Multiple Consciousness: The Context of a Black Feminist Ideology." *Signs* 14, no. 1 (1988): 42–72.

King, James D. "Single-Member Districts and the Representation of Women in American State Legislatures: The Effects of Electoral System Change." *State Politics & Policy Quarterly* 2, no. 2 (2002): 161–75. doi:10.2307/40421455.

Klobuchar, Amy. *The Senator Next Door: A Memoir from the Heartland.* New York: Henry Holt, 2015.

Koch, Jeffrey. "Candidate Gender and Women's Psychological Engagement in Politics." *American Politics Quarterly* 25, no. 1 (1997): 118–33. doi:10.1177/1532673X9702500107.

Koenig, Anne M., Alice H. Eagly, Abigail A. Mitchell, and Tiina Ristikari. "Are Leader Stereotypes Masculine? A Meta-Analysis of Three Research Paradigms." *Psychological Bulletin* 137, no. 4 (2011): 616–42. doi:10.1037/a0023557.

Krook, Mona Lena, and Pippa Norris. "Beyond Quotas: Strategies to Promote Gender Equality in Elected Office." *Political Studies* 62, no. 1 (2014): 2–20. doi:10.1111/1467-9248.12116.

Lawless, Jennifer L. "Politics of Presence? Congresswomen and Symbolic Representation." *Political Research Quarterly* 57, no. 1 (2004): 81–99. doi:10.1177/106591290405700107.

Lawless, Jennifer L., and Richard L. Fox. *It Still Takes A Candidate: Why Women Don't Run for Office.* New York: Cambridge University Press, 2010.

Lawless, Jennifer L., and Sean Theriault. "Nice Girls? Sex, Collegiality, and Cooperation in the U.S. Congress." Cambridge, MA: Political Parity, Hunt Alternatives Fund, 2016.

Layton, Lyndsey. "To Get Support for Education Bill, Senators Conjure Lost Art: Compromise." *Washington Post*, July 28, 2015. https://www.washingtonpost.com/local/education/senators-conjure-lost-art-to-get-support-for-education-bill-compromise/2015/07/28/c1bb953a-3177-11e5-97ae-30a30cca95d7_story.html.

Lee, Frances E. *Beyond Ideology: Politics, Principles, and Partisanship in the U. S. Senate.* Chicago: University Of Chicago Press, 2009.

———. "How Party Polarization Affects Governance." *Annual Review of Political Science* 18 (2015): 261–82. doi:10.1146/annurev-polisci-072012-113747.

———. *Insecure Majorities: Congress and the Perpetual Campaign.* Chicago: University of Chicago Press, 2016.

Levy, D., C. Tien, and R. Aved. "Do Differences Matter? Women Members of Congress and the Hyde Amendment." *Women & Politics* 23, no. 1–2 (2001): 105–27.

Lovenduski, Joni. "Gendering Research in Political Science." *Annual Review of Political Science* 1, no. 1 (1998): 333–56. doi:10.1146/annurev.polisci.1.1.333.

Lublin, David. *The Paradox of Representation: Racial Gerrymandering and Minority Interests in Congress*. Princeton, NJ: Princeton University Press, 1997.

MacDonald, Jason A., and Erin E. O'Brien. "Quasi-Experimental Design, Constituency, and Advancing Women's Interests: Reexamining the Influence of Gender on Substantive Representation." *Political Research Quarterly* 64, no. 2 (2011): 472–86.

Mackay, Fiona. *Love and Politics: Women Politicians and the Ethics of Care*. London: Bloomsbury Academic, 2001.

Madison, James. In *The Federalist Papers: A Collection of Essays Written in Favour of the New Constitution*. Coventry House Publishing, 1787.

Mandel, Ruth B. *In the Running: The New Woman Candidate*. Boston: Houghton Mifflin, 1981.

Mann, Thomas E., and Norman J. Ornstein, *The Broken Branch: How Congress Is Failing America and How to Get It Back on Track*. New York: Oxford University Press, 2006.

Manning, Jennifer. "Members of the 114th Congress: A Profile." Congressional Research Service, 2016. https://fas.org/sgp/crs/misc/R43869.pdf.

Mansbridge, Jane. "Rethinking Representation." *American Political Science Review* 97, no. 4 (2003): 515–28.

———. "Should Blacks Represent Blacks and Women Represent Women? A Contingent 'Yes.'" *Journal of Politics* 61, no. 3 (1999): 628–57.

Mayhew, David R. *Congress: The Electoral Connection*. New Haven, CT: Yale University Press, 1974.

McCall, Leslie. "The Complexity of Intersectionality." *Signs* 30, no. 3 (2005): 1771–1800.

McCarty, Nolan. "Polarization Is Real (and Asymmetric)." *Monkey Cage*, May 15, 2012. http://themonkeycage.org/2012/05/polarization-is-real-and-asymmetric/.

McCarty, Nolan, Keith T. Poole, and Howard Rosenthal. *Polarized America: The Dance of Ideology and Unequal Riches*. Cambridge, MA: MIT Press, 2006.

McKay, Joanna. "'Having It All?' Women MPs and Motherhood in Germany and the UK." *Parliamentary Affairs* 64, no. 4 (2011): 714–36. doi:10.1093/pa/gsr001.

Mill, John Stuart. *Considerations on Representative Government*, 1861.

Miller, Melissa K., and Jeffrey S. Peake. "Press Effects, Public Opinion, and Gender: Coverage of Sarah Palin's Vice-Presidential Campaign." *International Journal of Press/Politics* 18, no. 4 (2013): 482–507. doi:10.1177/1940161213495456.

Minta, Michael D. *Oversight: Representing the Interests of Blacks and Latinos in Congress*. Princeton, NJ: Princeton University Press, 2011.

Minta, Michael D., and Nadia E. Brown. "Intersecting Interests: Gender, Race, and Congressional Attention to Women's Issues." *Du Bois Review: Social Science Research on Race* 11, no. 2 (2014): 253–72. doi:10.1017/S1742058X14000186.

Mirabile, Francesca. "Chicago Isn't Close to Being the Gun Violence Capital of the United States." *Trace*, October 21, 2016. https://www.thetrace.org/2016/10/chicago-gun-violence-per-capita-rate/.

Mo, Cecilia Hyunjung. "The Consequences of Explicit and Implicit Gender Attitudes and Candidate Quality in the Calculations of Voters." *Political Behavior* 37, no. 2 (2015): 357–95. doi:10.1007/s11109-014-9274-4.

Monroe, Nathan W., Jason M. Roberts, and David W. Rohde, eds. *Why Not Parties? Party Effects in the United States Senate*. Chicago: University of Chicago Press, 2008.

Mundy, Liza. "The Secret History of Women in the Senate." *Politico Magazine*, February 2015. http://www.politico.com/magazine/story/2015/01/senate-women-secret-history-113908.

Newton-Small, Jay. "Women Are the Only Adults Left in Washington." *Time*, October 16, 2013. http://swampland.time.com/2013/10/16/women-are-the-only-adults-left-in-washington/

Niven, David, and Jeremy Zilber. "'How Does She Have Time for Kids and Congress?' Views on Gender and Media Coverage from House Offices." *Women and Politics* 23, no. 1–2 (2001): 147–64.

Norris, Pippa. "Women Politicians: Transforming Westminster?" In *Women in Politics*, edited by Joni Lovenduski and Pippa Norris, 91–104. Oxford: Oxford University Press, 1996.

Norton, Noelle H. "Uncovering the Dimensionality of Gender Voting in Congress." *Legislative Studies Quarterly* 24, no. 1 (1999): 65–86. doi:10.2307/440300.

Orey, Byron D'Andrá, Wendy Smooth, Kimberly S. Adams, and Kisha Harris-Clark. "Race and Gender Matter: Refining Models of Legislative Policy Making in State Legislatures." *Journal of Women, Politics & Policy* 28, no. 3–4 (2006): 97–119. doi:10.1300/J501v28n03_05.

Osborn, Tracy. *How Women Represent Women: Political Parties, Gender, and Representation in the State Legislatures*. New York: Oxford University Press, 2012.

———. "Women State Legislators and Representation: The Role of Political Parties and Institutions." *State and Local Government Review* 46, no. 2 (2014): 146–55.

Osborn, Tracy, and Jeanette Morehouse Mendez. "Speaking as Women: Women and Floor Speeches in the Senate." *Journal of Women, Politics & Policy* 31, no. 1 (2010): 1–21. doi:10.1080/15544770903501384.

Palmer, Barbara, and Dennis Michael Simon. *Breaking the Political Glass Ceiling: Women and Congressional Elections*, 2nd ed. New York: Routledge, 2008.

———. *Women and Congressional Elections: A Century of Change*. Boulder, CO: Lynne Rienner, 2012.

Palmieri, Sonia. "Gender-Sensitive Parliaments: A Global Review of Good Practice." Inter-Parliamentary Union, 2011. http://www.ipu.org/pdf/publications/gsp11-e.pdf.

Panagopoulos, Costas. "Boy Talk/Girl Talk." *Women & Politics* 26, no. 3–4 (2004): 131–55. doi:10.1300/J014v26n03_06.

Pearson, Kathryn. *Party Discipline in the U.S. House of Representatives*. Ann Arbor: University of Michigan Press, 2015.

Pearson, Kathryn, and Logan Dancey. "Elevating Women's Voices in Congress: Speech Participation in the House of Representatives." *Political Research Quarterly* 64, no. 4 (2011): 910–23.

Pearson, Kathryn, and Eric McGhee. "What It Takes to Win: Questioning 'Gender Neutral' Outcomes in U.S. House Elections." *Politics & Gender* 9, no. 4 (2013): 439–62. doi:10.1017/S1743923X13000433.

PerryUndem. "The State of the Union on Gender Equality, Sexism, and Women's Rights." January 17, 2017. https://www.scribd.com/document/336804316/PerryUndem-Gender-Equality-Report

Peters, Ronald M., and Cindy Simon Rosenthal. *Speaker Nancy Pelosi and the New American Politics.* New York: Oxford University Press, 2010.

Pew Research Center. "Partisanship and Political Animosity in 2016." Pew Research Center for the People and the Press, June 22, 2016. http://www.people-press.org/2016/06/22/partisanship-and-political-animosity-in-2016/.

———. "Political Polarization in the American Public." Pew Research Center for the People and the Press, June 12, 2014. http://www.people-press.org/2014/06/12/political-polarization-in-the-american-public/.

———. "Women and Leadership." Pew Research Center's Social & Demographic Trends Project, January 14, 2015. http://www.pewsocialtrends.org/2015/01/14/women-and-leadership/.

Phillips, Anne. *The Politics of Presence.* New York: Oxford University Press, 1995.

Pitkin, Hanna Fenichel. *The Concept of Representation.* Berkeley: University of California Press, 1967.

Poole, Keith T., and Howard Rosenthal. *Ideology and Congress: A Political Economic History of Roll Call Voting.* New York: Transaction Publishers, 2007.

Puwar, Nirmal. "Thinking About Making a Difference."*British Journal of Politics and International Relations.* 6 (2004): 65-80.

Rehfeld, Andrew. "Representation Rethought: On Trustees, Delegates, and Gyroscopes in the Study of Political Representation and Democracy." *American Political Science Review* 103, no. 2 (2009): 214–30.

Reingold, Beth. *Legislative Women: Getting Elected, Getting Ahead.* Boulder, CO: Lynne Rienner, 2008.

———. *Representing Women: Sex, Gender, and Legislative Behavior in Arizona and California.* Chapel Hill: University of North Carolina Press, 2000.

Reingold, Beth, and Jessica Harrell. "The Impact of Descriptive Representation on Women's Political Engagement: Does Party Matter?" *Political Research Quarterly* 63, no. 2 (2010): 280–94.

Reingold, Beth, and Adrienne R. Smith. "Welfare Policymaking and Intersections of Race, Ethnicity, and Gender in U.S. State Legislatures." *American Journal of Political Science* 56, no. 1 (2012): 131–47.

Rocca, Michael S., Gabriel R. Sanchez, and Jason L. Morin. "The Institutional Mobility of Minority Members of Congress." *Political Research Quarterly* 64, no. 4 (2011): 897–909. doi:10.1177/1065912910379225.

Rocha, Rene R., and Robert D. Wrinkle. "Gender, Ethnicity, and Support for Bilingual Education: Will Just Any Woman or Latino Do? A Contingent 'No.'" *Policy Studies Journal* 39, no. 2 (2011): 309–28. doi:10.1111/j.1541-0072.2011.00409.x.

Rohde, David W. *Parties and Leaders in the Postreform House.* Chicago: University of Chicago Press, 1991.

Rosenthal, Cindy Simon. *When Women Lead: Integrative Leadership in State Legislatures.* New York: Oxford University Press, 1998.

———, ed. *Women Transforming Congress.* Norman: University of Oklahoma Press, 2002.

Rouse, Stella M. *Latinos in the Legislative Process Interests and Influence*. New York: Cambridge University Press, 2013.

Rouse, Stella M., Michele Swers, and Michael David Parrott. "Gender, Race, and Coalition Building: Agenda Setting as a Mechanism for Collaboration among Minority Groups in Congress." Paper presented at the Annual Meeting of the American Political Science Association, Chicago, 2013.

Sanbonmatsu, Kira. *Democrats, Republicans, and the Politics of Women's Place*. Ann Arbor: University of Michigan Press, 2002.

———. "Gender-Related Political Knowledge and the Descriptive Representation of Women." *Political Behavior* 25, no. 4 (2003): 367–88.

———. "Representation by Gender and Parties." In *Political Women and American Democracy*, edited by Christina Wolbrecht, Karen Beckwith, and Lisa Baldez, 96–109. New York: Cambridge University Press, 2008.

———. *Where Women Run: Gender and Party in the American States*. Ann Arbor: University of Michigan Press, 2006.

Sanbonmatsu, Kira, and Kathleen Dolan. "Do Gender Stereotypes Transcend Party?" *Political Research Quarterly* 62, no. 3 (2009): 485–94.

Saward, Michael. "The Representative Claim." *Contemporary Political Theory* 5, no. 3 (2006).

Schneider, Judy. "House Standing Committee Chairs and Ranking Minority Members: Rules Governing Selection Procedures." Congressional Research Service, 2006. https://fas.org/sgp/crs/misc/RS21165.pdf

Schneider, Monica C. "Gender Bending: Candidate Strategy and Voter Response in a Marketing Age." Ph.D. dissertation, University of Minnesota, 2007.

Schneider, Monica C., and Angela L. Bos. "Measuring Stereotypes of Female Politicians." *Political Psychology* 35, no. 2 (2014): 245–66. doi:10.1111/pops.12040.

Schroeder, Patricia, and Olympia Snowe. "The Politics of Women's Health." In *The American Woman, 1994–1995: Where We Stand, Women and Health*, edited by Cynthia Costello and Anne J. Stone, 91–108. New York: Norton, 1994.

Schwindt-Bayer, Leslie A., and Renato Corbetta. "Gender Turnover and Roll-Call Voting in the U.S. House of Representatives." *Legislative Studies Quarterly* 29, no. 2 (2004): 215–29. doi:10.3162/036298004X201159.

Schwindt-Bayer, Leslie A., and William Mishler. "An Integrated Model of Women's Representation." *Journal of Politics* 67, no. 2 (2005): 407–28. doi:10.1111/j.1468-2508.2005.00323.x.

Shames, Shauna L. *Out of the Running: Why Millennials Reject Political Careers and Why It Matters*. New York: New York University Press, 2017.

Shogan, Colleen J. "Speaking Out: An Analysis of Democratic and Republican Woman-Invoked Rhetoric of the 105th Congress." *Women & Politics* 23, no. 1–2 (2001): 129–46.

Simon, Dennis M., and Barbara Palmer. "The Roll Call Behavior of Men and Women in the U.S. House of Representatives, 1937–2008." *Politics & Gender* 6, no. 2 (2010): 225–46. doi:10.1017/S1743923X1000005X.

Sinclair, Barbara. *Party Wars: Polarization and the Politics of National Policy Making*. Norman: University of Oklahoma Press, 2006.

————. *The Transformation of the U.S. Senate*. Baltimore: Johns Hopkins University Press, 1989.

————. *Unorthodox Lawmaking: New Legislative Processes in the U.S. Congress*, 4th ed. Washington, DC: CQ Press, 2012.

Singh, Robert. *The Congressional Black Caucus: Racial Politics in the U.S. Congress*. Thousand Oaks, CA: Sage, 1998.

Smooth, Wendy. "African American Women State Legislators: The Impact of Gender and Race on Legislative Influence." Ph.D. dissertation, University of Maryland, College Park, 2001.

————. "Gender, Race, and the Exercise of Power and Influence." In *Legislative Women: Getting Elected, Getting Ahead*, edited by Beth Reingold, 175–96. Boulder, CO: Lynne Rienner, 2008.

————. "Standing for Women? Which Women? The Substantive Representation of Women's Interests and the Research Imperative of Intersectionality." *Politics & Gender* 7, no. 3 (2011): 436–41. doi:10.1017/S1743923X11000225.

Stokes-Brown, Atiya Kai, and Kathleen Dolan. "Race, Gender, and Symbolic Representation: African American Female Candidates as Mobilizing Agents." *Journal of Elections, Public Opinion and Parties* 20, no. 4 (2010): 473–94. doi:10.1080/17457289.2010.511806.

Swain, Carol M. *Black Faces, Black Interests: The Representation of African Americans in Congress*. Cambridge, MA: Harvard University Press, 1995.

Swers, Michele L. *The Difference Women Make: The Policy Impact of Women in Congress*. Chicago: University of Chicago Press, 2002.

————. *Women in the Club: Gender and Policy Making in the Senate*. Chicago, IL: University of Chicago Press, 2013.

Swers, Michele L., and Christine C. Kim. "Replacing Sandra Day O'Connor: Gender and the Politics of Supreme Court Nominations." *Journal of Women, Politics & Policy* 34, no. 1 (2013): 23–48. doi:10.1080/1554477X.2013.747882.

Tate, Katherine. *Black Faces in the Mirror: African Americans and Their Representatives in the U.S. Congress*. Princeton, NJ: Princeton University Press, 2003.

————. *Concordance: Black Lawmaking in the U.S. Congress from Carter to Obama*. Ann Arbor: University of Michigan Press, 2014.

Theilmann, John, and A. L. Wilhite. "The Determinants of Individuals' Campaign Contributions to Congressional Campaigns." *American Politics Quarterly* 17, no. 3 (1989): 312–31. doi:10.1177/1532673X8901700305.

Theriault, Sean M. *Party Polarization in Congress*. New York: Cambridge University Press, 2008.

————. "Party Polarization in the US Congress: Member Replacement and Member Adaptation." *Party Politics* 12, no. 4 (2006): 483–503. doi:10.1177/1354068806064730.

————. *The Gingrich Senators: The Roots of Partisan Warfare in Congress*. New York: Oxford University Press, 2013.

Theriault, Sean M., and David W. Rohde. "The Gingrich Senators and Party Polarization in the U.S. Senate." *Journal of Politics* 73, no. 4 (2011): 1011–24. doi:10.1017/S0022381611000752.

Thomas, Sue. *How Women Legislate*. New York: Oxford University Press, 1994.

Thomas, Sue. "The Impact of Women on State Legislative Policies." *Journal of Politics* 53, no. 4 (1991): 958–76. doi: 10.2307/2131862.

Thomas, Sue, and Susan Welch. "The Impact of Gender on Activities and Priorities of State Legislators." *Western Political Quarterly* 44, no. 2 (1991): 445–56. doi:10.2307/448788.

Thomas, Sue, and Clyde Wilcox. *Women and Elective Office: Past, Present, and Future*, 3rd ed. New York: Oxford University Press, 2014.

Thomsen, Danielle. "Why So Few (Republican) Women? Explaining the Partisan Imbalance of Women in the US Congress." *Legislative Studies Quarterly* 40, no. 2 (2015): 295–323. doi:10.1111/lsq.12075.

Tillery, Alvin B. *Between Homeland and Motherland: Africa, U.S. Foreign Policy, and Black Leadership in America*. Ithaca, NY: Cornell University Press, 2011.

Trinko, Katrina. "Martha Roby, Working Mom." *National Review*, April 30, 2013. http://www.nationalreview.com/article/346947/martha-roby-working-mom-katrina-trinko.

Tronto, Joan. *Moral Boundaries: A Political Argument for an Ethic of Care*. Routledge, 1993.

Trounstine, Jessica, and Melody E. Valdini. "The Context Matters: The Effects of Single-Member versus At-Large Districts on City Council Diversity." *American Journal of Political Science* 52, no. 3 (2008): 554–69. doi:10.1111/j.1540-5907.2008.00329.x.

"2015 Vote Studies: Party Unity Remained Strong." *CQ Weekly*, February 8, 2016. http://library.cqpress.com.proxy.libraries.rutgers.edu/cqweekly/weeklyreport11 4000004830472.

"2016 Vote Studies: House GOP More Unified Than Ever." *CQ Weekly*, February 6, 2017. http://library.cqpress.com.proxy.libraries.rutgers.edu/cqweekly/weeklyreport11 5000005034993.

Tyson, Vanessa C. *Twists of Fate: Multiracial Coalitions and Minority Representation in the US House of Representatives*. New York: Oxford University Press, 2016.

Uhlaner, Carole Jean, and Kay Lehman Schlozman. "Candidate Gender and Congressional Campaign Receipts." *Journal of Politics* 48, no. 1 (1986): 30–50. doi:10.2307/2130923.

"Vital Statistics on Congress." *Brookings Institution*, 2017. https://www.brookings.edu/multi-chapter-report/vital-statistics-on-congress/

Volden, Craig, and Alan E. Wiseman. "Legislative Effectiveness in the US Senate." *Journal of Politics* 80, no, 2 (2018): 731–35. doi/10.1086/697121.

Volden, Craig, Alan E. Wiseman, and Dana E. Wittmer. "Why Are Women More Effective Members of Congress?" *American Journal of Political Science* 57, no. 2 (2013): 326–41. doi:10.1111/ajps.12010.

———. "Women's Issues and Their Fates in the US Congress." *Political Science Research and Methods* (2016): 1–18. doi:10.1017/psrm.2016.32.

Wallace, Sophia J. "Representing Latinos: Examining Descriptive and Substantive Representation in Congress." *Political Research Quarterly* 67, no. 4 (2014): 917–29. doi:10.2307/24371962.

Walsh, Katherine Cramer. "Enlarging Representation: Women Bringing Marginalized Perspectives to Floor Debate in the House of Representatives." In *Women Transforming Congress*, edited by Cindy Simon Rosenthal, 370–96. Norman: University of Oklahoma Press, 2002.

Warren, Mark. "Help, We're in a Living Hell and Don't Know How to Get Out." *Esquire*, October 15, 2014. http://www.esquire.com/news-politics/news/a23553/congress-living-hell-1114/.

Weisman, Jonathan, and Jennifer Steinhauer. "Senate Women Lead in Effort to Find Accord." *New York Times*, October 14, 2013. https://www.nytimes.com/2013/10/15/us/senate-women-lead-in-effort-to-find-accord.html.

Weissberg, Robert. "Collective vs. Dyadic Representation in Congress." *American Political Science Review* 72, no. 2 (June 1978): 535–47.

Welch, Susan. "Are Women More Liberal than Men in the U.S. Congress?" *Legislative Studies Quarterly* 10, no. 1 (1985): 125–34. doi:10.2307/440119.

Weldon, S. Laurel. "The Structure of Intersectionality: A Comparative Politics of Gender." *Politics & Gender* 2, no. 2 (2006): 235–48. doi:10.1017/S1743923X06231040.

Wilhite, Allen, and John Theilmann. "Women, Blacks, and PAC Discrimination." *Social Science Quarterly* 67, no. 2 (1986): 283.

Williams, Melissa S. *Voice, Trust, and Memory: Marginalized Groups and the Failings of Liberal Representation*. Princeton, NJ: Princeton University Press, 2000.

Wilson, Walter Clark. *From Inclusion to Influence: Latino Representation in Congress and Latino Political Incorporation in America*. Ann Arbor: University of Michigan Press, 2017.

Wolbrecht, Christina. "Female Legislators and the Women's Rights Agenda: From Feminine Mystique to Feminist Era." In *Women Transforming Congress*, edited by Cindy Simon Rosenthal, 179–97. Norman: University of Oklahoma Press, 2002.

———. *The Politics of Women's Rights: Parties, Positions, and Change*. Princeton, NJ: Princeton University Press, 2000.

Wolbrecht, Christina, and David E. Campbell. "Role Models Revisited: Youth, Novelty, and the Impact of Female Candidates." *Politics, Groups, and Identities* 5, no. 3 (2017): 418–34. doi:10.1080/21565503.2016.1268179.

Young, Iris Marion. "Gender as Seriality: Thinking about Women as a Social Collective." *Signs* 19, no. 3 (1994): 713–38.

INDEX

Figures, notes, and tables are indicated by "f," "n," and "t" following the page numbers.